The Future of the Welfare State

Edited by
Brigid Reynolds, s.m.
Seán Healy, s.m.a.
Micheál Collins

Social Justice Ireland

I.S.B.N. No: 978 1 907501 03 6
First Published: September 2010

Published by:
Social Justice Ireland
Working to build a just society

Social Justice Ireland
Arena House
Arena Road
Sandyford
Dublin 18
Ireland

Tel: 01-213 0724
e-mail: secretary@socialjustice.ie
website: **www.socialjustice.ie**

Sponsored by
AIB Investment Managers
AIB Investment House,
Percy Place,
Dublin 4.
Tel: (01) 661 7077
Fax: (01) 661 7038

TABLE OF CONTENTS

CONTRIBUTORS

Willem Adema is Chief Economist at the Social Policy Division, OECD (Organisation for Economic Cooperation and Development) Paris.

Tony Fahey is Professor of Social Policy and Head of School at the School of Applied Social Science, University College Dublin

Seán Healy is Director, Social Justice Ireland

Daniel O'Connell is with the Department of Learning, Society and Religious Education in Mary Immaculate College, University of Limerick.

Brigid Reynolds is Director, Social Justice Ireland

INTRODUCTION

The welfare state is not an end in itself. It is a means to an end – the well-being of all people. The future of the welfare state has been a topic of discussion and argument for more than 30 years on issues ranging from education to employment, from healthcare to social housing, from welfare rates to pensions to provision for people with disability. Some have claimed it cannot survive because the population is aging. Others have argued that globalisation will undermine it in due course. Recent economic upheavals and huge budget cutbacks in many countries have added to the questions faced by the welfare state.

Is the welfare state really under threat? Has the era of the welfare state passed? Will people continue to support it? What are the major challenges faced by the welfare state at this time? What impact does the welfare state have on reducing poverty? Can the necessary funding be provided? If the welfare state is to survive how should it adjust to the changing economic situation? What are the implications of demographic developments? What should be the core of the welfare state if it is to persist in the twenty first century? Can the nation state continue to be the basis for this kind of development model, this kind of social contract?

In these economically turbulent times it is essential to focus on the shape of the society we wish to see emerge. The welfare state has been in existence in Ireland for about a century. Do we wish to see it continue? If so, what form should it take? What are the key challenges it faces in Ireland? How might these be addressed effectively and efficiently? Should people's expectations of the welfare state change?

The chapters in this book, which were first presented at a policy conference on the topic of *The Future of the Welfare State*, seek to address some of the key questions and issues that emerge in this context.

This publication is the 22nd volume in this series organised and published by *Social Justice Ireland* (previously published by *CORI Justice*) which has sought to address these questions and issues on a day to day basis.

Tony Fahey's opening chapter provides an overview of the welfare state and addresses some key questions concerning its future. Willem Adema analyses the welfare state across selected OECD countries including Ireland, asks how much it really costs and how good it is in reducing poverty. Daniel O'Connell asks if there is a place for values-led debate and discourse in the public sphere in the shaping of public policy and proposes a core set of guidelines that should underpin such debate. Seán Healy and Brigid Reynolds focus on the purpose of the welfare state, the challenges it faces and what the core elements of a welfare state for the 21st century should be. They also address the key issues of financing and of responsibility.

Social Justice Ireland is concerned with issues of principles, paradigms and guiding values as well as with the specifics of problems and policies. It approaches all of these from a social justice perspective.

Social Justice Ireland is a recognised social partner within the Community and Voluntary pillar of social partners. In presenting this volume *we* do not attempt to cover all the questions that arise around this topic. This volume is offered as a contribution to the ongoing public debate around these and related issues.

Social Justice Ireland expresses its deep gratitude to the authors of the various chapters that follow. They contributed long hours and their obvious talent to preparing these chapters.

A special word of thanks also to the AIB Investment Managers whose financial assistance made this publication possible.

Brigid Reynolds
Seán Healy
Micheál Collins
September 21, 2010

1.

The future of the welfare state: An overview

Tony Fahey

Introduction

The welfare state has been in existence for about a century in Ireland. The introduction of old age pensions in 1908 and unemployment insurance in 1911 marked its birth (McCashin 2004: 3-27). Some state funded services long pre-dated this period – the National school system, for example, was founded in 1831. On a broad definition, therefore, the origin of state supports for the welfare of the population goes well back into the nineteenth century. However, it is common to think of provisions for maintaining people's incomes in times of need, conceived of as a matter of right rather than of charity, as at the heart of the welfare state. On that basis the first decade of the twentieth century witnessed sufficiently radical shifts in the direction of modern welfare provision for it to be counted as a founding period. Developments in this era were not peculiar to Ireland: the initiatives of 1908 and 1911 came from the UK government rather than from within Ireland and reflected the growing strength of the labour movement in Britain. They were in keeping with the widespread movement in leading western countries at that time to expand the state's welfare role: Germany led the way in the 1880s with the world's first system of state-backed social insurance for sickness, accidents, old age and invalidity, while the United States did not get on the same track until Roosevelt's New Deal of the 1930s (Flora and Alber 1981). The welfare state could thus be said to be entering its second century, as long as we take that to refer to something like its average duration across the western world as a whole rather than its exact duration in every country.

As the welfare state reaches this stage, the question we are concerned with here is what its future will be. I will address this question as it applies to the welfare state in general rather than in Ireland as it is worth trying to focus on the overall thrust of likely developments rather than dwell on the undoubtedly important issue of national variations. Taking a big-picture approach, then, we can ask if the best days of the welfare state are behind it, or if it has become a too firmly rooted part of modern societies for it to be easily dislodged. Will it take the same form in the future as we have become accustomed to in the past?

The present paper provides a three-fold answer to these questions:

- first, that the welfare state has become so well established and so tied into the fabric of modern life that it is extremely difficult to cut back – the welfare state is unlikely to be much *smaller* in the foreseeable future than it is today;
- second, the *progressivity* of the welfare state (its effectiveness in providing protection to the vulnerable rather than favour the well off) is less secure than its size: there are real risks that ever-present tendencies for the poor and marginalised to come second in welfare distribution will gain the upper hand;
- third, the very notion of what progressivity means is coming under new scrutiny in the light of cross-national inequalities and various movements towards cross-national integration, of which the European Union is a leading example. The issue here is whether the nation-state as the frame of reference for defining and understanding public welfare provision will continue to be as dominant and unquestioned in the coming century as it has been in the century just gone and what that means for what we would define as the ideal welfare state of the future.

Underlying these answers is a more general theme of the cross-cutting nature of forces affecting the welfare state and the consequent difficulty of detecting a single clear underlying direction of movement. So many things are happening at once that it is difficult to list and grasp them all, much less add them together and come up with a forecast of where the resulting balance of forces will lie.

Crisis and retrenchment?

The question of how big the welfare state should be has often been discussed over the past century. Supporters of the welfare state have often worried that it might be about to shrink, while opponents have often sought to bring that outcome about. As we in Ireland, like other peoples in the world, try to come to terms with the recession and financial upheaval of the past two years, talk of welfare cuts is in the air and the future of welfare provision seems particularly threatened at the present time. In dealing with this issue, we have to distinguish between short-term changes during recessions which are more-or-less automatic responses arising from the current structure of welfare provision (such as the increase in welfare payments for the unemployed as their numbers soar) and longer term structural changes which might alter the underlying nature or role of the welfare state. In the short-term, the recession has caused social expenditure to balloon in Ireland, as it has in many other countries, both in absolute terms and as a share of a national income. However, this tells us little about long-term prospects since the future direction of welfare provision will be the outcome of longer-term forces. It is the latter we will be concerned with here, and for guidance on this question, it is useful as a first step to look at past experience and see what that can tell us about where we are headed. Over the past century, there have been two episodes of crisis of a type and on a scale of what we are now experiencing – the depression of the 1930s and the long recession which followed the oil-price shock of 1973. What do they tell us about how the present crisis might affect the welfare state?

The 1930s depression
The value in referring briefly to the depression of the 1930s in this context is the reminder it gives us of the role of welfare spending as part of the *solution* to recession and of how widely that role was adopted and put into practice in the 1930s, even before Keynesian theories of macro-economic management provided a new orthodoxy on that question. Roughly speaking, in the first half of the 1930s the still-young and small systems of state welfare provision of that period come under severe pressure, often to the point of collapse. Economic contraction, soaring unemployment

and falling revenues in effect bankrupted services like Britain's system of unemployment insurance and led to economic chaos in Germany. However, there were other countries where social insurance principles continued to expand, and in many cases did so because of rather than in spite of the social and economic pressures created by the difficult economic problems of the time. The state stepped in to strengthen the fiscal base of social insurance in Britain as its original revenues from insurance contribution bases dried up. In the United States, the Social Security Act of 1935 in effect created the American welfare state (such as it ever was) and was a central component of Roosevelt's New Deal. In New Zealand, the Social Security Act of 1938 was hailed at the time as setting a new benchmark for social insurance provision (Lindert 1984).

At the same time, Keynes was building an intellectual case for the welfare state which presented it not as an altruistic support for the poor but as part of a package of policy instruments which states could use to keep the market economy on track and prevent recurrences of economic collapse. Welfare spending in his model served not only to protect the economically vulnerable but also to stimulate economic demand at times when private expenditure by firms and households dried up and locked economies into downward spirals of falling output and falling demand. In trying to account for the burgeoning of the welfare state after the Second World War, it is difficult to separate out the effects of the war itself from the groundwork that had been laid in the 1930s, but there is no doubt that the experience of depression and the failures of free-market capitalism in that period contributed to the groundswell of support among both political elites and the general public for state social provision that built up during the war. It is instructive in this context to recall that the Beveridge Report, which drew up the blueprint for the post-war welfare state in Britain and was an inspiration for similar efforts around the world, was initiated in 1941 and published in 1942 (Hills, Ditch and Glennerster 1994). The 'giant evils' of 'squalor, ignorance, want, idleness and disease' it sought to combat were of the 1930s and earlier decades rather than of the war itself. Beveridge had been involved in the design of social policy in Britain since 1908 and his thinking in the early 1940s on Britain's welfare state had thus been maturing for over three decades. Beveridge also emphasised the benefits of welfare provision for the competitiveness of the British economy and as a necessary element of general economic reconstruction.

In general, therefore, it is reasonable to say that the economic crisis of the 1930s was a major spur to the flowering of the welfare state which occurred after the war. It is well to keep in mind this generally pro-welfare outcome of the 1930s depression as we think of the possible consequences of the present financial crisis for the future of the welfare state.

The 1970s recession and the new right

Although the post-1973 recession was less severe than the depression of the 1930s, its portents for the welfare state seemed to have all of the negatives and none of the potential for a stronger public role that were present in the earlier crisis. By the early 1970s, the western world in general, and most western European countries especially, had experienced 'thirty glorious years' of the post-war welfare state. This was the period when there seemed to be no contradiction between strong economic growth and rapid extension of social provision, since both had expanded at an unprecedented rate since the 1950s (Lindert 1984). However, the economic shocks of the 1970s – the collapse of the Bretton Woods agreement in 1971 and the oil crisis of 1973 – brought this period to an end and gave rise to a new era of slow growth, high unemployment and industrial unrest. Most puzzlingly for champions of the then standard model of welfare capitalism, the period was marked by a combination of stagnation and inflation ('stagflation') which could not be accounted for by Keynesian economics and which challenged the intellectual consensus that had underpinned the state-market mix of welfare capitalism. The way was opened for the alternative 'monetarist' doctrine of Milton Friedman and the 'Chicago school of economics' to build a following. This doctrine highlighted control of the money supply rather demand management by government as the key instrument of macro-economic guidance. It advocated a minimal role for state intervention outside the field of monetary policy.

The election victories of Margaret Thatcher in Britain in 1979 and of Ronald Reagan in the United States in 1980 seemed to signal a triumph for this new approach. Both were swept into power on the back of attacks on high taxation and generous social provision, which they blamed as the causes of slow growth and high unemployment. Their pledge to roll back the state in favour of a stronger role for the free market seemed to herald a new era of retrenchment in social spending, while the historic champions of the welfare state, the trade unions and left-wing parties, were on the wane. It appeared that, in some ways, this period was the reverse of what had emerged in the 1930s and 1940s. Welfare provision in the 1970s and 1980s was not a new arrival on the scene which could be presented as offering a solution to the ills of the day. Intellectual radicalism came from the new right rather than the left, and the 'giant evils' portrayed by the new right as obstacles to progress had to do with indolence and lack of enterprise caused by the nanny state rather the old problems of destitution and diseases caused by the heartlessness of the market.

Against that background, the surprise of the period which followed is how resilient the system of social provision proved to be. Far from succeeding in cutting back on social spending, both Reagan and Thatcher either held it steady or allowed it to expand somewhat (see esp. Pierson 1994). Looking over the whole of the OECD and over the longer period from 1980 to 2005, the overall pattern was for social spending to continue to grow. In the UK, for example, gross social expenditure rose from 16.7 per cent of GDP in 1980 to 21.3 per cent in 2005. In the USA, the corresponding increase was from 13.1 per cent in 1980 to 15.9 per cent in 2005, while taking 24 OECD states together, the increase was from 16 per cent to 20.6 per cent (Adema and Ladaique 2009: 22-24; see also Obinger and Wagschal 2010: 336-7).

There has been a great deal of scholarly debate on how complete and accurate this picture of continued expansion is. The range, diversity and complexity of state social programmes are so great that it is difficult to summarise trends in individual components, much less add them all together to get an overall picture. In the case of social expenditure, for example, programmes come and go over time, the boundaries around what to include and exclude as relevant expenditure are often difficult to define, and tax-related factors such as tax claw-backs on gross expenditures and tax-breaks for private pensions and health insurance mean that actual net social expenditure can be very different from what gross expenditure data suggest (on these complexities, see Adema and Ladaique 2009). Some fields – such as supports for housing – are so complex to compute on a comparable basis across time and place that they are usually omitted from comparative data on welfare states (Fahey and Norris 2010). Thus even the more comprehensive attempts to measure the scale of the welfare state often have to overlook certain components.

These complexities have enabled some scholars to offer different interpretations of the durability of social provision over recent decades and to argue that in fact there has been 'more retrenchment than meets the eye' (Levy 2010: 558-61). Some individual instances of harsh cutback did occur (e.g. New Zealand in the 'mother of all budgets' in 1991); there were many shorter periods of regress that are lost sight of if long time comparisons are made, and in many cases apparent expansion concealed reductions in levels of benefit since rising unemployment, population ageing and changing family structures caused need to outstrip growth in provision (Korpi and Palme 2003, Starke 2008). Others have argued that to interpret developments along a single axis of expansion and contraction is too narrow since many important changes in welfare provision have had to do with redesign and recalibration of programmes rather than simple growth or decline. This is the case, for example, in regard to the interest in 'activation' which was added to programmes for the unemployed in the 1990s as governments sought to shift the emphasis of unemployment supports from income maintenance to training and incentives to return to work (Eichhorst and Memerijck 2010: 220-9).

Nevertheless, in spite of these qualifications, the picture of trends in the level of social provision in the aftermath of recession in the 1970s and growth of the new right in the 1980s is of resilience and durability rather than radical cutback. The extent of the welfare state may have differed between countries, it may have fluctuated somewhat over short periods and individual programmes may be subject either to contraction or expansion. But it proved surprisingly resistant to overall sustained reduction, even at the hands of political leaders who seemed to have secured a popular mandate for just that. Thus, the welfare state that took root and flourished in the first thirty years after the Second World War was often assaulted in the second thirty years that followed and was sometimes clipped back here and there, but it has just as often thrown out new shoots and nowhere has returned to the minimal levels of provision of its earliest years.

Why resilience?

In the light of this apparent resilience of the welfare state since the 1980s, researchers have tried to understand what protected it and made it seemingly immune to large reduction (Levy 2010). Many of the forces that caused it to grow in the early years (such as strong labour movements and the success of political parties with left-wing leanings) went into decline and new threats emerged from a resurgent new right, yet large-scale social provision persisted. Why was that so?

Part of the answer lies in basic changes in economic and demographic trends. As the era of full or nearly full employment came to an end in the 1970s, the resulting rise in unemployment put upward pressure on welfare spending. For many European countries in particular, high unemployment seemed to become a fixed part of the landscape in the 1980s and 1990s (Eichhorst and Hemericjk 2009). Population ageing also began to have an impact, as pension costs started out on a long rising trend that has not yet reached a plateau.

In addition to these underlying socio-demographic movements, a range of political factors served to protect the welfare state. The pioneering analysis of this issue by Pierson (1994) traced these factors to the political mobilisation of new interest groups that had grown up around the welfare state as it developed into a major feature of the institutional landscape. Some of these interests centred on the recipients of welfare benefits, of which the elderly in receipt of old age pensions were a particularly large and powerful example. However, it was not just the elderly: the growth of the welfare state in previous decades had meant that, taking all elements of social provision together, the share of the population that gained no benefit from it was small. Even voters who might be sympathetic to the general idea of a roll-back of the state were likely to resist it very strongly when it came to those aspects of public provision which benefited themselves.

Another large block of interests sympathetic to social provision formed on the provider side of the system, particularly in regard to services in fields such as education and health. An important role was played here by trade unions not so much as advocates of the interests of the working class in general but rather as protectors of jobs and working conditions for their own members in the public sector. Trade unions in general had gone into decline in western countries outside the Nordic regions since the 1970s, particularly in the new and expanding private services sectors of the economy, but rates of unionisation remained high in the public sector in most countries (Visser 2006). Public sector unions provided a powerful source of resistance to wage and job cuts in state social services and thus acted as a bulwark against reductions in spending in these areas of the welfare state.

In addition to the factors which acted directly in support of public social provision was the growing public doubt about the effectiveness of market alternatives (Glennerster 2010). Private pensions provide an important example since it was in the field of pensions that the Chicago school of economics had made a particularly strong case for the virtues of market-based over public provision. It also had its greatest real-life impact in the form of the wholly market-based pension system which was introduced in Chile in 1981 and was held up at the time as a model which other countries should follow.

However, over the past three decades private pension systems have run up against problems of coverage, cost and reliability that have raised as many question marks over their effectiveness as have been raised over any area of public sector provision, and these questions reached a new level during the recent financial crisis. A fundamental issue is their inability to make provision for the poor – the private pensions system in Chile never reached more than two-thirds of the population and in recent years has had to be supplemented by a public system directed at low-income households. Annual fees charged by the private pensions industry range from 0.5 to 2.0 per cent of fund assets and thus depress the real rate of return – and the more market competition there is, the higher the level of fees since contributors are more swayed by promotion and sales effort than by fees (Tapia and Yermo 2007). In addition, those relying on private pensions have had recent dramatic lessons in how unreliable they can be: before the recent financial crisis, the median funding level for 2,100 private pensions funds across 15 OECD countries was 13 per cent in deficit; by 2009, as a result of the crisis, that median deficit had increased to 26 per cent (OECD 2010: 9).

Protecting the vulnerable

The more inclusive and precise measurement of social expenditures that is now possible on the basis of the OECD data has shown that there is less difference in the size of welfare states across the OECD than had previously been thought: the strong role of private social expenditures and related tax breaks in some countries means that their welfare states are bigger than they seem, while the taxation levied on social welfare incomes in the more generous welfare states means that they are smaller than they seem (Adema and Ladaique 2009). A comparison between Denmark and the United States provides a good illustration (the following is based on Table 5.5 in Adema and Ladaique 2009). Using a traditional measure (gross social expenditure as a percentage of GDP), the Danish welfare state is 87 per cent larger than that of the United States. However, if we take account of the quite high taxes levied on welfare payments in Denmark and the generous tax breaks for pensions and health insurance allowed in the United States, the differential narrows a great deal – the Danish welfare state reduces to a 29 per cent size advantage over the United States. If in addition, account is taken of voluntary private expenditures on social services, which is very high in the United States and low in Denmark, the differential disappears altogether – total social expenditure according to the broadest measure used in OECD data is marginally higher in the United States than in Denmark.

However, to say that some welfare states are bigger than we had thought and others are smaller is not necessarily to say that they are also similar in how progressive they are. Precise measurement of the progressivity of a package of social programmes is impossible to achieve (Esping-Andersen and Myles, 2010), but nevertheless there are useful summary measures that go a long way towards capturing their overall distributive impact. A particularly important one is the poverty rate, which provides a metric for the effectiveness of the welfare state in achieving what some would regard as the most important of its core goals, namely, the protection of the economically vulnerable from basic inadequacies in living standards. According to this measure, states in the developed world continue to be quite different from each other and to differ very much along the lines of traditional measures of welfare effort. This pattern is shown in Figure 1, which plots poverty rates in OECD countries against a core traditional element of welfare spending, namely, gross expenditure on cash transfers for the working-age population (the focus here on the working-age population serves to keep to one side the impact of pensions systems where distributive effects often have a distinctive character). As this graph shows, levels of poverty vary widely and are closely related to the measure of welfare spending used. To take the Denmark-United States comparison mentioned earlier as an example, the poverty rate in the United States is roughly three times higher than in Denmark, while cash transfers to the working age population as a percentage of GDP are about four times higher in Denmark than in the United States.

Trends in poverty rates over time also enable us to assess the impact of the rise in social expenditures since the 1980s noted earlier. Here again there are problems of consistency and comparability in the available data, but insofar as a picture can be constructed, it suggests that poverty rates in OECD countries over the period 1985-2000 either remained stable or rose slightly, with very few instances of significant decline (Nolan and Marx 2009: 322). The dominance of stability and increase in poverty levels in most countries over this period could be interpreted to mean that the rise in social expenditures over the same period did not produce the kind of anti-poverty results that might have been expected of them. Such an interpretation would be consistent with the scepticism about the real significance of those increases among some critics, as outlined above – the 'more retrenchment that meets the eye' view. However, an alternative view is that inequalities in market incomes widened considerably in this period in most countries but disposable household incomes did not, or did so less consistently (Brandolini and Smeeding 2009). This would suggest that the equalising job to be done by public social expenditures increased over this period and that it represented a considerable success on the part of welfare states that there wasn't a considerably larger deterioration in poverty rates than actually occurred.

Figure 1. Cash benefits for working age population as % of GDP and poverty rates (<50% of median income) in OECD countries, 2005

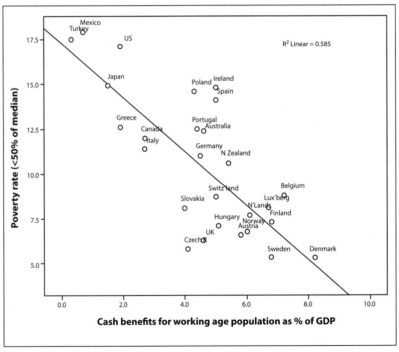

Source: OECD database

Progressive versus regressive programmes

In looking to the future of the welfare state in the light of these patterns, there is a strong case for arguing that we should be less concerned about overall size than about distributive impact. That in turn would require us to treat social expenditures not as a uniformly good thing but as a mix of progressive, regressive and neutral elements which could develop in different directions in the future. In looking at the resilience of the welfare state and its apparent immunity to radical cutback outlined earlier, then, we would have to ask where the greatest resilience lay across these types of elements and what factors were more supportive of the progressive as opposed to the regressive or neutral elements.

Such an exercise is beyond the scope of this paper, but a few points can be made. The first is that certain elements of public social expenditure broadly defined are inherently either regressive or neutral – they are incapable of being progressive. This is most true of 'tax breaks for a social purpose', which are of benefit only to those earning taxable income – and usually the more taxable income they earn, the greater the benefit they can derive from these measures. The prominence of measures of this kind in the United States, along with the private social expenditures they stimulate, is the main reason why the US system of social expenditure seems bigger on a comprehensive measurement than it appears in standard measurement – but also the main reason why the positive distributive impact of American social expenditure remains relatively small no matter what measurement is used. In that context, the pressure to restructure taxation in the light of the sudden deterioration in the fiscal situation in most countries as a result of the financial crisis is an important turning point. It offers the opportunity for champions of welfare distribution to highlight regressive tax expenditures as a particular area for reform and as an area where hard-pressed finance ministries could seek to raise additional revenue.

A second and related point that can be made is that the stance of the public system towards private social expenditures also has important effects on the types of resilience that is present in welfare states. Broadly speaking, a public-private mix of the American type is more effective in harnessing private sector interests to the defence of social expenditures – but not necessarily in a benign way from a social distribution point of view. Such interests, acting on the provider side of the private social services in fields such as private health care, private pensions and owner-occupied housing, typically strive to maintain public subsidisation of those services through the tax system and resist attempts to reform such subsidies in a more progressive direction. This is one area, therefore, where resilience in the current structures of the welfare state is not necessarily a good thing. However, it is also an area where the appeal of market solutions has been dented by the financial crisis and where the ground for a stronger public role in welfare distribution is more fertile than it has been for many decades.

A final point we can make about prospects for greater progressivity in welfare distribution is the vigilance that needs to be exerted over social provision that is more wholly contained within the public system. The problem here is that public provision can be and often is regressive. A good example is provided by pension systems in some parts of Europe, particularly in the Mediterranean countries. Here, public pensions have tended to be constructed on an insider-outsider basis in such a way that those in secure long-term employment (quite often in the public sector) enjoy generous pension benefits, while those in the secondary labour market have weaker entitlements.

Welfare States and Nation States

I will turn now briefly to my final and most uncertain theme – the future of the nation state as the platform for the welfare state. Twentieth century systems of welfare distribution, as is well recognised, had their economic foundation in the free market and we constantly debate how welfare institutions and market institutions should interact. Less attention is paid to the political dimension of the welfare state in the nation state or to the question of how welfare institutions should relate to the polities which underpin them. Lack of interest in this topic arises largely because the nation state has become such a taken-for-granted element of the global – and especially the European – landscape. The welfare state in its earliest forms was created by European imperial powers, principally Germany and Britain. But its maturation and full development came about with the end of empire and the emergence of the relatively small and ethnically homogenous nation state as the standard political formation in Europe. One might argue, in fact, that the character of Europe as a continent of small, highly bounded, ethnically distinct and internally homogenous nation states was a foundation of the 'European social model': welfare solidarity was an expression of national solidarity and a means by which national solidarity was built up. Its highly successful impact in that regard is evident in the taken-for-granted character it now possesses in Europe (on these issues, see esp. Bartolini 2005 and Ferrera 2005).

European fragmentation – its proliferation of small to medium-sized nation states – has been coming into question for European political elites since the earliest days of the European movement in the 1950s. Europe's competitors since that time have been large, multi-ethnic continental scale states – in the 1950s, the United States and the Soviet Union, today with rising powers like China, India and Brazil added to the mix. The European project is in part a peace process designed to ensure that European states will never again assault each other as they did in the first half of the twentieth century. But it is also a power process by which the larger states in Europe – now merely mid-sized states by global standards – have sought to come together, gather in their smaller neighbours and together create a polity and an economy that will large and united enough to hold its place in the world.

The long, slow and halting process of European integration has encountered one of its many crises – possibly its worst ever crisis – in the current phase of financial upheaval. The painfully built up single market and the monetary union which seeks to further it are teetering on the brink of collapse, with the financial problems of the Greek government having provided a flashpoint (and with Ireland's problems not far behind). There is now a widely held view that the EU must now move either forwards or backwards: it must integrate more – that is, transfer further sovereignty from member states to the European level – or slip back into fragmentation.

The welfare state is a core focus in debates on these issues. The retention of national control over social policy has been a cardinal principle of European integration. For European publics, the idea that welfare responsibilities should cross national frontiers has been inconceivable (witness the recent fury among German voters at the idea that German taxes might be used to shore up Greek pensions). As we talk of the future of the welfare state, we automatically think in national terms – we talk of distribution *within* states, not between states. Real household incomes among the Polish middle classes are only about half of what we in Ireland would count as the poverty threshold. The Polish poor, not to speak of the poor in Romania and Bulgaria, are even further removed from what we would count as a basic living standard. So far, it has been possible for us to talk of our welfare state without taking either German financing or east European social need into account. But we are also now becoming aware that these factors could well loom larger in the future: a European polity with European powers of taxation and distribution might have to become part of the context in which the next phase of evolution of welfare states will take place.

Conclusion

The central message to be drawn from the reflections presented in this chapter is that current conditions leave the future of the welfare state relatively open. Financial turmoil and economic slowdown are now exerting a great deal of pressure on public social expenditures. There are also long-term forces at work, such as population ageing, widening inequalities in market incomes and sustained periods of relatively high unemployment, which pose difficulties for welfare states. However, the balance between market and state which public social provision represents is shaped not only by problems on the state side. Of equal significance is what is happening in the market. Here of course what has to be noted about the present crisis is that, echoing the experience of the 1930s, it is a crisis of the market rather than of the state, and the role of the state as rescuer of last resort for market institutions is now evident in ways that it has not been since the middle of the twentieth century. The global economy has thus been catapulted into a new era of state activism, to a degree and in ways that were wholly unexpected as recently as 2007.

As far as welfare distribution is concerned, a further lesson of recent decades is that state activism is not always progressive and protective of the vulnerable – but equally that it often is. Which of these routes the state takes over the coming decades is a matter of politics in which the weight of political forces is not yet set in any clear direction. It all is to play for. As that play is worked out, there is a particular political challenge for European welfare states in how they relate to each other. The European social model has usually been defined as a distinctively European commitment to social solidarity but it could equally be characterised by the fragmentation of Europe into a multiplicity of states, each with its own jealously guarded control over its welfare system. Whether that fragmentation can continue into the future is one of the looming question marks now emerging over the European tradition of highly bounded national welfare states.

References

Adema, W. and M. Ladaique (2009), "How Expensive is the Welfare State?: Gross and Net Indicators in the OECD Social Expenditure Database (SOCX)", *OECD Social,Employment and Migration Working Papers*, No. 92, OECD Publishing

Bartolini, S. (2005) *Restructuring Europe: Centre Formation, System Building, and Political Structuring between the Nation State and the European Union*. Oxford: Oxford University Press

Brandolini, Andrea and Tim Smeeding, 2009. 'Income inequality in OECD countries', in W. Salverda, B. Nolan and T. Smeeding (eds) *The Oxford Handbook of Economic Inequality*. Oxford: Oxford University Press

Eichhorst, Werner and Anton Hemerijck. 2010. 'Welfare and employment: A European dilemma?' pp. 201-36 in J Alber and N Gilbert (eds.) *United In diversity? Comparing Social Models in Europe and America*. Oxford: Oxford University Press.

Esping-Andersen, Gosta and John Myles (2009) 'Economic Inequality and the Welfare State', pp. 549-574 in W. Salverda, B. Nolan and T. Smeeding (eds) *The Oxford Handbook of Economic Inequality*. Oxford: Oxford University Press.

Fahey, Tony and Michelle Norris (2010) 'Housing', pp. 519-32 in Francis G Castles, Stephan Leibfried, Jane Lewis, Herbert Obinger and Christopher Pierson (eds.) *Oxford Handbook of the Welfare State*. Oxford: Oxford University Press.

Ferrera, Maurizio (2005) *The Boundaries of Welfare: European Integration and the New Spatial Politics of Social Protection*. Oxford: Oxford University Press.

Flora, Peter, and Alber, Jens, 1981. Modernization, democratization, and the development of welfare states in Western Europe, pp. 37-80 in Peter Flora and Arnold J. Heidenheimer (eds.) *The Development of Welfare States in Europe and America*, New Brunswick, NJ: Transaction Books.

Glennerster, Howard (2010) 'The Sustainability of Western Welfare States', pp. 689-702 in Francis G Castles, Stephan Leibfried, Jane Lewis, Herbert Obinger and Christopher Pierson (eds.) *Oxford Handbook of the Welfare State*. Oxford: Oxford University Press.

Hills, John, John Ditch and Howard Glennerster. 1994. *Beveridge and Social Security. An international Retrospective.* Oxford: Clarendon Press.

Korpi, Walter and Joachim Palme. 2003. New politics and class politics in the context of austerity and globalization: Welfare state regress in 18 countries, 1975–1995. *American Political Science Review,* 97 (3): 425–46

Levy, Jonah H. 2010. 'Welfare state rentrenchment', pp. 552-65 in Francis G Castles, Stephan Leibfried, Jane Lewis, Herbert Obinger and Christopher Pierson (eds.) *Oxford Handbook of the Welfare State.* Oxford: Oxford University Press.

Lindert, Peter H. 2004. Growing Public. Social Spending and Economic Growth Since the Eighteenth Century, 2 vols. Cambridge: Cambridge University Press.

McCashin, Anthony. 2004. *Social Security in Ireland.* Dublin: Gill and Macmillan.

Nolan, Brian and Iwe Marx (2009) 'Economic Inequality, Poverty and Social Exclusion', pp. 315-341 in W. Salverda, B. Nolan and T. Smeeding (eds) *The Oxford Handbook of Economic Inequality.* Oxford: Oxford University Press.

Obinger, Herbert and Uwe Wagschal. 2010. 'Social expenditures and revenues', pp. 333-352 in Francis G Castles, Stephan Leibfried, Jane Lewis, Herbert Obinger and Christopher Pierson (eds.) *Oxford Handbook of the Welfare State.* Oxford: Oxford University Press.

OECD 2010. *Pension Markets in Focus* July, Issue 7.

Pierson, Paul. 1994. *Dismantling the Welfare State? Reagan, Thatcher, and the Politics of Retrenchment.* Cambridge: Cambridge University Press.

Starke, Peter. 2008. *Radical Welfare State Retrenchment: A Comparative Analysis.* Basingstoke: Palgrave Macmillan.

Tapia, Waldo and Juan Yermo. 2007. 'Fees in Individual Account Pensions Systems: A cross-country comparison' OECD Working Paper on Insurance and Private Pensions No. 27, OECD: Financial Affairs Division, Directorate for Financial and Enterprise Affairs

Visser, Jelle. 2006. 'Union membership statistics in 24 countries' *Monthly Labor Review,* January 2006: 38-49

World Bank Independent Evaluation Group, 2006. *Pension Reform: How to Strengthen World Bank Assistance.* Washington,DC: WorldBank. Available at http://lnweb90.worldbank.org/OED/OEDDocLib.nsf/OEDSearch?OpenForm

2

The Welfare State across Selected OECD Countries: How much does it really cost and how good is it in reducing poverty?

Willem Adema[1]

This chapter argues that the conventional measures of public spending are incomplete measures of welfare state effort. They can be improved upon by accounting for private social spending and the effects that tax systems have on social expenditure: direct taxation of benefit income; indirect taxation of consumption by benefit-recipients; and the award tax breaks with a social purpose. There are significant differences in the extent to which private spending and tax systems affect levels of social support, so accounting for these issues is crucial to international comparisons of the welfare state.

Public and private social expenditure programmes may also have different redistributive effects. However, cross-national differences in redistribution are not just related to individual programme design, but also to the overall level of social spending, and the nature of tax systems. Net spending indicators may give a better idea of "true" levels of social spending they do not cover employer social security contributions and private pension contributions which limit their use for assessing re-distribution in tax/benefit systems. In particular, research on the redistributive nature of employer social security contributions would be a most welcome addition to the expanding areas of social welfare research.

---

[1] Willem Adema is a senior economist in the OECD Social Policy Division. He is indebted to Pauline Fron and Maxime Ladaique for statistical support, and he thanks Dominic Richardson for helpful comments. The views expressed in this paper cannot be attributed to the OECD or its Member governments; they are the responsibility of the author alone.

Outline of chapter

Bilbiography

Tables

Boxes

Charts

1. Introduction

1. The welfare state is once again in the spotlight. In the aftermath of the financial crisis that unfolded in 2008/9 public budgets are being reconsidered with an eye on potential savings. Since public welfare spending constitute almost half of general government spending, it is not surprising that social spending programmes are being re-assessed.

2. But what is social welfare? Is it largely public provided or does the private sector play a role? How is it measured, what is included and what not? Most analyses on the size of the welfare state are based on social expenditure data as on public budgets, and relating this spending aggregate to gross domestic product (GDP) then gives a comparison of the size of welfare states across countries. Such an analysis has many advantages, not least that it allows for a detailed examination of different social spending programmes. But it has its shortcomings: it ignores the effect of tax systems as well as private social spending.

3. Tax systems can significantly affect the degree to which expenditure budgets reflect true public social effort. In particular, account should be taken of: direct taxation of benefit income; indirect taxation of consumption out of benefit income; fiscal supports to households that are similar to cash benefits; and, tax breaks to encourage individuals and/or commercial and non-commercial entities to provide social support (e.g. through favourable tax treatment of private pension contributions or tax breaks to charities). Accounting for these effects of the tax system on budgetary allocations with a social purpose leads to indicators of net, *after tax*, public social expenditure.

4. Furthermore, public authorities are also instrumental in generating delivery of social benefits by the private sector. Most directly, governments can mandate individuals to take up certain types of insurance, or employers to provide pension coverage or continued (partial) wage payment in case of sickness. Governments can also

stimulate private provision of benefits or take-up of insurance through favourable fiscal treatment of such arrangements. In all, through regulation and fiscal stimulation governments affect redistribution within private sector arrangements, thereby enhancing their social nature.

5. Inevitably, the analysis of social expenditure starts with outlining methodological concepts. This section is kept short, and may therefore appear somewhat dense: for more detail the interested reader is referred to Adema and Ladaique (2009). On the basis of new and preliminary data in the *OECD Social Expenditure database* (SOCX), the paper then provides new data on gross public and private social expenditure, and indicators on the effect of the tax system on social expenditure (OECD, 2010a). The different public and private spending measures, as adjusted for the effect of taxation on social spending are then considered in view of poverty outcomes, and the paper concludes with considering the overall effect of tax and cash transfers on the redistributive nature of welfare systems.

2. Setting the scene: what is the social domain?

6. The OECD defines social expenditures as:
    "The provision by public and private institutions of benefits to, and financial contributions targeted at, households and individuals in order to provide support during circumstances which adversely affect their welfare, provided that the provision of the benefits and financial contributions constitutes neither a direct payment for a particular good or service nor an individual contract or transfer."

7. Since only benefits provided by institutions are included in the social expenditure definition, transfers between households – albeit of a social nature, are not in the social domain (Adema, and Ladaique, 2009).

8. There are two main criteria which have to be simultaneously satisfied

for an expenditure item to be classified as social in SOCX. First, the benefits have to be intended to address one or more social purposes. Second, programmes regulating the provision of benefits have to involve either a) inter-personal redistribution, or b) compulsory participation

2.1 Social purposes

9. Expenditures with a social purpose towards circumstances that adversely affect welfare include: *Old-age benefits* – pensions and home-help and residential services for the elderly; *Survivor benefits* – pensions and funeral payments; *Incapacity-related benefits* – disability benefits and services, employee sickness payments; *Health expenditure* – spending on in- and out-patient care, medical goods, and prevention; *Family benefits*[3] – child allowances and credits, supports for early childhood care and education[4], income support during leave, sole-parent benefits; *Active Labour Market Policies* – employment services, training, youth measures, subsidised employment, employment measures for the disabled; *Unemployment benefits* – unemployment compensation, early retirement for labour market reasons; *Housing*[5]– housing allowances

---

[3] SOCX does not include public supports for married couples, as there is no international consensus on whether marriage support is a social policy objective or not. Such support can be substantial, and in some countries married couples are viewed as the appropriate unit for taxation (OECD, 2006).

[4] To improve comparisons of public spending on early childhood and education supports, indicators have been adjusted for cross-national differences in the compulsory age of entry into primary school (which vary from age 5 to 7 across the OECD). Expenditures concerns formal supports for children age 0 to and including 5 years of age (OECD, 2010b, *OECD Family database*).

[5] Rent subsidies are considered social, as is residential support for the elderly, disabled and other population groups (as recorded under Old-age, Incapacity-related benefits, etc.). Mortgage relief for low-income households has some similarities with such programmes. However, it is unclear up to what level of income, or what level of property value, such support should be considered social. Relevant thresholds differ across countries, and, in any case, cross-nationally comparable data is not available. Therefore, mortgage relief and capital subsidies towards construction of housing are not considered here.

and rent subsidies; and, *Other contingencies*, other support measures, including non-categorical cash benefits to low-income households, legal aid, supports towards substance abuse, etc.

10. The detailed recording of spending data in SOCX allow for a thorough assessment of quality whilst limiting the risk of double counting. There remain some gaps in data quality, particularly in areas which are the remit of local government. For example, expenditure data on early childhood care and education services or social assistance benefits in federal countries as Canada and Switzerland are deemed of lesser quality than in most OECD countries.

11. SOCX includes data on the magnitude of private social spending across the OECD, but this data is nevertheless deemed of lesser quality than information on budgetary allocations for social support.

2.2 *Compulsion and/or inter-personal redistribution.*

12. Expenditure programmes are considered 'social' if participation is compulsory[6] and/or if they involve inter-personal redistribution of resources among programme participants; in other words, if entitlements are not the result of direct market transactions by individuals given their individual risk profiles. The provision of social services (by public authorities and/or non-government organisations) and social insurance and social assistance programmes practically always involves redistribution across households. Such programmes are either financed through general taxation or social security contributions, which lead to the redistribution of resources across the population or within population groups (*e.g.* all members of an unemployment insurance fund).

---

[6] In theory, it is possible that public and private pension programmes do not involve redistribution of resources across households, but only over time. However, if participation is compulsory that reflects a policy judgement that coverage of these plans is desirable, and hence, these programmes are considered social.

13. Inter-personal redistribution in private programmes is often introduced by government regulation or fiscal intervention. Governments may force individuals and/or employers to take up protection provisions regardless of their risk-profiles or the prevailing market prices. For example, through risk-sharing (*e.g.* through forcing insurance companies to have one price for both sick and healthy people) public policy can subsidise sick people, and thus ensure redistribution between households. Public fiscal intervention to stimulate private take-up on a collective or individual basis also means that the take-up decision is not fully determined by the individual risk-profile or prevalent market prices (the same holds for social benefits derived from collective agreements or taken out by employers on a collective basis). There is a high degree of similarity between legally-stipulated private arrangements and tax-advantaged plans.

2.3 Public, private social and exclusively private expenditure

14. The distinction between public and private social protection is made on the basis of whoever controls the relevant financial flows; public institutions or private bodies. Public social spending concerns programmes whose financing is controlled by different levels of government and social security funds, as income support payments. All social benefits not provided by general government are considered 'private'.

15. Private social benefits can be categorized in two broad groups. First, there are mandatory private social benefits, including legally stipulated employment-related incapacity-related cash transfers, such as sickness, disability and occupational injury benefits and, pensions derived from mandatory contributions. Second, there is a range of voluntary private social expenditure items, including: social services provided by NGOs, employer-provided income support during child-related leave or sickness, and pensions derived from employer contributions or fiscally advantaged individual contributions (as in the National Accounts, SOCX records pensions

paid to former civil servants through autonomous funds as a private spending item, e.g. Denmark, Sweden and the United Kingdom).

16. Take-up of individual insurance, even with a social purpose, is a matter for the persons concerned, and premiums are based on the individual preferences and the individual risk profile. For example, if someone takes out private pension insurance which is actuarially fair, then there is no *ex ante* redistribution across households. The insurance company sets the price so that the individual can expect to receive back in compensation payments exactly what it costs him or her. Such spending is not considered social, but 'exclusively private'. Table 1 summarizes which expenditures are social and which are not.

Table 1: Categorisation of benefits with a social purpose [1,2]

	Public		Private	
	Mandatory	*Voluntary*	*Mandatory*	*Voluntary*
Redistribution	Means-tested benefits, social insurance benefits	Voluntary participation in public insurance programmes. Self-employed 'opting in' to obtain insurance coverage.	Employer-provided sickness benefits, benefits accruing from mandatory contributions to, for example, pension or disability insurance.	Tax-advantaged benefits, *e.g.* individual retirement accounts, occupational pensions, employer-provided health plans
No redistribution	Benefits from government managed individual saving schemes		Non tax-advantaged actuarially fair pension benefits	*Exclusively private*: Benefits accruing from insurance plans bought at market prices given individual preferences.

(1) By definition transfers between individuals, also when of a social nature, are not considered to be within the social domain.
(2) The shaded cells reflect benefits that are NOT classified as social.

3. The size of the welfare state: indicators on social spending

3.1 Public social spending before taxation

17. Since 1980, gross public social expenditure has increased from about
16.0% to 20.6% of GDP in 2003/4 before falling back to 20% on
average across the 30 OECD countries (Chart 1). Experiences differ
across OECD countries, but on average, public social spending-to-
GDP ratios increased most significantly in the early 1980s, early
1990s and, again in the beginning of this millennium, when the
average public spending-to-GDP increased by almost 1.5% of GDP
from 2000 to 2003. Except for Denmark, Ireland, and Sweden,
spending-to-GDP ratios were considerably higher in 2007 than they
were in 1980 in most selected countries[7]. During the 1980s social
spending-to-GDP ratios in Ireland reached 20%, but with sustained
GDP-growth outpacing spending increments, spending-to-GDP
ratios have oscillated around 15 percentage points until 2008. In
2008/9, the contraction in GDP and the increase in unemployment
and social assistance spending will have led to a marked increase of
social spending-to-GDP ratios in most OECD countries (Box 1).

18. On average across the OECD, spending on cash benefits (11.3% of
GDP) is 3 percentage points higher than spending on health and social
services (Chart 2). Public pension transfers to the retired population
and survivors at 7.2% of GDP and public spending on health care
services at 6.1% of GDP are the largest spending items. By comparison,

---

[7] At the time of writing, work on updating OECD gross and net social expenditure
indicators was ongoing. The data concern 2007, as estimates on taxation of benefits
income become available two to three years after the relevant year. Because of this
as well as presentation reasons, in parts of the paper the analysis has been restricted
to a limited group of OECD countries, broadly representing the different groupings
of welfare systems and the geographical spread of OECD countries. The selected
countries included Ireland, the larger European countries, France, Germany, Italy
and the United Kingdom, two Nordic countries (Denmark and Sweden) as well as
Japan and the United States.

public spending on income transfers to the working-age population is on average considerably lower across the OECD at just over 4.1% of GDP in 2007, while spending on social service other than health is around 2.2% of GDP. Only Nordic countries spend considerable more, because of the comprehensive system of early childhood care and education supports as well as services for the elderly.

19. Cross-national variation in social spending is considerable, in particular for public pension expenditure. Public pension spending is highest in France, Germany and Italy and much lower in the US, Denmark, the UK and Ireland. The reasons for this are many and include: the relative importance of in-kind benefit provision to the elderly (Denmark); low gross mandatory pension benefit replacement rates in Ireland, the UK and the US (OECD, 2009a); the US and particularly Ireland have old-age dependency rates well below the OECD average (OECD, 2009b); and, the relative importance of private pensions (see below).

3.2 Private social expenditure

20. In terms of benefits paid and services delivered private pension payments are the largest private social expenditure item across the OECD area at almost 2% of GDP. Health services covered by private health insurers amount to almost 5.5% of GDP and 1.5% of GDP in France. Employer-provided sick-pay is most important in Germany and Sweden. Social services by NGOs are important, but these organisations are not obliged to report to central agencies. Hence, there is no comprehensive dataset on the magnitude of social benefits provided by NGOs.

> **Box 1. Austerity measures and family and child policies: an initial overview**
>
> Over the years, the unfolding ageing of populations has led to pension reform in many OECD countries. Frequently, such reform involved increasing retirement ages, as part of a more general drive to put pension systems on a more financially sustainable footing (OECD, 2009a).
>
> The financial crisis which started to unfold in 2008 has put welfare programmes under more pressure, although initially many European governments increased the generosity (in terms of eligibility criteria, and/or duration, and/or supplementary payments) of income supports for unemployed low-income families (Richardson, 2010).
>
> In the area of family policy (including child allowances, fiscal supports for families, income support during leave, and family services including early childhood care and education supports), many European governments are planning austerity measures. Austerity packages have been approved or are under approval in Denmark, Germany, Greece, Ireland, Italy, Portugal, Spain and the United Kingdom. Austerity packages have been announced in Estonia, France, Hungary, Luxembourg, and Slovenia. Discussions are ongoing following elections in Belgium, the Czech Republic, Finland, the Netherlands, the Slovak Republic and Sweden. There are no austerity measures in the family policy area in Poland and Austria; indeed, in Austria family supports were increased in response to the unfolding crisis.
>
> Family policy supports in both Korea and notably Japan are being extended with the aim to support families to have more children (OECD, 2007). In the US the "Recovery Act" included special measures extending family policies to the working poor including in-work benefits and the Earned Income Tax Credit. Australia plans to roll out paid parental leave supports in 2011. Following elections in New Zealand plans to extend free early childhood care and education services to 2-year olds have been shelved, and reform to limit unconditional income support for sole parents to when children are in primary school is being considered.
>
> Thus far, most of the measures are of a temporary nature, the few benefits that have been scrapped altogether include the first child tax break in Estonia, and the baby / maternity / trust fund / health grants in Spain and the UK. Up to now, there has been no reform which added an income or means-test to universal benefits (Richardson, 2010).

Chart 1: Social expenditure has increased significantly since 1980

Public social expenditure-to-GDP ratio, 1980-2007, preliminary data

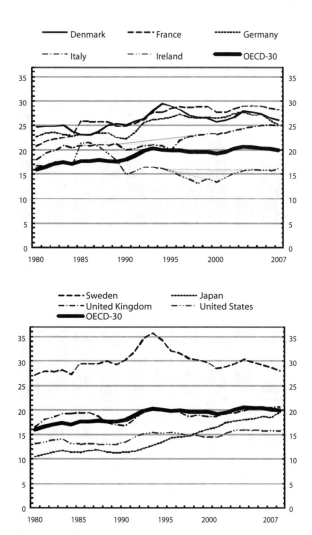

Source: OECD (2010a), *OECD Social Expenditure database.*

Chart 2: In terms of spending are pensions and health the most important social policy areas?

Public social expenditure by broad social policy area, in percentage of GDP in 2007, preliminary data

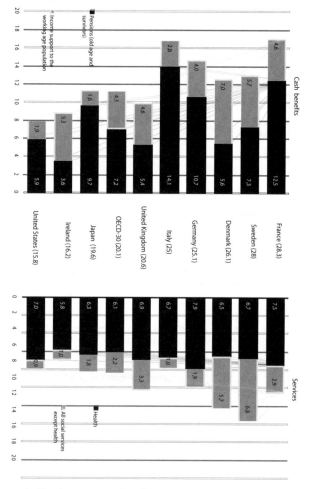

Countries are ranked by decreasing order of public social expenditure as a percentage of GDP. Spending on Active Labour Market Programs (ALMPs) cannot be split by cash/services breakdown; they are however included in the total public spending-to-GDP ratios shown in brackets.

Source: OECD (2010a), OECD Social Expenditure database, preliminary data.

The Future of the Welfare State

Chart 3: Private social expenditure largely concerns pensions across the OECD, but not in France, Germany or the US

Private social expenditure by broad social policy area, in percentage of GDP in 2007, preliminary data

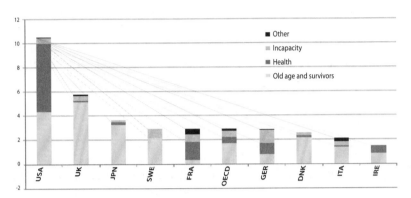

Source: OECD (2010a), OECD Social Expenditure database, preliminary data.

21. Already in the mid-1990s, the value of spending on private pension benefits in Ireland amounted to around 1% of GDP (Hughes and Whelan, 1995). Available data indicate that the spending-to-GDP ratio had not increased much until 2007. This suggests that spending on tax expenditures on pensions (See Table 2 below and Hughes, 2008) is about as high as spending on current private pension payments.

3.3 The tax system and social spending

22. Taxation, including social security contributions, is used to finance social support (OECD, 2009c), and the manner in which this is done influences the redistributive effects of tax/benefit systems (OECD, 2008). Tax systems also affect levels of social expenditure, and broadly speaking they do so through direct and indirect taxation of

benefit income, and the provision of social supports through the tax system, so-called tax breaks with a social purpose.

23. There is a range of methodological and measurement issues involved in the estimation of the effects of tax systems on social expenditure. This discussion is not presented here, but can be found in Adema and Ladaique (2009). For our purposes here, it suffices to say that generally, the quality of estimates on the size of taxation of benefit income and tax breaks with a social purpose is considered lower than the quality of information on public social expenditure.

3.3.1. Clawing back benefit income through direct and indirect taxation

24. Tax systems are also used to claw back social support in two ways. First, through *direct taxation of benefit income*, Governments levying income tax and social security contributions on cash transfers to beneficiaries. Second, benefit income is provided to finance consumption of goods and services by recipients and consumption is subject to indirect taxation.

25. The extent to which benefit income is taxed varies hugely across countries, and thus affects international comparisons of social support. For example, in Sweden a sole parent with two children on unemployment benefit who previously was on average earnings, pays about 20% of his/ her income to the government through income taxation and social security contributions, whereas unemployment benefit income in Germany and Japan is not subject to taxation (OECD, 2010c). This means that in net terms, i.e. after tax, differences in aggregate spending on unemployment benefits between Sweden and Germany and Japan are not as large as suggested by gross spending indicators. Apart from variation across countries, different benefits are also taxed differently. Child benefits, social assistance and housing support are generally not taxed across the OECD; pensions and income support payments during periods

of child-related leave, sickness and invalidity are often part of taxable income.

26. Taxation of consumption using benefit income is lowest in non-European OECD countries, since indirect tax rates are lower. Adema and Ladaique (2009) estimated that in 2005, on average indirect tax rates on consumption in Japan (6.6%) and the US (4.3%) were very low compared to Sweden (20.5%), Ireland (21%) and Denmark (25.9%). Consequently, in non-European countries with limited indirect taxation, gross spending levels can also be relatively low to generate the same net income level for benefit recipients in European countries.

27. At just below 5% of GDP at factor cost in 2007, direct taxation of benefit income (including private transfers) is particularly high in large welfare states such as Denmark and Sweden, three times as high as the OECD average at 1.7% (Chart 4). Direct tax on public benefit income is 0.5% of GDP or less in Japan and Ireland. Indirect taxation of consumption out of benefit income is around 3 to 3.5% of GDP in Denmark, France and Sweden, and about 2.5% of GDP in the other selected European countries. In Japan and the US it amounted to 1 percentage point of GDP or less.

28. Taken together, through direct and indirect taxation of benefit income Danish and Swedish Exchequers claw back about 8 percentage points of GDPfc, while this is about 3 to 5 percentage points of GDPfc in other European countries, and less than 2% of GDPfc in Japan and the US.

Chart 4: Benefit income in Denmark and Sweden is taxed heavily

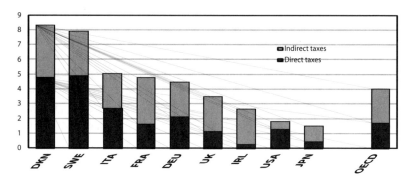

Direct and Indirect tax of benefit income, percentage of GDP at factor costs, 2007, preliminary data

Data for the United States refer to 2005. Data for indirect taxes refer to 2005
GDP at market prices is the most frequently used indicator on the size of an economy.
However, net social spending indicators are better related to GDP at factor cost, because
both Net spending indicators and GDPfc are adjusted for the value of indirect taxation.
Source: OECD (2010a), OECD Social Expenditure database, preliminary data.

3.3.2. Providing social support through the tax system

29. The tax system can be used to directly provide social support to clients, and this delivery channel is often used to support families with children, most notably in France, Germany and the United States (Chart 5). In Germany in 2007 tax relief for children amounted to EUR 36.6 billion of which EUR 20.9 was off-set against tax liabilities and EUR 15.7 billion paid out in transfer income. Similarly, in 2005, the cost of the Earned Income Tax Credit in the US amounted to USD 43.2 billion, of which USD 5.0 billion off-setting tax liabilities of clients and USD 38.2 billion in cash payments. In many OECD countries, support for families with children is also embedded in the tax unit. In France, fiscal support towards children through a variety of fiscal measures (including the 'Quotient Familial') amounted to EUR 13.6 billion in 2007. In all, the role of the

tax system in providing family support was most pronounced in France, Germany and the United States with fiscal benefits towards families amounting to around 1% of GDPfc.

Chart 5: Tax breaks with a social purpose are most important in France, Germany and the US

Tax breaks with a social purpose (excluding pensions), 2007, preliminary data

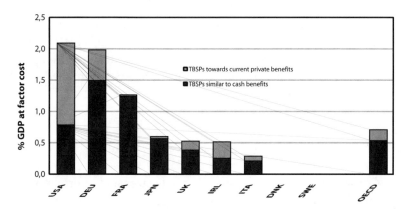

Data for the United States refer to 2005. Data for indirect taxes refer to 2005
Source: OECD (2010a), OECD Social Expenditure database, preliminary data.

30. Governments also use the tax system to stimulate the take-up of private protection insurance coverage by individuals and/or employment-related plans. These tax breaks can be categorised in two broad groups. First, there are 'Tax breaks towards *current* private social benefits', *i.e.* favourable tax treatment aimed at stimulating the provision of private social benefits in the current year such as voluntary private unemployment coverage or private health insurance. This type of tax break is important in Germany (where about 18% of the population is covered by private health insurance) and, particularly in the US where the exclusion of employer

contributions for medical insurance premiums and medical care amounted to about 1.0% of GDP (Chart 5).

31. Second, there are tax breaks towards pensions. These are important, but there is, as yet, no comparable data set available on the value of tax breaks for pensions. Favourable tax treatment of pensions can be in three different forms: tax exemptions for contributions to private pensions; tax relief for investment income of capitalised pension funds; and tax relief for pension benefits. These three forms of support should be netted out against each other according to a common methodology to facilitate international comparison. However, at present such a data set does not exist. Consequently, the information which is available has been included in Table 2 (below) as a memorandum item. Nevertheless, it is clear that fiscal supports for private pensions are important in Germany, Japan, the United States and Ireland.

3.3.3. From gross public to net total social expenditure

32. Considering gross public spending indicators and information on the effects of the tax system on social spending gives an indicator of *net current public social expenditure*. This indicator gives an impression of the real magnitude of budgetary efforts in the social field. Also considering information on private social spending and taxation of such benefit income identifies that proportion of an economy's domestic production to which recipients of social benefits can lay claim: *net total (public and private) social expenditure*.

33. At about one-third of GDPfc gross public spending is highest in France and Sweden among the countries selected here as well as across the OECD. Gross spending is lowest in Ireland (19%) and the US at 17% of GDPfc.

34. In most countries, governments claw back more money through direct and indirect taxation of public transfer income than they

award in tax advantages for social purposes. Hence, net public spending is often lower than gross amounts. But the effect of tax systems varies considerably across countries. For example, in France net public social expenditure, is close to 30% of GDPfc, only 3 percentage points below gross spending levels. This is because direct taxation of benefit income in France is limited, while French policy (as in Germany) also makes intensive use of fiscal supports for families. By contrast, net public social spending is around a quarter of GDPfc in Denmark and Sweden

35. In the United States, gross public spending is actually lower than net public spending, because they tax benefit income at very low rates, but use their tax system relatively intensively to deliver social support directly or indirectly subsidise its private provision.

36. Pulling together all the information on public and private social benefits and the importance of tax systems facilitates comparisons of net total social expenditure. This proportion is highest at 33% of GDPfc in France. Denmark, Germany, Italy, the United Kingdom and the United States all spend about 25 to 29% of GDPfc on social effort. Total social spending is around 24% of GDPfc in Japan and on (a preliminary) average across the OECD. Total social spending is considerably lower in Ireland at 18%, but as noted that does not include an estimate on private pension expenditure. The similarity of net spending levels is driven by including private social spending, particularly in the UK and the US, and the relatively high level of direct and indirect taxation on income transfers and ensuing in European countries vis-à-vis non-European countries

Table 2: From gross public to net total social spending, 2007

Social expenditure, in percentage of GDP at factor cost, 2007, preliminary data

	DNK	FR	GER	IRL	ITL	JPN	SWE	UK	US	OECD
1 Gross public social expenditure	30.7	33.0	28.1	18.9	28.8	21.3	32.9	23.9	17.1	24.3
Direct taxes and social contributions	3.8	1.6	1.5	0.2	2.5	0.4	4.1	0.3	0.5	1.5
2 Net cash direct public social expenditure	26.9	31.3	26.6	18.6	26.3	20.8	28.8	23.2	16.6	
Indirect taxes (on cash benefits)	3.0	2.8	2.0	2.1	2.1	0.8	2.5	1.5	0.4	2.0
3 Net direct public social expenditure	23.8	28.5	24.6	16.5	24.2	20.1	26.3	21.6	16.2	21.5
+T1 TBSPs similar to cash benefits	0.0	1.2	1.5	0.3	0.2	0.5	0.5	0.7	0.8	0.6
Indirect taxes	0.0	0.2	0.2	0.1	0.0	0.0	0.3	0.7	0.0	
4 Net TBSPs similar to cash benefits	0.0	1.0	1.3	0.2	0.2	0.5	0.5	0.9	0.8	0.5
+T2 TBSPs towards current private benefits	0.0	0.0	0.4	0.3	0.1	0.0	0.5	0.3	1.8	
5 Net TBSPs (not including pensions)	0.0	1.1	1.8	0.5	0.3	0.5	0.3	0.7	2.6	0.6
6 Net current public social expenditure	23.8	29.7	26.4	17.0	24.5	20.6	26.6	22.8	18.8	21.8
7 Gross mandatory private soc. Exp.	0.3	0.4	1.2	0.0	1.4	0.6	0.3	0.7	0.4	0.4
Direct taxes and social contributions	0.1	0.1	0.4	0.0	0.2	0.0	0.1	0.1	0.0	
Indirect taxes	0.0	0.0	0.1	0.0	0.2	0.0	0.1	0.0	0.0	
8 Net current mand. private soc. exp.	0.1	0.3	0.7	0.0	0.7	0.6	0.1	0.5	0.4	2.5
9 Net publicly mandated soc. exp. [6+8][b]	24.0	29.9	27.1	16.9	25.8	21.2	26.3	22.5	18.4	
10 Gross voluntary private soc. exp.	2.7	3.0	2.0	1.7	1.6	3.3	3.0	7.8	10.6	2.5
Direct taxes and social contributions	0.9	0.1	0.2	0.2	0.0	0.2	0.6	0.7	0.6	0.6
Indirect taxes	0.4	0.1	0.1	0.1	0.0	0.0	0.5	0.3	0.2	
11 Net current voluntary private soc. exp.	1.4	2.8	1.7	1.5	0.6	3.1	1.9	6.3	9.8	
12 Net current private soc. exp. [8+11]	1.6	3.2	2.4	1.5	2.0	3.7	2.1	7.0	10.2	2.1
13 Net total social expenditure [6+12-T2][c]	25.4	32.9	28.3	18.2	26.4	24.3	28.5	29.4	27.2	23.8
Memorandum items										
TBSPs towards pensions[d]	:	0.0	0.9	1.4	0.0	0.8	0.0	:	0.9	:

Data for the United States refer to 2005. Data for indirect taxes refer to 2005.

GDP at market prices is the most frequently used indicator on the size of an economy. However, net social spending indicators are better related to GDP at factor cost, because both Net spending indicators and GDPfc are adjusted for the value of indirect taxation.

Source: OECD (2010a), OECD Social Expenditure database, preliminary data.

4 Re-distribution of income

4.1. Social expenditure indicators and income poverty

37. Considered together the social expenditure and income poverty outcomes (as measured in terms of disposable income) provide an indication of the redistributive power of social expenditures. Chart 6 shows poverty rates as cross-plotted against gross public social expenditure (Panel A); gross private social expenditure (Panel B); net public social expenditure (Panel C) and net total social expenditure (Panel D) using preliminary data on income poverty (based on EU-SILC for EU countries) and social expenditure for 26 OECD countries.[8]

38. The picture emerges that gross public expenditures are effective in reducing poverty, while private social expenditures have the opposite effect. Furthermore, once account has been taken of the effect of taxation on benefit income and tax breaks with a social purpose, the linkage between net public social spending and poverty is much smaller than for gross spending, and almost disappears when net total social expenditures is considered (see also Castles and Obinger, 2007; Goudswaard and Caminada, 2009; and, Caminada, Goudswaard and Koster (2010)). [9]

---

[8] Outcomes for Korea and Mexico have been excluded from the analysis here for reasons of robustness. These are countries with relatively low public spending and above average poverty rates (Chile would be similar) and are thus statistical outliers.

[9] These four indicators of social expenditure can also be linked with indicators on poverty reduction (differences in poverty rates at market income and poverty rates at disposable income) or indicators on the reduction of inequality (the Gini coefficient measured at market prices and the Gini–coefficient at disposable income) and generate similar results (not reported here). Gross public social spending reduces further poverty reduction and reduces inequality, with weaker effects for net public and total social expenditure, while private spending as measured here, is associated with reduced poverty reduction and reduced income inequality. However, it seems inappropriate to link private social spending and changes in poverty and income inequality at market income and disposable income, as private transfers are included in market income, and thus do not affect the difference between market income and disposable income in the way public spending does.

Chart 6: Income poverty and different indicators of social expenditure

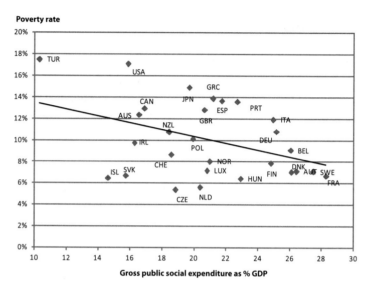

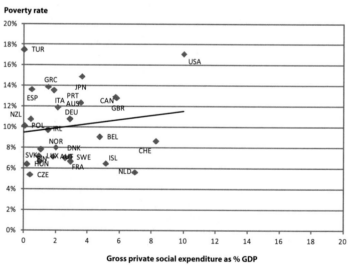

Chart 6: Poverty and different indicators of social expenditure (continued)

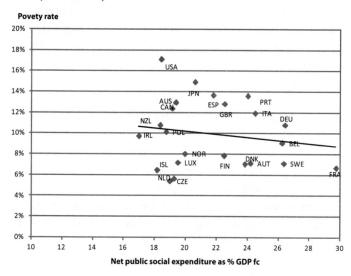

Povety rate

Net public social expenditure as % GDP fc

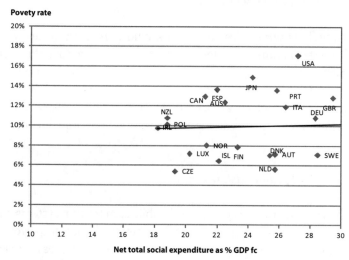

Povety rate

Net total social expenditure as % GDP fc

The income poverty rate is measured against the usual threshold of 50% of median equivalized household income.

Source: EU-SILC and preliminary OECD data on poverty and income distribution and social expenditure.

39. Poverty indicators are income-based and are limited in the sense that they do not account for differences in access to services across the population. That is a drawback, but not one which invalidates the use of poverty rates. However, there are different items that are not covered in the indicators of social expenditure whose omission is likely to affect the results, including (see Adema and Whiteford, 2010, for more detail):

- Private social spending by charities: more comprehensive data on such spending would enhance the distributive effect of private spending.
- Personal income tax and social security contributions by workers not in receipt of benefit income, are not covered in the analysis.
- Employer social security contributions are not covered in the calculations; these are insignificant in Denmark while they account for more than a quarter of tax revenue in France (OECD, 2009c).
- Employer contributions to pension and other employer-provided supports are not covered.

Household surveys are used to look at how broad categories of public transfer income are allocated to households across the income distribution, although often not on a programme by programme basis. However, employer contributions to public and private social benefits are not covered by these surveys, and little is therefore known about their redistributive effect on household incomes.

4.2 Taxes and public cash transfers

40. Considering the effect of tax and public cash transfer systems, rather than social expenditure levels, is a better, though imperfect (see below), way of looking at the redistribution of resources in societies.

41. Table 3 illustrates the nature of redistribution towards people in the lowest quintile of the income distribution, and does so by separately identifying the role of gross public transfers (the first three columns)

and then taxes and social security contributions (data for 2007/8 is not yet available). The role of cash transfers in supporting the income of people in the bottom quintile is computed by first estimating the average ratio of cash transfers as a percentage of household disposable income measured in income surveys (Column A); second, by calculating how much of this share goes to the poorest 20% of the population (Column B); and finally, by multiplying the size of spending by the progressivity of its distribution to calculate gross benefits accruing to people at the lower end of the distribution (divided by 100, in Column C). The same procedure is used to calculate how much tax is paid by people at the lower end of the distribution, while the difference between the two values (in Column G) represents the "net" cash transfers to the lowest income quintile.

42. The results in Table 3 include:

1. Further evidence corroborating the finding that Anglophone countries pay less generous transfers, place a limited tax burden on low-income families, and in these countries the value of the public transfers to people in the lowest quintile (Column C) is at least 15 times that of the household taxes they pay (Column F). By contrast, Denmark and Sweden transfer large amounts of gross benefits to low-income people but also levy a significant amount of household taxes on them.

2. Public cash transfers are more targeted to the poorest 20% of the population in Denmark, Ireland and the United Kingdom (where the lowest income quintile receive more than 30% of all transfers, and; in this sense the level of targeting is roughly similar in Sweden, and the United States).

3. There are large differences in the overall size of the redistribution towards low income households: this ranges from almost 6% of household disposable income in Denmark and Sweden, to values of around 2% in Japan and the United States (Column G).

Table 3: Denmark, Ireland and Sweden are successful in transferring public social spending to low-income groups

Redistribution through cash transfers and household taxes towards low-income groups, mid-2000s

	Gross public transfers paid to households			Direct taxes and social security contributions paid by households			
	A. Average ratio of household disposable income	B. Share of public transfers paid to lowest quintile	C. Transfers to lowest quintile (A*B/100)	D. Average ratio of household disposable income	E. Share of taxes paid by lowest quintile	F. Taxes from lowest quintile (D*E/100)	G. Net transfers to lowest quintile (C-F)
Denmark	25.6	36.0	9.2	52.5	6.1	3.2	6.0
France	32.9	16.2	5.3	26.0	5.6	1.5	3.9
Germany	28.2	17.4	4.9	35.5	2.1	0.7	4.2
Ireland	17.7	30.8	5.4	19.4	0.9	0.2	5.3
Italy	29.2	12.6	3.7	30.2	1.8	0.6	3.1
Japan	19.7	15.9	3.1	19.7	6.0	1.2	2.0
Sweden	32.7	25.9	8.5	43.2	6.5	2.8	5.7
United Kingdom	14.5	31.4	4.6	24.1	1.7	0.4	4.1
United States	9.4	24.8	2.3	25.6	1.6	0.4	1.9
OECD-23	22.0	24.4	5.4	28.3	4.2	1.2	4.2

Note: Values in Columns A and D are the ratios of public transfers and household taxes, respectively, in the disposable income of the entire population; Columns B and E show the shares of public transfers and household taxes received and paid, respectively, by people of the bottom quintile of the population. Data refer to the mid-2000s for all countries.
Source: OECD (2008), *Growing Unequal?*

43. Thus, redistribution as measured in Table 3 depends on size of spending, the targeted nature of the social protection programme, and the progressivity in the tax system. Table 3 underestimates redistribution in Denmark and Sweden as it does not capture the redistributive effects of tax-financed provision of social services to different population groups. And Chart 2 showed that both these countries spend much more on public social services for the elderly, and early childhood care and education facilities for families of working age than the other countries (and most other OECD countries).

5. Conclusions

44. Conventional measures of public spending are incomplete measures of welfare state effort. They can be improved upon by taking account of private social expenditures which are legally mandated or financially stimulated by government intervention. Furthermore, account should be taken of: tax advantages for social purposes (*e.g.* child tax allowances); direct taxation of benefit income; and indirect taxation of consumption by benefit-recipients.

45. There are significant differences across countries in the extent to which social policy goals are pursued through the tax system or in the role of private provision within national social protection systems. These differences point to substantial variance in the redistributional nature of social systems. Some private social programmes may generate a more limited re-distribution of resources than public ones, and tax advantages towards private pension and health plans are more likely than not to benefit the relatively well-to-do. Private employment-related social benefits mostly re-allocate income between the (formerly) employed population, and the same holds largely true for fiscally-advantaged individual or group retirement plans. Cross-national differences in redistribution are not just related to individual programme design, but also to the overall level of social spending. Income re-distribution

in a high public spending country such as Denmark tends to be larger than in, for example, the US, where private social spending plays a much more substantial role.

46. Although net after-tax measures of social expenditure give a better idea of levels of social effort, important items are missing from the net spending framework, which limit their use for assessing re-distribution in tax/benefit systems. Arguably, most important is the lack of good information on employer social security contributions and private pension contributions and their redistributive effect, and innovative studies in this regard would be a very welcome contribution to social research.

47. Finally, the financial crisis which started to unfold in 2008 will exert further pressure on social spending. Initially, many countries extended income supports to help those affected by the crisis, but in an increasing number of European countries austerity packages are being introduced that will limit access to social welfare provisions. The challenge will be to cut smartly and spend wisely: public welfare programmes will be re-assessed on their efficiency in providing support to people, supporting people of working-age back to work and investing in human capital the moment it matters most.

Bilbiography

Adema, W. and M. Ladaique (2009), "How Expensive is the Welfare State? Gross and Net Indicators on the OECD Social Expenditure Database (SOCX)", Social, Employment and Migration Working Papers, No. 92, OECD, Paris (www.oecd.org/els/workingpapers).

Adema, W and P. Whiteford (2010), "Chapter 9: Public and Private Social Welfare", In Castles *et al*, (Eds), *The Oxford Handbook of the Welfare State*, Oxford University Press.

Caminada, K., K. Goudswaard, and F. Koster (2010), "Social Income Transfers and Poverty Alleviation in OECD Countries", *Leiden Law School, Department of Economics Research memorandum 2010.01*, Universiteit van Leiden

Castles, F.G. and H. Obinger (2007), "Social expenditure and the politics of redistribution", *Journal of European Social Policy*, August 2007; 17: 206 - 222

Goudswaard, K. and K. Caminada (2009), "The redistributive effect of public and private social programmes: a cross-country empirical analysis", *International Social Security Review*, Vol.63, 1/2010, pp. 1-19.

Gauthier, A. (2010) *The Impact of the Economic Crisis on Family Policies in the European Union*. European Commission, Employment, Social Affairs and Equal Opportunities DG. Downloaded at http://ec.europa.eu/employment_social/emplweb/families/admintool/ userfiles/file/Final%20revised.pdf, July 2010.

Hughes. G (2008), "The case for a Universal State Pension: Lessons from New Zealand for Ireland's Green paper on Ireland", Social Justice Ireland (www.socialjustice.ie/sites/default/files/file/socialpolicy08/chapter7.pdf).

Hughes, G and B.J. Whelan (1995), *Occupational and Personal Pension Coverage*, 1995, the Economic and Social Research Institute, Dublin.

OECD (2006), *OECD Taxing Wages 2004-2005*, OECD, Paris.

OECD (2007a), *Babies and Bosses, Reconciling Work and Family Life, - A Synthesis of findings for*

OECD countries, OECD, Paris (www.oecd.org/els/social/family).

OECD (2008), *Growing Unequal: Income distribution and Poverty in OECD Countries*, OECD, Paris (www.oecd.org/els/social/inequality).

OECD (2009a), *Pensions at a Glance*, OECD, Paris.

OECD (2009b), *Society at a Glance: OECD Social Indicators 2008*, OECD, Paris.

OECD (2009c), *Revenue Statistics 1965 -2008*, OECD, Paris

OECD (2010a), *OECD Social Expenditure database 1980 – 2007*, OECD, Paris (www.oecd.org/els/social/expenditure), *forthcoming.*

OECD (2010b), *OECD Family database*, OECD, Paris (www.oecd.org/els/social/family/database).

OECD (2010c), "OECD Tax-Benefit Models", OECD, Paris (www.oecd.org/els/social/workincentives).

Richardson, D. (2010), "Child and Family Policies in a Time of Economic Crisis", Children and Society, *forthcoming.*

3.

Shaping Public Policy: Is there a place for values-led debate and discourse in the public sphere?

Daniel O'Connell

Introduction

This paper argues that there ought to be a place for values-led debate and discourse in the public sphere. It uses faith communities as a focus for developing its position. The paper outlines the importance of our public lives and the values of civil society as a buffer against the encroachment of the state and the market, and it points out the contribution of faith-communities to this endeavour. In analysing faith communities it outlines the reasons for the public presence of the Christian faith tradition, an inherently public religion. It goes on to explore the issues around justifying participation by faith-communities in public debate and the legitimate role of government in this process. It outlines three approaches to public participation by a particular faith community that is in keeping with the principles established earlier in the paper and extrapolates from these some suggestions for all who participate in the public sphere.

Civil Society and Public Life

There are many meanings to the word 'public'. At a very basic level, the public refers to all the people in a society. It makes sense to say something like: 'In the eyes of the public, she did the right thing'. But it can also refer to distinct groups of people within a society who share a common interest. We can have the theatre going public, the Cosmo reading public, or the football public. This happens when people gather around shared interests, perhaps objects, other people or movements. Finally, when used as an adjective, public describes openness and accessibility. A public hospital is there for all, a public park can be shared by everyone and a public good, such as a clean environment, is in the common interest.

Just as a public can refer to everyone, a particular interest group, or be used as an adjective, it is important to note that there are different sorts of publics. Alastair Hannay, in *On the Public*, makes this point tellingly when he asks: "Did Roman citizens form a public? Was there ever an Iraqi public? What about present day China?"[10] If someone were to answer 'yes' to any of these questions, then we need to wonder if the use of the word public in these cases has the same meaning as when we refer to the public in Ireland today? And if not, what is the difference?

Being a public is more than having freedom to move about in public spaces as one wishes or to gather as an audience around a common interest. Both of these could have been enjoyed by the Romans. Rather, an essential element "includes the freedom to influence public debate." [11] The opportunity to participate in matters of common concern goes to the heart of a democratic society. A healthy public life helps political institutions to become accountable. It pre-exists political life and allows people to gather casually in a myriad of places throughout society, where they form common lives, where they reflect and feel and debate and disagree about issues of concern to them. This is essential if politics is not to be a 'theatre of illusion', with the real work going on backstage. "Public life creates community which both establishes legitimate government and holds it accountable to what people want".[12] This is in keeping with the Latin meaning of the word public – *publius*, the people. It is the realm governed by the people and the source of the republic – *Res Publica* – 'things of the public.'

---

[10]   Alastair Hannay, *On the Public* (London ; New York: Routledge, 2005), 3.

[11]   Ibid., 19.

[12]   Parker J. Palmer, *The Company of Strangers : Christians and the Renewal of America's Public Life* (New York: Crossroad, 1981), 23.

Public and Private

I return to the idea of the public as all the people we meet in our daily lives, those we know but most of all, those we don't know. Parker Palmer in *The Company of Strangers* describes it very well when he says that:

> The word 'public' as I understand it contains a vision of our oneness, our unity, our interdependence upon one another. Despite the fact that we are strangers to one another—and will stay stranger for the most part—we occupy a common space, share common resources, have common opportunities, and must somehow learn to live together. To acknowledge that one is a member of the public is to recognize that we are members of one another.[13]

This vision must do battle with the turn to the 'private' that is so popular today. There is not a great deal of value placed on being 'members of one another.' Rather, we attempt to carve out our own space in society, one protecting us from unwanted interference from others and the state. Our self-understanding is attracted by the notions of individuality and autonomy. In the midst of strangers, complexity and ambiguity, people understandably seek refuge and security in the private realm of life. It is the place where we can 'really be ourselves.'

There is a danger if we see these two spheres in oppositional terms, the private and the public. We need both, a healthy private life and a healthy public life. Hannah Arendt, in *The Human Condition,* points out one of the dangers in an overly privatised life. She warns that:

> [t]o live an entirely private life means above all to be deprived of things essential to a truly human life: to be deprived of the reality that comes from being seen and heard by others, to be deprived of an 'objective' relationship with them that comes from being related to and separated from them through the intermediary of a common world of things.[14]

---

[13] Ibid., 19.
[14] Hannah Arendt, *The Human Condition,* 2 ed. (Chicago: University of Chicago Press, 1986), 58.

An appreciation of how we are all connected, hearkening back to Palmer's view of our interdependence, is essential. We need to be open to other perspectives, insights and ways of living in the world. This is not an easy thing to do – hence the attraction of a private life. Such openness can be difficult to realise, for it might challenge our own assumptions about what we value and force us to take responsibility for what we believe and how we act in a new way. If this is to be a possibility, we need a healthy private life; we need to feel safe in some place, secure and at home. Arendt also supports such a view, warning against too much time being spent in public, in the presence of others, for life will become shallow.[15] She appreciates the need for places that are 'hidden' from the light of publicity if there is to be depth to our lives. But the opposite is also true; the quality of our private lives is also contingent on the quality of our public lives.

A poor public life will negatively impact on the quality of one's private life. Take the example of security. If the public areas in our neighbourhood become unsafe, then our freedom is curtailed and simple tasks like walking to the shops for the newspaper become a worry. There are a number of important aspects to a healthy public life. It is an environment for learning. It is here that "we are reminded that the foundation of life together is not the intimacy of friends but the capacity of strangers to share a common territory, common resources, and common problems — without ever becoming friends."[16]

Public life allows for countless opportunities to meet with the 'other'. In a study of lives committed to the common good, Laurent Daloz et al., in their book *Common Fire, Lives of Commitment in a Complex World*, found that "constructive engagements with otherness was the single most critical element undergirding commitment to the common good in the lives we studied."[17] Everyone in the study described at least one significant experience at some point during their formative years when they

---

[15] Ibid., 71.
[16] Palmer, 31.
[17] Laurent A. Parks Daloz, Cheryl Hollman Keen, James P. Keen, Sharon Parks Daloz, *Common Fire: Leading Lives of Commitment in a Complex World* (Boston: Beacon Press, 1996), 215.

developed a strong attachment with someone previously viewed as 'other' than themselves. The authors found that where people crossed boundaries in liberating and transformative ways, they came to a deeply held conviction that *everyone counts*.[18] This does not *necessarily* happen in public life but it does provide a context for it to take place. These sorts of encounters are not always pleasant or easy. It is in meeting others with whom we disagree, disapprove, or even fear a little, that real transformation can take place.

Public life also provides needed respites and refreshment. There are all sorts of places in the public that help us get through the day – shops, cafes, community centres, faith communities, hairdressers, blogs, social networking sites, bars and theatres. It operates as a centre of communication. It allows for communication between diverse individuals and groups. Finally, public life helps with the creation of cosmopolitans, places where different cultures and ethnicities mix freely, in mutual appreciation for one another. The very fact of living and moving in public life among strangers, does seem, over time to create tolerance and appreciation towards others. There are, of course, many exceptions to this, but public life allows space for human diversity to be openly expressed. And as a consequence, "one of the most critical uses of the public realm is its capacity to teach its residents about tolerance—its capacity to transform its residents into cosmopolitans."[19]

Civil Society

A dimension of public life that contributes towards a healthy balance between the public and private dimension of human existence together is called 'civil society.' It is composed of those 'secondary institutions' or 'mediating structures' that stand between the person and the state on the one hand and the person and the market on the other. Civil society includes families, voluntary and community organisations, religious

---

[18] Ibid., 76.
[19] Lyn H. Lofland, *The Public Realm : Exploring the City's Quintessential Social Territory* (Hawthorne, N.Y.: Aldine de Gruyter, 1998), 237.

institutions, NGOs and neighbourhoods.[20] People are embedded in a host of groups and communities at any one time. They might be members of their own families, socialise with their friends, are members of the local football club, nominal members of their church, sing with a choral society, and do some work with a local charitable organisation.

When thinking of civil society, it is important to remember that it is not a homogenous sphere of society. There is great diversity in it and this is the cause of some tension. In order to be effective at the level of social policy, the sector needs to find a balance between presenting a common set of beliefs and finding a space for the diversity of the sector. A vibrant "civil society is one that provides a space for a diverse range of voices to be heard and where different interests and opinions are respected."[21] But all that goes on in civil society is not positive. For example, racist communities are members of civil society and at times, require the intervention of the state. Although there is great emphasis on the importance of community and belonging in civil society, we need to pay careful attention to what sorts of communities are at work. Communities rich in social capital can be formed in opposition to issues such as immigration or social inclusion. We need to acknowledge the shadow side to civil society.

Civil society shapes identity

At a very fundamental level, the relationships, groups, associations, and communities in civil society shape the kinds of persons we are and will become. In civil society, it is not monetary exchange (the market) or the coercive use of power (the state) that creates and sustains relationships and gives them meaning. Rather it is a commitment to a common purpose characterised by qualities such as love, friendship, loyalty, faithfulness, and trust that is essential here. Civil society fosters pre-political virtues such

---

[20] Don E. Eberly, "The Quest for Civil Society," in *Building a Community of Citizens: Civil Society in the 21st Century*, ed. Don E. Eberly (Lanham: University Press of America, 1994), xxv.

[21] Siobhan Daly, "Mapping Civil Society in the Republic of Ireland," *Community Development Journal* 43, no. 2 (2008): 74.

as civility, integrity, honesty, reliability. These sorts of values are essential to the market and the state. They both need consumers and citizens who are, among other things, trustworthy, honest, loyal, self-controlled, and fair. It is in civil society that these virtues are learned in such a way that they become 'habits of the heart.' It is ironic to think that both the market and the state rely on the sorts of qualities that are produced in civil society and at the same time, they both undermine the very conditions that make their own existence possible. Ties of trust and solidarity are essential to markets – but the market does not foster these sorts of qualities. The state relies on communities to keep it at the service of all the people but it does not foster these conditions on its own.

Such virtues are not learned in an abstract fashion. They are cultivated in the give and take of relationships in specific communities of civil society, which are themselves shaped by the surrounding culture and public institutions. Aristotle pointed this out in the *Nicomachean Ethics*. He saw that the brave were found where bravery was honoured. When the Greeks were at war, it helped to have people who were willing to fight. To recruit soldiers, they built statues to their brave heroes, and they told stories of their great deeds. Children grew up influenced by these sorts of traditions and so were more inclined to follow in the footsteps of those that their community honoured. The same dynamic is at work in the cultivation of all sorts of other qualities, such as trust, compassion, and forgiveness. Bellah et al., in *Habits of the Heart*, refer to these sorts of communities as 'communities of memory.'

The communities of memory that tie us to the past also turn us toward the future as communities of hope. They carry a context of meaning that can allow us to connect our aspirations for ourselves and those closest to us with the aspirations of a larger whole and see our own efforts as being, in part, contributions to the common good.[22] This is a question of "having the social systems, institutions, and environments on which we all depend, work in a manner that benefits all people."[23]

---

[22] Robert N Bellah and others, *Habits of the Heart : Individualism and Commitment in American Life* (New York: Harper & Row, 1985), 153.

[23] Sean Healy and Brigid Reynolds, "Making Choices - Choosing Futures, a Question of Paradigms," in *Making Choices - Choosing Futures: Ireland at a Crossroads* (Dublin: CORI Justice, 2008), 45.

Importance of civil society

Gordon Brown, former British Prime Minister, states:
> My intuition was and still remains that modern politics has been dominated by two entities, the individual and the state. They are embodied in two institutions, namely markets and governments. The shared assumption has been that between them they hold the answer to all social problems. The right prefers the market. The left prefers the state. Both however have found themselves faced with social problems that have resisted all attempts at a solution.[24]

Brown's implicit point is that civil society is essential. In the relationships, institutions, and structures that characterise this dimension of society, people discover the bonds of love and trust, they hear and participate in the collective stories of which they are a part and in which their lives make sense, and they belong to communities of memory where they learn the importance of solidarity and the common good. This takes place through the sharing of common interests, working with others on common projects such as the Tidy Towns competition or through membership of the local football club. Collectively, it is here that the language of 'we' is learned along with the language of 'I'. In civil society, people learn moral literacy, the give and take of rights and responsibilities, and the importance of honesty and fairness. This learning takes place through a myriad of relationships that people are a part of from the cradle to the grave.

Although Tocqueville never used the phrase 'social capital', he understood the importance of those relationships that produced it—families, religious bodies, associations of all kinds—in forming democratic values and habits, and facilitating citizen participation that could influence and moderate the power of government. Finally, Bellah et al., also remind us that along with providing a check on the function and power of the state, these mediating institutions that constitute civil society are "the only alternative we as a nation have ever had, or are likely to discover, to the dominance of business leaders."[25]

---

[24] Jonathan Sacks, *The Politics of Hope* (London: Vintage, 2000), xiv.
[25] Bellah and others, 212.

The Public Sphere

Communication is essential to civil society. People need opportunities to share information, opinion, values and ideas. The public sphere is the metaphor used to refer to this dynamic. According to Jürgen Habermas, it is a "domain of our social life where such a thing as public opinion can be formed [where] citizens...deal with matters of general interest without being subject to coercion...[to] express and publicize their views."[26] It is where and how people find out what is happening in their communities and the world around them. It is the forum in which they see the news, read the papers and magazines, surf the web, blog, podcast, look at television, listen to the radio and so on. But the public sphere is not just a forum for information; it is a space for participation on issues that are of interest to people. They go to meetings, participate in online blogs, write books, articles, journals, submit letters to newspapers, talk on the radio, produce music and theatre, participate in conferences, demonstrations and protests. This sort of participation gives rise to public opinion and helps shape consensus about how to live together. The public sphere is not unlike a public notice board where private citizens can publish their views on a whole range of ideas, not just political, but economic, social, and cultural. The important dimension of all this is how debate becomes public. Circulation is an important feature of this context. "Anything that addresses a public is meant to undergo circulation."[27] The public sphere ought to be characterised by conversation and a diversity of positions.[28] Alan McKee says "We hear a story on the news, then we talk about it with friends; we exchange ideas on email groups, down at the pub, at the hairdresser; we telephone a talkback radio station, write a letter to a magazine, stop buying a newspaper because we disagree with its political stance." [29]

---

[26] As quoted in Alan McKee, *The Public Sphere : An Introduction* (Cambridge ; New York, NY: Cambridge University Press, 2004), 4.

[27] Michael Warner, *Publics and Counterpublics* (New York Zone Books, 2002), 91.

[28] David Tracy has much that is helpful to understand about the dynamics of conversation in *Plurality and Ambiguity: Hermeneutics, Religion, Hope* (Chicago: University of Chicago Press, 1994); and Hans Georg Gadamer, Joel Weinsheimer, and Donald G. Marshall, *Truth and Method*, 2nd, rev. ed., Continuum Impacts (London; New York: Continuum, 2004).

[29] McKee, 5.

Charles Taylor in *Modern Social Imaginaries* points out two important features of the public sphere. It is independent of the political and it has a force of legitimacy.[30] In other words, it can lend credence or credibility to particular perspectives or social arrangements. It is in the public sphere that the public have somewhere to stand that is outside of the political and gives a perspective from which to reflect on society. Political society is founded on the consent of those bound to it. The government must always seek the consent of those governed. And when the public come to a common mind on important matters, through debate and critical reflection, government is obliged to listen to it. "The public sphere is, then, a locus in which rational views are elaborated that should guide government."[31] But the public sphere is more than an instrument to guide government. It is, at its best, a humanising place,[32] where relationships are built across differences, where perspectives are enlarged, and questions about what it means to live a good life are explored and behaviour changed accordingly. The public sphere is a place of contestation.[33]

Habermas believes that there were two essential characteristics to the public sphere. It depends upon both quality of discourse and quality of participation. These are foundational to the public sphere.

A strong public life is essential for the overall cohesion of society and well-being of the person-in-community. Civil society plays a critical role in finding the right balance between the public and private dimensions of our lives. It is the place in society—outside of the state and the market—where civic virtues are taught and interests are acted upon in organized and meaningful ways. Participation in the public sphere itself is essential

---

[30] Charles Taylor, *Modern Social Imaginaries.*, Public Planet Books (Durham: Duke University Press, 2004), 87.

[31] Ibid., 89.

[32] This does not mean that it is always pleasant or enjoyable, but it can build community, consensus, and enlarge our sense of 'we' and improve our sense of 'I' at the same time, see Hannah Arendt, *The Human Condition*, 2nd ed. Chicago: University of Chicago Press, 1986.

[33] This is a phrase used by Jose Casanova to refer to the public as the place in which ideas are contested with one another, see José Casanova, *Public Religions in the Modern World.* Chicago: University of Chicago Press, 1994.

The Future of the Welfare State

if members of the public are not to become passive in the face of the state and simply consumers in response to the market. It is in the public sphere that ideas are generated, contested, accepted or rejected, and these in turn shape identity, understanding, and action.

Religion and Society

There is much discussion about the appropriate place of religious traditions in the public sphere. In the next sections of this chapter, I will explore the relationship between religion and society, its contribution to civil society, the internal logic for the public presence of the Catholic Christian community in the public sphere and three forms this 'public' presence can take.

The relationship between religion and society can be characterised by two very different points of view.[34] The first can be called the 'inclusive' position. It holds that Jerusalem does have something to say to Athens and that it is appropriate for people of faith to bring the social significance of their religious traditions to bear on public issues.

The other view, sometimes referred to as the exclusive position, suggests that religion and religious beliefs are best kept at home or within the church. People who hold this view are conscious of the pluralistic nature of societies today. Since there are many different religious beliefs present in society, they fear that the public involvement of religion will inevitably lead to a loss of freedom for some or the imposition of an agenda that is religiously based, thus compromising the neutrality of the state. Behind these fears is the assumption that religion in public inevitably leads to conflict and division.[35] Our history testifies well to such concerns.

---

[34] See Kent Greenawalt, "Religion and American Political Judgments," *Wake Forest Law Review* 36, no. 219 (2001).

[35] For more about people's fears concerning the negative dimension of religion in public see Kristin E. Heyer, *Prophetic & Public : The Social Witness of U.S. Catholicism* (Washington, D.C.: Georgetown University Press, 2006), Chapter 1; Martin E. Marty and Jonathan Moore, *Politics, Religion, and the Common Good : Advancing a Distinctly American Conversation About Religion's Role in Our Shared Life* (San Francisco: Jossey-Bass Publishers, 2000), 23-41.

The two ways of framing the relationship between religion and society just outlined need more nuance. Religion is not simply a set of convictions that one can bring to bear on issues of public significance. "It is a considerably more dynamic and multidimensional reality than the term 'convictions' might suggest."[36] It is part of the identity of the person and community. It is one of the 'ways' that people make sense of the world in which they live. It shapes how some people see, feel, understand, judge, and act in society. Therefore, it is not so easy to deliberately bring religion into the public sphere (in many ways it is already 'with' people from a religious background, whether they know it or not). This is equally true when one is expected to leave religious beliefs behind in one's private lives (which aspect gets left behind, and how much of one's identity is to be excluded from the public sphere, how does one separate religious convictions from one's values?). The resolution to such issues will depend on the prevailing cultural assumptions about what is the most appropriate place for religious expression and these vary from place to place.

Contribution of Religion to Society

Much of the discussion about religion and society concerns the influence of religion on the working of government and policy issues. This is a very narrow focus and one that misses much of how this relationship actually takes place. David Hollenbach reframes this conversation in a very helpful way. He goes beyond the direct impact of religion on policy choices and explores the more indirect and subtle ways that religion influences politics and society at large. He emphasises the importance of intermediary associations in realising human dignity and the value of civil society as a counter weight to the market on the one hand and the state on the other. "Society is composed of a rich and overlapping set of human communities such as families, neighbourhoods, churches, labour unions, corporations, professional associations, credit unions, co-operatives, universities, and a host of other associations."[37] These overlapping communities, their identity and values, give rise to particular political environments. And it is here, in and among these different communities, that religion has its greatest influence.

---

[36] David Hollenbach, "Contexts of the Political Role of Religion: Civil Society and Culture," *San Diego Law Review* 30, no. 4 (1993): 878.
[37] Ibid.: 884.

Churches make a significant contribution to the qualities of civil society. The fact of religious freedom—something that is essential in the development of democracies—draws attention to the importance of this right for other diverse groups to organize and participate in society.

The right to religious freedom allows religious traditions to be resources to democratic states through their teaching of compassion, love of neighbour, their myths and stories, imagination and source of civic skills.[38] Martin Marty fleshes out the contribution of religion, at its best, to society. He says that one of the positive elements of religious discourse in public is that it reveals the hidden motivations and assumptions of one's conversation partners. "A republic would be better off if everyone brought into the open whatever motivates and impels the citizens to decide and to act."[39] Marty outlines many other contributions of religion to society. He points out how religion can help bring perspective and point to the limits of politics; it can help combat apathy; its communities are practiced and durable; it contributes to conversations about the common good, and can draw on overlooked resources such as community, tradition, memory, intuition, affection and hope; religion provides a voice for the voiceless; encourages dealing positively with the other; provides stamina for dealing with crisis and offers chances for renewal.[40] Habermas recognises this contribution of religion to society and suggests that the liberal state

> has an interest in unleashing religious voices in the political public sphere, and in the political participation of religious organisations as well. It must not discourage religious persons and communities from also expressing themselves politically as such, for it cannot know whether secular society would not otherwise cut itself off from key resources for the creation of meaning and identity.[41]

---

[38] Ibid.: 888.
[39] Marty and Moore, 47.
[40] See Chapter 2 in Marty and Moore.
[41] Jürgen Habermas, "Religion and the Public Sphere," *European Journal of Philosophy* 14, no. 1 (2006): 10.

Another way to look at the contribution of religion to society is to recognize the social capital it generates. According to sociologist John A. Coleman, religion generates "an inordinate amount" of social capital.[42] Active citizenship relies on social capital. People who are connected to others in bonds that are characterised by trust and reciprocity are more likely to vote and engage in volunteer activity. And if they belong to churches, they are significantly more likely to vote and give money to others.[43] In their sociological survey, *Voice and Equality: Civic Voluntarism in American Politics*, Sidney Verba, et al., found participation in churches sows seeds of political activism and facilitates political participation in the United States.[44] This is because churches offer three key resources that increase the likelihood of political and civic participation in society. First, people learn transferable skills, such as public speaking, setting and running a meeting, writing a memo and raising money. These are the sorts of things that make the transition to wider participation much easier. Second, the churches provide dense networks of relationships among a wide variety of organisations; this makes it all the more likely that someone will be 'asked' to become involved in something more. And finally, churches give people a sense of their own power and ability to make a difference.[45] *Voice and Equality* provides evidence of the importance of churches to civil society and democracy. Coleman sums it up by saying that "The churches make our society more participatory, more egalitarian and more communitarian than it would be without them." [46]

---

[42] John A Coleman, "Compassion, Solidarity and Empowerment: The Ethical Contribution of Religion to Society," *Journal of Religion in the Social Services* 19, no. 2 (1999): 12.

[43] Ibid.: 13.

[44] Sidney Verba, Kay Lehman Schlozman, and Henry E. Brady, *Voice and Equality : Civic Voluntarism in American Politics* (Cambridge: Harvard University Press, 1995), 9.

[45] See Coleman: 13-14.

[46] Ibid.: 14.

These findings are confirmed by a later survey conducted by the John F. Kennedy School of Government at Harvard. A 2001 survey entitled the "Social Capital Community Benchmark Survey," found that

> religiously engaged people are more likely than religiously disengaged people to be involved in civic groups of all sorts, to vote, to be active in community affairs, to give blood, to trust other people (from shopkeepers to neighbours), to know the names of public officials, to socialise with friends and neighbours, and even simply to have a wider circle of friends. [47]

Finally, the public role of Christianity and the Catholic Church in particular, has been noted for their contribution to building up democracy throughout the world since Vatican II. Samuel Huntington illustrates how more than thirty countries in Europe, Asia, and Latin America moved from authoritarianism to democracy between 1974 and 1989. He points out that most of the population in them is Catholic and that their culture has been shaped by Catholicism in significant ways.[48]

It can be difficult to recognise this contribution when we are living with the knowledge of the unspeakable harm done to children in the care of the Catholic Church. The subsequent mismanagement and cover up by Church authorities compound this shocking and abominable practice. So much so, that there are many who cannot contemplate any sort of contribution to the public good by the Catholic Church.

That said, we must remember that the Church is made up of millions of good people and religious organisation, who in their day to day activities, generate much needed social capital and teach necessary civic skills that are required by functioning democracies. They shape and influence the

---

[47] John F. Kennedy School of Government, "Social Capital Community Benchmark Survey" http://www.ksg.harvard.edu/saguaro/communitysurvey/index.html (accessed 30 October 2007).

[48] As found in David Hollenbach, *The Common Good and Christian Ethics*, New Studies in Christian Ethics 22 (Cambridge, UK ; New York: Cambridge University Press, 2002), 98.

---

culture of a society in thousands of ways. Religious values and arguments that take place in the public sphere, that shape the imagination and vision of communities and persons, also filter up into the working of government by a process of osmosis. There is a symbiotic relationship between what happens in the background culture of a society and the apparatus of the state. But what is the theological warrant for such an engagement of religion and society? Why doesn't the Catholic Church simply look after its members and leave the public sphere to others?

Social Mission of the Catholic Church

The Catholic Christian tradition is inherently public. There is no choice for its members but to allow its vision, beliefs and convictions into the public sphere. There is no separation between love of God and love of neighbour. They are the two sides of the same coin. Catholic Christians are called to show love to their neighbours through the practice of justice and compassion, most especially to their neighbours who are poor, vulnerable and excluded. This social mission goes to the heart of the very identity of the Catholic Church.

At Vatican II, a dualistic view of the world and the confinement of religion to the private domain of one's life is described by *Gaudium et Spes* as one of the "more serious errors of our age."[49] One of the ways to avoid such an error is to re-examine the relationship between the religious and social mission of the church. These two dimensions do not exist independently of one another – rather, they are constitutive and indispensable to one another. It is not possible to find something 'essential' in each so that a clear distinction can be made between them. Rather, we need to allow for a complex intersection between them – one that is in constant motion and creative tension. Theologian Francis Schüssler Fiorenza offers a helpful analogy. If we are asked to define what it means to be human, we

---

[49] Vatican II, "Gaudium Et Spes," in *Catholic Social Thought: The Documentary Heritage*, ed. David J. O'Brien and Thomas A. Shannon (New York: Orbis Books, 1999), #43.

might say that our rationality is what makes us different from animals. But that answer would not be sufficient on its own. We would need to add something about our emotions and the fact that we are embodied. In this way, we inevitably show how there is some overlap between what it means to be human and what it means to be animal. The same is true for the social mission of the church. The religious dimension does not stand alone; it criss-crosses with economic, political, social, and cultural dimensions of life. Attempts at exclusive descriptions inevitably lead to distortions. Fiorenza suggests that the "religious and social mission of the church relate to each other not in a singular or essential manner but with overlapping and crisscrossing characteristics."[50] They are dialectical, in that the religious and social constantly *affirm, question,* and *enhance* each other. The religious mission criss-crosses with the humanisation of the world in which we live. This is not only a social task but rather is also "a sacred task for a vision of the world and humanity, as created and redeemed by God in an eschatological hope and promise."[51]

Gaudium et Spes [52]

Prior to the Vatican II there was a great deal of work being done by theologians to overcome a theology separated from ordinary life and share with the world "an intellectually rich and spiritually powerful Christian vision."[53] This new effort in theology sought to overcome the dualistic eschatological vision of life that had come to characterise the practice of

---

[50] Francis Schüssler Fiorenza, "Social Mission of Church," in *The New Dictionary of Catholic Social Thought*, ed. Judith A. Dwyer (Minnesota: The Liturgical Press, 1994).

[51] Ibid., 167.

[52] *The Pastoral Constitution on the Church in the Modern World*, a key document of Vatican II known as *Gaudium et Spes* (from the opening lines of the document, meaning, joy and hope).

[53] J. Bryan Hehir, "The Church in the World : Responding to the Call of the Council," in *Faith and the Intellectual Life: Marianist Award Lectures*, ed. James L. Heft (Notre Dame: University of Notre Dame Press, 1996), 107.

---

faith. It wanted to move the church from being 'over against' the world, to a place where it was in conversation with social movements, both learning from society and teaching out of its own tradition and wisdom. This was an enormous shift; for so long Catholicism had defined itself over and against three movements: the Protestant Reformation, the Democratic Revolution, and the Enlightenment.[54] Now the church was placing itself 'in' the world, not over and against it but in it. "The joys and the hopes, the griefs and the anxieties of the men (sic) of this age, especially those who are poor or in any way afflicted, these too are the joys and hopes, the griefs and anxieties of the followers of Christ." [55]

In *Gaudium et Spes*, the church starts with examining the 'signs of the times', i.e. to the world. This listening is done in light of a particular biblical anthropology (view of the human person), eschatology (end times), ecclesiology (nature of the church) and Christology (understandings of Jesus Christ and his mission to the world).[56] This shift in the church's relationship to the world has been described as being from a juridical conception of the church's role to an anthropological one.[57] This is one of the central theological shifts that places the social mission at the heart of the church. Significantly, the person is now seen as the place of intersection between the church and the world. *Gaudium et Spes* says "The role and competence of the Church being what it is, she must in no way be confused with the political community, nor bound to any political system. For she is at once a sign and safeguard of the transcendence of the human person."[58] This text captures the essence of how *Gaudium et Spes* understands the relationship of the church to the world. It takes the central theme of social teaching – the protection of human dignity – and gives it ecclesial standing.[59] Bryan Hehir puts it this way: "The reason why the

---

[54] J. Bryan Hehir, "The Social Role of the Church: Leo XIII, Vatican II and John Paul II," in *Catholic Social Thought and the New World Order*, ed. Oliver F and John W. Houck Williams (Notre Dame: University of Notre Dame Press, 1993), 37.

[55] Vatican II, #1.

[56] David Hollenbach, "Gaudium Et Spes," in *Modern Catholic Social Teaching: Commentaries and Interpretations*, ed. Kenneth R. Himes (Washington DC: Georgetown University Press, 2004), 273.

[57] Hehir, "The Church in the World : Responding to the Call of the Council," 113.

[58] Vatican II, #76.

[59] Hehir, "The Social Role of the Church: Leo XIII, Vatican II and John Paul II," 37.

church enters public or social ministry is to protect the transcendent dignity of the human person."[60] The decisive shift of this text was to locate the defence of the human person at the centre of Catholic ecclesiology and this moved the social ministry from the margins of the church to its centre.

Gaudium et Spes outlines four principles concerning the relationship of the Catholic Church to the world:

1. the ministry of the church is religious in nature and it has no political charism or ambition;
2. the religious mission is to seek the reign of God, this is its purpose and the church serves this aim;
3. the religious mission touches all parts of life; there is no part removed from God's reigning power;
4. finally, there are economic (resources), political (power), social (relationships) and cultural (meaning) consequences to the gospel – the church seeks to fulfil its religious mission by asking its members to uphold human dignity, promote human rights, contribute to the unity of the human family and help people make meaning in their lives.[61]

Dignitatis Humanae[62]

The social mission is realisable because of the recasting of the church–state relationship that took place in *Dignitatis Humanae*, Vatican II's *Declaration on Religious Freedom*. Since the seventeenth century, the

---

[60] J. Bryan Hehir, "Church-State and Church-World: The Ecclesiological Implications," *Catholic Theological Society of America* 41 (1986): 57.

[61] See Ibid; Hehir, "The Social Role of the Church: Leo XIII, Vatican II and John Paul II."; Hehir, "The Church in the World : Responding to the Call of the Council."; Hollenbach, "Gaudium Et Spes."

[62] *Declaration on Religious Freedom*, another key document from Vatican II. *Dignitatis Humane* comes from the first line of the document, meaning Dignity of the Human Person.

Catholic Church believed it should be accorded special status in society by the state and that the coercive power of the state should be used to promote Catholic faith. However, *Dignitatis Humanae* replaced this belief with three principles. The first accepted the reality of religious pluralism in society and that religious freedom is a human right and should be protected by civil law. The second accepts the secular nature of the state – that it is not divinely constituted nor so ordered – rather, it has its own constitution and is limited by the law on the use of force. The third concerns the freedom of the church to be itself, without particular favour from the state.[63] This last principle creates a challenge for the church, in that, without any favouritism from the state, it is only as good as its witness. Sociologist José Casanova sees in this differentiation of the church from the state an opportunity for the church to "come fully into its own, specialising in 'its own religious' function and either dropping or losing many other 'nonreligious' functions it had accumulated and could no longer meet efficiently."[64]

Dignitatis Humanae has helped depoliticise the church-state relationship and *Gaudium et Spes* is responsible for putting the social mission of the church at the centre of its identity. Taken together, their legacy has been, as Hehir puts it, "to plunge the church more deeply into the political arena precisely because the protection of human dignity and the promotion of human rights in fact happen in a political context."[65] Although this can sound very unreligious and very political, we must remember the context. The church is focused on improving the dignity of the person, building up solidarity among the human community, and with caring for creation. It has this purpose because by its nature it is to "continue to make present in history God's salvation in Jesus Christ." [66]

---

[63] See Hehir, "Church-State and Church-World: The Ecclesiological Implications," 1-2.

[64] José Casanova, *Public Religions in the Modern World* (Chicago: University of Chicago Press, 1994), 21.

[65] Hehir, "Church-State and Church-World: The Ecclesiological Implications," 58.

[66] Fiorenza, 156.

Implications of Vatican II

The work done at Vatican II regarding the church's social mission meant three things. First, the social mission became central to the nature of the church. It is no longer an optional task on the margins to be engaged with from time to time, before or after evangelisation. Second, the church has a right to work in freedom from political systems in society, expecting no favours from the state, while acknowledging the secular nature of the state. And finally, Vatican II has provided the theological basis for the church's legitimate engagement with the world.

The work the Council did on articulating theological principles that brought the social mission of the church to the centre of its identity was solidified in the 1971 and 1975 synodal documents, *Justitia in Mundo* and *Evangelii Nuntiandi*. In the now famous statement of the bishops in 1971, there is no doubt about the centrality of the social mission, "Action on behalf of justice and participation in the transformation of the world fully appear to us as a constitutive dimension of the preaching of the Gospel, or, in other words, of the Church's mission for the redemption of the human race and its liberation from every oppressive situation."[67] However one understands the use of the word 'constitutive',[68] there is no doubt that its use places the social mission at the heart of the identity and purpose of the church in and to the world. The concern for justice must be a part of all the dimensions of Christian life, and every aspect of the Church's ministries should help promote social justice and the dignity of the person in community.

---

[67] Synod of Bishops, "Justitia in Mundo," in *Catholic Social Thought: The Documentary Heritage*, ed. David J. O'Brien and Thomas A. Shannon (New York: Orbis Books, 1999), #6.

[68] Kenneth Himes, O.F.M. asks if the bishops were "putting the work of justice on a par with the preaching of the Word and the celebration of the sacraments as being definitive of the Church? Or were the bishops simply making the point that working for justice is not merely an ethical implication of discipleship but something at the very heart of Christian life?" see Kenneth R. Himes O.F.M., "Commentary on Justitia in Mundo (Justice in the World)," in *Modern Catholic Social Teaching: Commentaries and Interpretations*, ed. Kenneth R. Himes O.F.M. (Washington, D.C.: Georgetown University Press, 2005), 341.

The duty to work for social liberation is central to Christian evangelisation. However, there are dangers if there is too much emphasis on liberation, with only a horizontal view of the world. *Evangelii Nuntiandi* warns against the reduction of the Good News, the politicisation of the Christian message, the over identification of religion with the struggle for liberation, and a danger of forgetting about the importance of attitudinal change.[69] These are helpful provisos in finding the right balance in the overlapping and crisscrossing characteristics that make up the church's social mission.

It is one thing in principle to articulate the reasons for the Catholic Christian Church's involvement in the world, it is another to see how it is and ought to be done in practice. We will now explore some of the challenges and tensions facing the Church and faith communities in participating in the public sphere and working for social change in liberal democratic systems.

Faith-communities: being public

In a secular state, religion becomes invisible at the political level, even when still prevalent at the personal level. Secular governments and politicians do not invoke scriptures or religious authorities to defend their policies. Instead they speak to principles and concerns that all the population can share irrespective of their beliefs or non-belief.[70]

The legitimacy of a law, which the whole of society must adhere to, rests on the understanding and agreement of all. Only secular reasons can achieve this end. The explanation and justification of a law must be readily accessible to everyone in the society, religious and secular alike. One of the fears that drives some secular liberals to exclude faith-communities and religious discourse from the public sphere is the prospect that a law

---

[69] Pope Paul VI, "Evangelii Nuntiandi," in *Catholic Social Thought: The Documentary Heritage*, ed. David J. O'Brien and Thomas A. Shannon (New York: Orbis Books, 1999), #32, #33, #35, #36.

[70] Julian Baggini, "The Rise, Fall and Rise Again of Secularism," *Public Policy Research* 12, no. 4 (2006): 204-212.

or policy imposed on all, will emerge and be justified by a belief from a particular religious tradition. This has happened in the past in this society and some are afraid that it might happen again, despite the advance of Modernity and separation of church and state. Consequently, an emerging assumption is that it is best to confine faith-communities and religious discourse to the realm of the personal and private dimensions of life. This will minimise conflict in the public sphere, prevent against the possibility of religious privilege and bullying inappropriately impinging on the state, and ensure a level playing field for all, regardless of creed.

For instance, Minister of Environment, John Gormley, might share some of this concern, when he said, in response to the Catholic Church's public participation in the Civil Partnership debate:

> Well, first of all I must say I was taken aback when I heard the news this morning. I thought we had left the era of Church interference behind us and I'm speaking as someone who recognises that the Church has made a contribution to this country but really it should concentrate its efforts on looking after the spiritual needs of its flock and not intrude into temporal or state matters.[71]

When Minister Gormley refers to the Church here – it seems he is referring to the Bishops of the Catholic Church, the Church hierarchy. I wonder if he would say the same for Social Justice Ireland, Trocaire, or the St Vincent de Paul Society? They are also motivated by the Christian tradition and attempt to shape public policy from a Christian values perspective.

For instance, *Social Justice Ireland*, previously *Cori Justice*, have sought to bring the Christian tradition, particularly its understanding of justice, to bear on the quality of life in our society and world, particularly for those on the margins. They believe that public debate needs to include exploration of values – the ones stated and the ones operative. They say,

---

[71] John Gormley, News at One, RTE, 17th June, 2010.

Our fears are easier to admit than our values. Do we as a people accept a two-tier society in fact, while deriding it in principle? This dualism in our values allows us to continue with the status quo, which, in reality, means that it is okay to exclude almost one sixth of the population from the mainstream of life of our society, while substantial resources and opportunities are channelled towards other groups in society.[72]

Such a juxtaposing of reality and stated values can be found just as jarring when applied to the Catholic community as when applied to the wider society in Ireland today. However, the point remains. The introduction of values into public debate is much needed.

Social Justice Ireland believes that "engaging in activity to influence public policy and to generate structural change is answering the call to transform society which is a constitutive dimension of the Gospel."[73] Over the past twenty years they have sought to translate Christian values into a language that is persuasive and reasonable to the public at large. They have done this through the use of accurate social analysis, credible alternatives and effective pathways from the present to the future. This combination is core to their work. It recognises the importance of speaking in "a language appropriate to the particular audience whether religious, secular, academic, policy maker or general public."[74] When speaking to government, they speak the language of social policy, when speaking to economists, they speak in an economic language, and when speaking to church, they speak in a language of faith. This is one of their great strengths – they 'communicate according to the mode of the receiver.' They are multilingual, non-sectarian and expect no special favour from

---

[72] Sean Healy and Brigid Reynolds, *Planning for Progress and Fairness, Policies to Ensure Economic Development, Social Equity and Sustainability*, Socio-Economic Review 2008 (Dublin: Cori Justice, 2008), 215.

[73] Sean Healy S.M.A. and Brigid Reynolds S.M., "Spirituality" http://www.cori.ie/Justice/Spirituality/45-Spirituality/120-Spirituality (accessed 1st February 2008).

[74] Social Justice Ireland, "About Us" http://www.socialjustice.ie/content/about-us (accessed 30th July 2010).

the state. The quality of their argument, their ability to work in partnership, openness about their motivation, and willingness to change when the evidence suggests it, all contribute to their effective participation in the public sphere. "We believe a public debate is urgently needed around the issues of progress, paradigms and policy, around the future that is to be built and the choices that need to be made now if the world is to move towards that future."[75] Clearly, such a debate is much needed today.

Public justification for policy or laws

A core principle—that needs to be appreciated by all who participate in the public sphere—is that executive and legislative decisions need to be at the service of the public good – this is the purpose of the state. Such decisions must be justified in a language that is available to everyone – regardless of whether they actually agree with the particular measure or not. It would be wholly inappropriate for an organ of the state to justify a new piece of legislation or social policy with recourse to a particular faith tradition, or simply because the St Vincent de Paul Society sought it. The use of Christian Scriptures to justify new levels of social welfare payments, on behalf of the Department of Social Protection would be inappropriate in our democracy. It would not be acceptable if the Irish Government were to justify a new law concerning environmental protection through reference to recommendations from the World Council of Churches. Those sources are neither available nor intelligible to all and so are inappropriate for use by the state. The reasons given would be more like confessions of faith rather than reasons that every citizen could find intelligible and the possible basis for law. If the justifications for law and policy appear to the public as unintelligible and impositions from particular religious traditions, the legitimacy of the law will be undermined and the political order will rightly be called into question. The nature of the reasons given to justify law and policy, on behalf of the state, is the key issue here. Habermas puts it this way: "In a secular state only those

---

[75] Healy and Reynolds, "Making Choices - Choosing Futures, a Question of Paradigms," 60.

political decisions are taken to be legitimate as can be impartially justified in the light of generally accessible reasons, in other words, equally justified vis-à-vis religious and non-religious citizens and citizens of different confessions."[76] Churches and faith-communities who participate in the public sphere must remember this and act as if they know it.

Appropriate level of involvement in public debate for faith-communities

While this principal has widespread acceptance in any functioning democracy, the appropriate level of involvement of faith-communities and religious discourse in wider society is more contested and complex. Ought faith communities to have a view on social and economic issues? If so, should they confine their voices to their own membership or is it legitimate for them to engage in public and political debate about these issues? And if debate is legitimate, what sort of language is appropriate? Can they use religious language or must it be a form of language that includes everyone, a form of public reasoning? These are important questions and suggest a place for faith-communities and religious discourse somewhere between the sacristy and the state. Some of these questions have been addressed earlier in this chapter. However, the issue of language is an important one.

There is a danger with too much care and attention being given to ensuring that the justification for policies and laws is equally accessible to all. While this is an essential dimension to our democracy, we ought not to let this principle stifle debate at the deliberative dimension of policy and law making. Perhaps there is room in this dimension for people to disclose some of their motivations for caring about particular issues – what values are behind the protection of human dignity and the environment? Some will draw strength from beliefs embedded in secular sources – others, from religious tradition(s). While there are opponents to

---

[76] Jurgan Habermas, "Religion and the Public Sphere," *European Journal of Philosophy* 14, no. 1 (2006): 5.

such an exercise, AC Grayling, Richard Dawkins and Christopher Hitchens, there are also emerging proponents, even ones that have shifted their position on this issue. Jürgen Habermas changed his position, believing now that there is wisdom in religious traditions that modern democratic societies could benefit from. He believes that there is a place for religious voices and traditions in the public sphere. Another voice is that of atheist and secularist Julian Baggini. He says that:

> Traditional secularism...has to go. In its place must be a public domain in which religion is allowed back in. The idea is not to create conflicts of belief but to allow disagreements to be resolved openly, without people feeling the need to deny differences in the fundamental convictions that shape their views. The secret of harmonious society in which different religious and non-religious beliefs are held is not for everyone to remain silent on the things that divide us, but discuss differences openly in a spirit of mutual respect and understanding. [77]

It is important that we try to allow disagreements to be resolved openly rather than on remaining silent on what divides us. In Ireland, there are new worldviews, values and principles at work in our communities and society. These need to be talked about, explored and open to public scrutiny. While there are all sorts of disagreements about what is truth, the nature of the human person, role of the state, human rights and responsibilities, we still must share this island together, we must learn, in the midst of differences, to live together. "Uncovering the underpinning values and having them discussed, scrutinised and evaluated is crucial if there is to be any agreement or consensus on what constitutes real progress."[78] How are we to deal with competing worldviews, to show respect to one another and reach consensus where possible? I suggest that excluding the participation of faith communities and the voice of religious language, while making for a less conflictual public sphere, is not the way to move forward. Rather, if those who participated in the public sphere

---

[77] Julian Baggini, "The Rise, Fall, and Rise Again of Secularism," *Public Policy Review* 12, no. 4 (2006): 210.

[78] Healy and Reynolds, "Making Choices - Choosing Futures, a Question of Paradigms," 41.

were encouraged to disclose the values behind their views, then the quality of participation and debate might improve.

In this approach, in the realm of the public sphere, there ought to be room for people or groups to bring their faith traditions into conversation with particular issues in a more overt manner. What is the advantage of such an approach? Firstly, it provides important opportunities for religious groups to participate in the public forum, partly because it allows for the use of religious language. This helps minimise sectarianism and promotes a tolerant public sphere. It also allows for the possibility of new voices, insights, challenges to the status quo. The inclusion of, for instance, the Evangelical, Catholic, Muslim and Hindu voices in the Irish public sphere allows it to represent in reality the members of society, reflecting the plurality of our country.

Appropriate use of language

The issue of language is a complex one. The challenges arising from the use of religious language will depend on a variety of circumstances. Much will depend on the context, the intentions of the speaker or group, what it is that the audience hears and/or experiences and how the participants relate what they hear to their own world view. For instance, if a member of a faith community were appearing on Frontline with Pat Kenny, to talk about care for the homeless, they need to think about their audience and the appropriate use of language in that context. Are they trying to raise consciousness about the plight of the excluded, push for a piece of legislation, call the government to account on a particular issue, and/or explain why it is that Islam requires Muslims to reach out to those who are homeless. The nature of the audience, coupled with the speaker's own intention should be instructive on what sort of language to use. Would it be helpful to quote from the Koran and tell the audience about the five pillars of faith? There is little use in speaking in a manner that might resonate with one's constituency but is misunderstood by one's immediate audience. In such circumstances, along with political debates, confessional self-restraint will be the norm. Jonathan Chaplain points out that:

"harnessing faith-based reasoning to the task of discerning the public good will already discourage a great deal of possibly inappropriate faith-based language." [79]

Strategy of Avoidance

Those who favour the use of liberal public reason and the confinement of faith-communities and religious discourse to the personal and private spheres of life, sometimes do so out of a sense of respect for others. They believe that the bringing of values rooted in religious and moral traditions into public discussion in a pluralistic society will only lead to conflict and disagreement, and the respectful thing to do is to avoid what will fracture and harm relationships. Accordingly, politics, policy and the law ought not to be mixed up with religious and moral arguments. This is a legitimate concern. However, this concern, motivated out of respect, often just leads to avoidance. It is an avoidance of the deeper moral and value issues behind policy and legislation. For the idea of a neutral state is really just a chimera. It is a fiction. Behind laws and underneath policy there are implicit views, often unarticulated, about the good life – what it means to live well. If these deeper questions are removed from public debate, there is a loss to our discourse. The evacuation of the public debate of the values dimension can also lead to resentment and a backlash from excluded communities and voices. Respect in this instance can can also mean leaving the moral intuitions of our interlocutors undisturbed and unexplored. But is this really respectful? I suggest not. Avoidance is not respectful, even if done for the best of reasons. Michael Sandel suggests that:

A more robust public engagement with our moral disagreements could provide a stronger, not a weaker, basis for mutual respect. Rather than avoid the moral and religious convictions that our fellow citizens bring to public life, we should attend to them more directly—sometimes by

---

[79] Jonathan Chaplin, *Talking God: The Legitimacy of Religious Public Reasoning* (London: Theos, 2008), 65.

challenging and contesting them, sometimes by listening to and learning from them...A politics of moral engagement is not only a more inspiring ideal than a politics of avoidance. It is also a more promising basis for a just society.[80]

Candour in representation, restraint in decision[81]

'Candour in representation, restraint in decision' might be a useful phrase to remember regarding the appropriate limits of participation and debate in the public sphere. My proposal is that citizens ought to be allowed to bring their faith convictions into the public sphere, engage in political debate and if they wish, use religious language. However, it must be remembered that statements that simply "assert the truth of a faith-based viewpoint without going on to unpack the public good reasons flowing from them, or without acknowledging the presence of other sincerely-held perspectives, will generally not be persuasive."[82] Stating religious beliefs on their own rarely persuades – if faith-communities want to influence public policy and the law, they need to give good public reasons for the validity of the views they hold. While it is appropriate for faith-communities to offer religious reasons for their policy proposals in civil society and deliberative forums of the state, it is not so for the state when justifying its own reasons for the adoption of policy or law. We do not expect our government to quote from the Koran or our judges to base a judgement on the sacred texts of Hindus.

While I suggest there ought to be a place for faith communities in the public sphere, who speak of values rooted in particular religious traditions – there ought also to be room for people who articulate other points of view to uncover their own values, the roots of their views and insight. What are the narratives and myths that give rise to particular positions

---

[80] Michael J. Sandel, *Justice : What's the Right Thing to Do?*, 1st ed. (New York: Farrar, Straus and Giroux, 2009), 268-269.
[81] Chaplin, 58ff.
[82] Ibid., 61.

being taken on issues in our communities? What is it that informs our own viewpoints? The advantage of such an approach is that it would lead to an improvement in the public sphere itself, in the forum – that it is not only concerned about particular issues of policy but about relationships and community – understanding and appreciating one's conversation partners. Such an approach might also help the participants not to adopt an immediate reflexive position to an issue. Rather, they might be invited to pause and wonder what it is about the present situation that challenges one's own worldview. Is there truth in the viewpoint of the other? Can I give it its best interpretation? Or am I just waiting for them to slip up or make the usual points before I pounce on them, making my own usual points – where is the learning, the relating, the fostering of the public sphere itself? Daly and Cobb put it this way:

> One of the central limitations of academic disciplines in contributing to wisdom is their professed aim of value neutrality. That there is here a large element of self-deception has been pointed out frequently and convincingly. The ideal of value neutrality is itself a value that is generally highly favourable to the status quo. More objectivity is in fact obtained by bringing values out into the open and discussing them than by denying their formative presence in the disciplines... as long as the disciplines discourage any interest in values on the part of their practitioners, they inevitably discourage the ordering of study of the solution to human problems.[83]

While the exploration of values and conversation is important, there comes a point when representative deliberation comes to an end and an executive or legislative decision is taken on behalf of the state. When this happens, the state needs to justify its decision through the use of reasons that affirm the public good. These reasons need to be understood and accessible to all citizens. It might be difficult to find exactly where this line is drawn, and there will be differences of opinion about that, but the fact remains, there is a limit to the use of religious language and the influence of faith-communities in our society. There comes a point where one must show restraint and trust in the executive and legislative dimensions of our society.

---

[83] Herman Daly and John Cobb, *For the Common Good* (London: Merlin Press, 1990), 131.

In the next section, I outline three modes of participating in the public sphere by faith-communities in Ireland today.

Faith-communities in the public sphere – 3 approaches

Cardinal Bernardin wrote that the 'how' or the 'style' of the church's engagement in public life is crucial to the outcome.[84] I believe it is possible to see three different 'styles' at work today in Ireland. One places great emphasis on persuasion and dialogue, one believes in taking a more prophetic stance and another, which is difficult to categorize, places much of its effort in shaping the law of the church and the law of the land.[85] Before I describe these, it is useful to remember that there is quite a bit of overlap between them. At their best, they can complement one another. Also, depending on the context, one 'style' might be more appropriate than another.

A conversational approach

The first approach, drawn from Vatican II, emphasises that the church be in dialogue with the world.[86] This is a two way relationship, where the church has something to learn from the world and something to offer the world. The reciprocal nature of the relationship is fostered by "the clear recognition of the intrinsic value and validity of secular institutions and secular disciplines."[87] This view allows the church to engage in authentic

---

[84] Joseph Bernardin, "The Public Life and Witness of the Church," *America* (1996): 18.

[85] To apply more classic types to these categories, the first category described by Niebuhr as Christ the Transformer of Culture, the second could also fit here or could be described, along with the third category as Christ against Culture, see Niebuhr, *Christ and Culture*; also the first category could be described as 'church' and the second and third one as 'sect', see Ernst Troeltsch, *The Social Teaching of the Christian Churches*, 2 Vols (New York: Harper Torchbooks, 1960).

[86] See especially *Gaudium et Spes* and *Dignitatis Humanae* in David J. O'Brien and Thomas A. Shannon, *Catholic Social Thought : The Documentary Heritage* (Maryknoll, N.Y.: Orbis Books, 1992).

[87] Hehir, "The Church in the World : Responding to the Call of the Council," 112.

conversation – for without an openness to learning something from others, there can be no real dialogue. The organisations, communities and people who find a home in this category value persuasion as a means of communicating Gospel values. They seek to communicate the wisdom of tradition in a credible and engaging way – appealing to the intellect, desires, and innate sense of goodness and justice in people. This style, which is respectful of the variety of ways that people of goodwill interpret their faith, is committed to the process of transformation that takes place incrementally over long periods of time. It does not see itself as having definitive answers to give to the world. Rather it is more of a "catalyst moving the public argument to grapple with questions of moral values, ethical principles and the human and religious meaning of policy choices."[88] In this way, it can help shape public opinion, values, and influence the culture. This influence on culture is the approach favoured by David Hollenbach.[89] He says, "Far better and more likely to succeed would be a church strategy of persuasion that operates on the cultural rather than the legal level."[90] Such an approach requires patience, courage, wisdom and humility. [91]

To such an approach, there are some necessary cautions. There is the danger that involvement with the public will lead to accommodation and co-option with the values of the world, thereby diluting the imperatives of the Christian message. Persuasion can take time and this is something that many people who suffer injustice and exclusion do not have; they need help immediately. And so, there is also a need for something more immediate, and at times, confrontational.

---

[88] Hehir, "Church-State and Church-World: The Ecclesiological Implications," 64.
[89] David Hollenbach, "Catholicism and American Political Culture: Confrontation, Accommodation, or Transformation," in *Inculturation and the Church in North America*, ed. T. Frank Kennedy S.J. (New York: The Crossroad Publishing Company, 2006).
[90] Ibid., 20.
[91] For further reading on the 'how' of theology in the public sphere see Dan O'Connell, "Religious Education and the Public Sphere," *The Furrow* 57, no. 7/8 (2006).

A prophetic approach

This leads to the second approach, which can be broadly categorized as prophetic. It seeks to persuade by witness and being uncompromising in its demands for social justice. This approach has deep roots in both the Christian and Hebrew scriptures. According to Abraham Heschel, "the prophet was someone who said No to his (sic) society, condemning its habits and assumptions, its complacency, waywardness, and syncretism."[92] The prophets were steeped in the justice of Yahweh and as a consequence were acutely aware of the presence of injustice and oppression within society. This awareness was nearly unbearable for them. They felt the pain of those excluded, the anger and compassion of Yahweh, and lived in the fissure between the prevailing culture of oppression and Yahweh's desire for justice. According to Walter Brueggemann, the task of the prophet is to "nurture, nourish, and evoke a consciousness and perception alternative to the dominant community around us."[93] This consciousness is to accomplish two things. Firstly, it is to use criticism in dismantling the dominant consciousness and secondly, it is to energize people through a vision of what is possible here and now. Those who are poor and powerless are at the heart of such an approach. It lifts up their lives, juxtaposing how things are for them and how things are for the rest of us. It seeks to transform the dominant consciousness that sustains inequality and social exclusion, often in jarring and confrontational ways.

A critique of this approach concerns its danger of politicizing the Gospel by getting too involved in politics and the work for social justice. At times, it can lose connection with its own religious traditions. Such an approach can be polarising; you are either with us or against us – there is no middle ground. It often deals in broad strokes about issues of social justice and "[D]istinction, qualifications, and contending opinions are not the prophet's stock in trade."[94] This tendency can lead to work on single issues,

---

[92] Abraham Joshua Heschel, *The Prophets* (New York: Perennial, 2001), xxix.
[93] Walter Brueggemann, *The Prophetic Imagination*, 2nd ed. (Minneapolis: Fortress Press, 2001), 3.
[94] J. Bryan Hehir, "Can the Church Convincingly Engage American Culture," *Church* (2004): 7.

which perpetuate single issue politics, fragmenting further the political process, and distorting the particular religious tradition one belongs to – making it equivalent to the issue at hand.

A juridical approach

The third approach can be seen at work in debates concerning such issues as abortion, euthanasia, stem cell research, cloning, gay marriage and adoption of children by gay parents. It is characterised by an oppositional stance on these issues. Within this category, there is a desire and a drive for clear and radical Gospel teaching. Its proponents will argue that their stance is to protect the vulnerable or promote some public good. It is reminiscent of the 'Christ against Culture' category as outlined by H. Richard Niebuhr in *Christ and Culture*. Those who favour this approach seek to use legislation to further their mission. This is quite a different method from the one outlined in the first category, which seeks to influence the culture, which may in turn influence the law. This group aims to shape the law and so influence the culture. They believe it is reasonable to use the coercive power of the state to help shape the values and habits of citizens in society. They appreciate the educative qualities of the law. [95]

Those who question this approach believe that it is alienating of church members and of society in general, and in the end is counterproductive. It does not appreciate the complexity of issues, nor the intricacies involved in working for social change. Referring to the mission of the church in working for justice and human rights, Hollenbach believes it will be compromised "by misdirected appeals to the coercive power of the state and by failure to make carefully reasoned and persuasive contributions on these matters in the cultural debates of the United States today."[96] Another danger with this juridical approach is that at some stage, Catholicism appears as only a "collection of prohibitions."[97] John Waters,

---

[95] Hollenbach, "Catholicism and American Political Culture: Confrontation, Accommodation, or Transformation," 17.
[96] Ibid., 22.
[97] John Waters, "Hearing Only Pious Cliches," *The Irish Times*, 22nd October 2007.

writing in *The Irish Times*, makes the point that if the culture perceives the church as being interested only in prohibitions, then regardless of what is said, it will not be heard properly. The danger then is that people only hear "pious regurgitation of what always sounds like clichés. The meaning shorts out on the circuit board of collective understanding, with its crisscrossing wires of prejudice, hostility, assumed knowledge, ideology and rote learning."[98] If the church places too much emphasis on using the coercive arm of the state to realise its mission, especially in a pluralistic context, there is every chance that people - both within and outside the church - will not be open to hearing or being in conversation with the church about what it means to live well today. They will associate the church with rules, prohibitions and the imposition of the law.

Implications for Values-led Debate and Discourse in the Public Sphere

Thus far in the paper, I have argued that civil society makes an important contribution to the wellbeing of our shared lives, the Catholic Christian church, for all its failings, makes a contribution to the quality of civil society in a variety of ways, a key aspect of civil society relies on a public sphere that is inclusive and participative. I have argued that there ought to be a place for voices motivated by religious traditions in the public sphere and that respect in the discourse requires room for alternative visions of the good. I believe it is in our interest to cultivate public conversations that are value led, where reasons are offered for positions held that go beneath the usual sound-bite. Public discourse is inherently respectful when it engages others at this level, despite the difficulty. Regardless of the friction it can cause, we need to develop a way of engaging with alternative views of the good that try to explore deeply the values behind the vision. It is my hope that this will minimise the amount of talking we do 'at' one another and improve our chances of talking 'to' one another.

---

[98] Ibid.

While this paper has concentrated on faith communities and some of the issues concerning their participation in public discourse, it can, I believe, offer some suggestions for all who participate in the public sphere today.

• At the heart of the paper is a keen awareness and appreciation of one's audience and the importance of communicating in a language that the other can understand. People and groups need to be at least bi-lingual. They need to have another language than that of their own constituency. As mentioned earlier, *Social Justice Ireland* moves between languages depending on the context. While this sounds straightforward enough, it is quite a difficult thing to do in practise. The ability to articulate one's values in a language that can be heard and understood by one's interlocutors requires a deep understanding of those values in the first place and the skill to do the translation, without anything being 'lost in translation'. Faith communities would do well to learn this lesson if they want to avoid the danger of simply speaking to themselves.

• If one is to be taken seriously in the public sphere, one's views need to be based on sound social analysis, for what we see will determine our response. Our 'seeing' needs to be carefully done, with as much expertise as we can muster. Our view must be based on sure footing, using evidence and experience, to ground our arguments.

• Participants in the public sphere need to find ways to articulate their values – not just assert their opinions. This would foster greater depth and respect in public discourse. Regardless of being located within a religious or a secular tradition, everyone is working from some value base – some of it might be conscious, while another part of it might simply be based on uncontested assumptions. This is true for all participants. The uncovering, discovering and articulation of these values can lead to greater honesty in the discourse and this is a key component in our learning how to live well with our differences.

• Values led discourse inevitably reveals one's vision of how things ought to be. Participants in the public sphere would do well to be realistic about what is possible from their vision in this particular setting, at this particular stage in our history. As *Social Justice Ireland* says, 'credible alternatives' are key. It goes on to suggest that the credibility of one's participation will be enhanced if one can suggest 'alternative pathways' to get from where we are to where we wish to go. It is one thing to decry what is happening in our world, it is another to suggest ways forward; something much needed in public discourse.

• There must be room in the public sphere, at appropriate levels, for all sorts of voices and visions. Voices from religious traditions might have some insight into how things are now (the naming of this present reality), how they might be in the future and how we might move from where we are to where we want to go. These voices, because they are a part of faith communities ought not to be excluded from public debate simply because they are rooted in religious traditions. To do this might cut us off from 'key resources for the creation of meaning and identity' as Habermas has warned.

• Participants in the public sphere, who are trying to influence social policy and/or the law of the land, need to appreciate the wisdom of 'candour in representation, restraint in decision'. When participants know that their interlocutors understand these limits, greater trust can emerge between them. They will not suspect one another of trying to unfairly influence the process or seeking some sort of privileged relationship with the state.

• The issue of respect was referred to in the paper earlier and it is an important quality for the well-being of the public sphere itself. The extent of participation will depend in part on how people actually participate. When the value of respect underlies robust and strong debate the overall well being of the forum will be enhanced. There is a danger if groups use the public sphere without consideration of the well-being of the very mechanism that affords them the opportunity to be public in the first place.

• The quality of dialogue is also critical. Good dialogue involves speaking 'with' another and not just 'at' them. It is a paradigm that appreciates the contribution of the other, and presumes that there is learning to be found in the conversation and encounter, for all the participants. Such a disposition will allow for partnerships and coalitions, essential if power is needed to engage with mechanisms of the state or the influence of the market.

- Efforts to uncover, discover and even recover values in public debate are crucial. They will allow for a greater congruence between what we say, how we act and what we believe.

- A participative, informative, and energetic public sphere is in the interest of the state. The state needs the legitimacy that is derived from the workings of the public sphere. Therefore, it ought to respect the nature of the deliberations that take place there and where appropriate, give practical support to its well-being.

Conclusion

This paper has argued that an inclusive public sphere is a public good. As Ireland changes, we are well advised to find appropriate mechanisms to include voices from different traditions: religious and secular. It is important that we try to allow disagreements to be resolved openly rather than on becoming silent on what divides us. These mechanisms ought to foster in participants a way to articulate their values, the sources of their positions and opinions. This will offer the possibility of greater understanding between the groups holding divergent positions. While their world views may diverge on different social issues, a strong, inclusive, participative public sphere is an appropriate forum for mutually enriching public debate and a contribution to civil society.

Bibliography

Arendt, Hannah. *The Human Condition.* 2 ed. Chicago: University of Chicago Press, 1986.

Baggini, Julian. "The Rise, Fall, and Rise Again of Secularism." *Public Policy Review* 12, no. 4 (2006): 204-212.

Baggini, Julian "The Rise, Fall and Rise Again of Secularism." *Public Policy Research* 12, no. 4 (2006): 204-212.

Bellah, Robert N, Richard Madsen, William M. Sullivan, Ann Swidler, and Steven M. Tipton. *Habits of the Heart : Individualism and Commitment in American Life.* New York: Harper & Row, 1985.

Bernardin, Joseph. "The Public Life and Witness of the Church." *America* (1996).

Brueggemann, Walter. *The Prophetic Imagination.* 2nd ed. Minneapolis: Fortress Press, 2001.

Casanova, José. *Public Religions in the Modern World.* Chicago: University of Chicago Press, 1994.

Chaplin, Jonathan. *Talking God: The Legitimacy of Religious Public Reasoning.* London: Theos, 2008.

Coleman, John A. "Compassion, Solidarity and Empowerment: The Ethical Contribution of Religion to Society." *Journal of Religion in the Social Services* 19, no. 2 (1999): 7-20.

Daly, Herman, and John Cobb. *For the Common Good.* London: Merlin Press, 1990.

Daly, Siobhan. "Mapping Civil Society in the Republic of Ireland." *Community Development Journal* 43, no. 2 (2008): 157-176.

Eberly, Don E. "The Quest for Civil Society." In *Building a Community of Citizens: Civil Society in the 21st Century*, ed. Don E. Eberly, xvii-xlviii. Lanham: University Press of America, 1994.

Fiorenza, Francis Schüssler. "Social Mission of Church." In *The New Dictionary of Catholic Social Thought*, ed. Judith A. Dwyer, 151-170. Minnesota: The Liturgical Press, 1994.

Greenawalt, Kent. "Religion and American Political Judgments." *Wake Forest Law Review* 36, no. 219 (2001): 401-422.

Habermas, Jurgan. "Religion and the Public Sphere." *European Journal of Philosophy* 14, no. 1 (2006): 5.

Habermas, Jürgen "Religion and the Public Sphere." *European Journal of Philosophy* 14, no. 1 (2006): 1-25.

Hannay, Alastair. *On the Public*. London ; New York: Routledge, 2005.

Healy S.M.A., Sean, and Brigid Reynolds S.M., "Spirituality" http://www.cori.ie/Justice/Spirituality/45-Spirituality/120-Spirituality (accessed 1st February 2008).

Healy, Sean, and Brigid Reynolds. "Making Choices - Choosing Futures, a Question of Paradigms." In *Making Choices - Choosing Futures: Ireland at a Crossroads*. Dublin: CORI Justice, 2008.

_____. *Planning for Progress and Fairness, Policies to Ensure Economic Development, Social Equity and Sustainability* Socio-Economic Review 2008. Dublin: Cori Justice, 2008.

Hehir, J. Bryan. "Church-State and Church-World: The Ecclesiological Implications." *Catholic Theological Society of America* 41 (1986): 54-74.

_____. "The Social Role of the Church: Leo XIII, Vatican II and John Paul II." In *Catholic Social Thought and the New World Order*, ed.

Oliver F and John W. Houck Williams. Notre Dame: University of Notre Dame Press, 1993.

_____. "The Church in the World : Responding to the Call of the Council." In *Faith and the Intellectual Life: Marianist Award Lectures*, ed. James L. Heft, 101-119. Notre Dame: University of Notre Dame Press, 1996.

_____. "Can the Church Convincingly Engage American Culture." *Church* (2004): 5-10.

Heschel, Abraham Joshua. *The Prophets*. New York: Perennial, 2001.

Heyer, Kristin E. *Prophetic & Public : The Social Witness of U.S. Catholicism*. Washington, D.C.: Georgetown University Press, 2006.

Himes O.F.M., Kenneth R. "Commentary on Justitia in Mundo (Justice in the World)." In *Modern Catholic Social Teaching: Commentaries and Interpretations*, ed. Kenneth R. Himes O.F.M., 333-362. Washington, D.C.: Georgetown University Press, 2005.

Hollenbach, David. "Contexts of the Political Role of Religion: Civil Society and Culture." *San Diego Law Review* 30, no. 4 (1993): 877-901.

_____. *The Common Good and Christian Ethics* New Studies in Christian Ethics 22. Cambridge, UK ; New York: Cambridge University Press, 2002.

_____. "Gaudium Et Spes." In *Modern Catholic Social Teaching: Commentaries and Interpretations*, ed. Kenneth R. Himes, 266-291. Washington DC: Georgetown University Press, 2004.

_____. "Catholicism and American Political Culture: Confrontation, Accommodation, or Transformation." In *Inculturation and the Church in North America*, ed. T. Frank Kennedy S.J., 7-22. New York: The Crossroad Publishing Company, 2006.

Kennedy School of Government, John F., "Social Capital Community Benchmark Survey" http://www.ksg.harvard.edu/saguaro/communitysurvey/index.html (accessed 30 October 2007).

Lofland, Lyn H. *The Public Realm : Exploring the City's Quintessential Social Territory*. Hawthorne, N.Y.: Aldine de Gruyter, 1998.

Marty, Martin E., and Jonathan Moore. *Politics, Religion, and the Common Good : Advancing a Distinctly American Conversation About Religion's Role in Our Shared Life*. San Francisco: Jossey-Bass Publishers, 2000.

McKee, Alan. *The Public Sphere : An Introduction*. Cambridge ; New York, NY: Cambridge University Press, 2004.

O'Brien, David J., and Thomas A. Shannon. *Catholic Social Thought : The Documentary Heritage*. Maryknoll, N.Y.: Orbis Books, 1992.

O'Connell, Dan. "Religious Education and the Public Sphere." *The Furrow* 57, no. 7/8 (2006): 391-402.

Palmer, Parker J. *The Company of Strangers : Christians and the Renewal of America's Public Life*. New York: Crossroad, 1981.

Pope Paul VI. "Evangelii Nuntiandi." In *Catholic Social Thought: The Documentary Heritage*, ed. David J. O'Brien and Thomas A. Shannon, 301-345. New York: Orbis Books, 1999.

Sacks, Jonathan. *The Politics of Hope*. London: Vintage, 2000.

Sandel, Michael J. *Justice : What's the Right Thing to Do?* 1st ed. New York: Farrar, Straus and Giroux, 2009.

Social Justice Ireland, "About Us" http://www.socialjustice.ie/content/about-us (accessed 30th July 2010).

Synod of Bishops. "Justitia in Mundo." In *Catholic Social Thought: The Documentary Heritage*, ed. David J. O'Brien and Thomas A. Shannon, 287-300. New York: Orbis Books, 1999.

Taylor, Charles. *Modern Social Imaginaries*. Public Planet Books. Durham: Duke University Press, 2004.

Troeltsch, Ernst. *The Social Teaching of the Christian Churches, 2 Vols.* New York: Harper Torchbooks, 1960.

Vatican II. "Gaudium Et Spes." In *Catholic Social Thought: The Documentary Heritage*, ed. David J. O'Brien and Thomas A. Shannon, 166-237. New York: Orbis Books, 1999.

Verba, Sidney, Kay Lehman Schlozman, and Henry E. Brady. *Voice and Equality: Civic Voluntarism in American Politics*. Cambridge: Harvard University Press, 1995.

Warner, Michael. *Publics and Counterpublics*. New York Zone Books, 2002.

Waters, John. "Hearing Only Pious Cliches." *The Irish Times*, 22nd October 2007.

4.

Shaping the future of the welfare state – What are the challenges and how might they be addressed?

Seán Healy and Brigid Reynolds

The welfare state is not an end in itself. It is a means to an end. In reflecting on the future of the welfare state, therefore, it is important to address the issue of purpose: if there is to be a welfare state what should its purpose be? To serve that purpose what should be the shape of the welfare state in the future? What are the challenges faced by the welfare state in seeking to achieve that purpose? What should be the key components of the welfare state in the twenty first century if it's to achieve its purpose? What additional challenges does the production of these key components present to governments, societies and individuals? These are the questions we seek to address in this chapter. Needless to say we will not be able to address all these questions comprehensively. However, we set out what we consider to be some of the core elements of the answers to each of these questions.

A question of purpose

In recent years the issue of well-being has been the subject of much discussion and debate. Many reports have been produced by significant bodies in the policy-making process internationally and in Ireland. These include reports by the Organisation for Economic Cooperation and Development (OECD), the New Economics Foundation (NEF), the Commission on the Measurement of Economic Performance and Social Progress (CMEPSP) and in Ireland, the National Economic and Social Council (NESC). These reports have all identified the importance of well-being for all societies and recognised that the purpose of public policy is ultimately to ensure the well-being of its members. Particular policies in specific economic, social, cultural, political or environmental areas are all measured by their ultimate capacity to contribute to the well-being of the members of society.

These reports and studies have identified a range of issues closely related to well-being. These include the issue of progress: what is progress and how should it be measured? What contributes to and what damages well-being? What should be the inter-relationship between the human and the ecological systems? How important is economic growth and how should it be measured? How are economic growth, progress, the environment and well-being interrelated?

Flowing from these discussions there has been an emerging series of questions concerning the obligation on societies to promote the well-being of their members. Do societies have such an obligation? How can the answer to such a question be decided? If such an obligation exists, what are the implications of this obligation? What are the criteria by which this obligation is determined? Who should be involved in this discussion and who should make the final decisions? How can these be monitored on an ongoing basis? How can directions be adjusted in light of emerging evidence?

A recent report by The National Economic and Social Council (NESC) defined well-being as follows: "A person's well-being relates to their physical, social and mental state. It requires that basic needs are met, that people have a sense of purpose, that they feel able to achieve important goals, to participate in society and to live the lives they value and have reason to value." (NESC 2009, p.xiii)[99] This is the wellbeing that *Social Justice Ireland* and the present authors would like for all members of all societies.

Spiritual;
Curriculum

---

[99] A summary of this report is included as a chapter in a previous volume in this series: Healy and Reynolds, 2009. That chapter was written by Helen Johnston of NESC who was the principal author of the report.

As far back as Plato it was recognised that the person grows and develops in the context of society. "Society originates because the individual is not self-sufficient, but has many needs which he can't supply himself"[100] (cited in George, V. 2010, p6). Down through the ages various philosophies and social arrangements have been proposed to meet the felt need in societies to fulfil their perceived obligations to their members. These varied from Aristotle's position of favouring private ownership but common use of property to ensure the dire needs of people were met, to the emphasis of both Plato and Aristotle that education should be free and compulsory, to Cicero's discussion of equality, to the early Christian emphasis on sharing and forming community.[101]

In more recent times the dignity of the person has been enshrined in The Universal Declaration of Human Rights which states: "All human beings are born free and equal in dignity and rights. They are endowed with reason and conscience and should act towards one another in a spirit of brotherhood." This core value is also at the heart of the Catholic Social Thought tradition. *Social Justice Ireland* and the authors in particular, support the values of both these traditions. We advocate that the dignity of each and every person must be recognised, acknowledged and promoted effectively. This implies that society's structures, institutions and laws should exist for the authentic development of the person.

The right of the individual to freedom and personal development is limited by the rights of other people. This leads to the second core value, namely, the common good. As we noted earlier the concept of the 'common good' originated over two thousand years ago in the writings of Plato, Aristotle and Cicero. More recently, the philosopher John Rawls defined the common good as "certain general conditions that are…equally to everyone's advantage" (Rawls, 1971 p.246). *Social Justice Ireland* understands the term 'common good' as "the sum of those conditions of social life by which individuals, families and groups can achieve their own

---

[100] (Plato, in Lee 1987, p58, cited in George, V. 2010, p6)
[101] For an interesting review of the historical development of welfare see George, V. (2010), *Major Thinkers in Welfare: Contemporary Issues in Historical Perspective*, Bristol, The Policy Press.

fulfilment in a relatively thorough and ready way" (Gaudium et Spes no.74). This understanding recognises the fact that the person develops their potential in the context of society where the needs and rights of all members and groups are respected. The common good, then, consists primarily of having the social systems, institutions and environments on which we all depend, work in a manner that benefits all people simultaneously and in solidarity. The NESC study referred to already states that "at a societal level, a belief in a 'common good' has been shown to contribute to the overall well-being of society. This requires a level of recognition of rights and responsibilities, empathy with others and values of citizenship" (NESC, 2009, p.32).

Common good

This raises the issue of resources. The goods of the planet are for the use of all people – not just the present generation; they are also for the use of generations still to come. The present generation must recognise it has a responsibility to ensure that it does not damage but rather enhances the goods of the planet that it hands on – be they economic, cultural, social or environmental. The structural arrangements regarding the ownership, use, accumulation and distribution of goods are disputed areas. However it must be recognised that these arrangements have a major impact on how society is shaped and how it supports the well-being of each of its members in solidarity with others.

In recent years many people have argued that the market will resolve these issues. They believe that following the economic recession the market is the only mechanism that can restore a sense of social obligation and develop a viable response to the questions raised above. Consequently, they argue that the primary focus of government policy should be to support and encourage business efficiency through the social, economic, cultural and political structures of society. This is an ideology that gives primacy to the economy. It believes that people should serve the economy, not vice versa.

On the other hand many others have argued that an untrammelled market undermines any reasonable attempt to shape society in the interest of securing every person's well-being. They believe that human dignity and human development are critically important as it is the right of every individual to realise his or her potential and aspirations. They look at history and say that the market has created inequalities rather than enhanced solidarity; that it has given huge priority to creating what is superfluous rather than redistributing necessities.

It is clear from what we have written already that the authors believe that the economy should serve people and not the other way around. However, it is very important to note that we do not reject the market or the social role of private enterprises or profit or finance and so on and their capacities to contribute positively to the well-being of society and its members. Rather, we believe that the market should be at the service of people and that all can contribute to deciding the aims and choosing the priorities that ensure that the market in its various manifestations is at the service of securing every person's well-being.

The welfare state

Down through the ages societies have struggled with these issues and responded to the challenge of securing and supporting the well-being of their members in a variety of ways. One approach to securing everyone's well-being has been the development of the welfare state. There has been an ongoing debate on the future of the welfare state for the best part of 30 years. Developments such as faltering economies, changing demographics, globalisation and many more have fuelled these debates at different times. There is general agreement in the literature that the welfare state has been changing in terms of both its purpose (ends) and its means. However, whether or not developments have been positive or negative is disputed. Some have concluded that the welfare state has been very effective at resisting attempts to reduce its scope (Mishra, 1990; Pierson, 1994; Timonen, 2003). Others argue that there has been substantial reduction in the welfare state in recent decades (Bryson, 1992; Leonard, 1997; Jamrozik, 2001).

In the year 2000 the European Union agreed a new strategy to become 'the most competitive and dynamic knowledge-based economy in the world capable of sustainable economic growth with more and better jobs and greater social cohesion'. The European social model was to be developed through investing in people and developing an active and dynamic welfare state. This was seen as crucial by the European Council so as to secure Europe's place in the knowledge economy and to ensure that the so-called new economy did not exacerbate social problems such as unemployment, social exclusion and poverty. This approach, known as the *Lisbon Strategy*, was substantially amended at its half-way point in 2005 and by its conclusion date in 2010 had clearly failed to deliver on either its economic or social goals. A new strategy was put in its place in 2010 called *Strategy 2020*. While it contains targets on poverty, education, jobs and the environment, there is little confidence that it will get to grips with some of the major challenges that face the welfare state at this moment in history.

Through all of this period however, many countries increased their social spending. Between 1980 and 2005 the 'Anglo-Saxon' countries along with other low-spend countries increased their social spending by about one fifth (as a percentage of GDP). Scandinavian countries were starting from a much higher base but they increased their spending by a similar amount. Japan increased its social spending by 75 per cent (principally to meet the needs of its aging population). The Mediterranean countries, which lagged behind other EU countries, had the fastest growing welfare states. Greece, Spain, Portugal and Italy increased their welfare effort by two-thirds in this period. Other countries in Western Europe saw their spending grow at a more modest rate. On average gross public expenditure on welfare across OECD countries increased from 16 per cent of GDP in 1980 to 21 per cent in 2005 (Adema and Ladaique 2009).

Another development that needs to be noted in this context is that spending on social policy rose as a share of public spending across the Western world in the second half of the twentieth century. Spending on defence was reduced as a proportion of public spending and industrial subsidies were reduced as major basic industries were privatised.

Overall, however, there is no doubt that the welfare state is under pressure, that it has changed and developed in the past and that it will do so again in the future. The broader context has been changing rapidly and this has produced a wide range of challenges which the welfare state now faces. We reflect on some of these.

Key Challenges

The welfare state is facing key challenges at a range of different levels today. These include:

- The economic level: is the welfare state fiscally sustainable in the long-term?

- The political level: can the welfare state be sustained in the current political climate?

- The meaning (cultural) level: is the welfare state sustainable from a moral perspective?

- The social level: is the welfare state a place in which people wish to live in the years ahead?

We look at each of these challenges in turn.

The economic dimension: is the welfare state fiscally sustainable in the long-term?

The past few years have produced a major economic upheaval across the world. There have been banking crises, budget crises and economic crises. The basis of the world's core economic model has fallen apart. The tax-payer has had to pay huge amounts of money to rescue financial institutions while, at the same time, many governments (including Ireland) have made huge cuts in funding for social services and infrastructure.

But the issue of whether or not the welfare state is fiscally sustainable in the long-term was already being addressed long before these recent series of crises exacerbated the situation. Governments had, for example, been introducing (or increasing) charges in healthcare systems. Likewise some governments reduced the levels of pensions to which people were entitled. Over the past two decades the levels of expected pension payments had been reduced by a quarter in the EU. However this was of little significance for Ireland which never had generous pension entitlements along EU lines (except for the wealthy who could provide for their own pensions and who got very generous tax breaks to fund these).

Changes introduced in recent years, however, may not be even close to being sufficient to address the fiscal sustainability challenge. The future may well see a regular recurrence of similar financial crises if international regulatory systems are not put into place or are not effective in policing the irresponsibility and criminal behaviour of the international banking system. If this is the situation that emerges then the stability and growth of modern economies will be under serious pressure. Their capacity for financing the welfare state will be precarious. This capacity is going to be tested in the medium term as the huge debt incurred by states in rescuing their financial sectors in recent years will put government budgets under pressure.

The political dimension: can the welfare state be sustained in the current political climate?

Macro-sociological studies have highlighted the importance of the political dimension in the evolution of the welfare state (for example, Oyen, 1986; Orenstein, 2000; Rys 2010). If it is to be maintained and developed in the long-term then it has to be politically acceptable to a wide range of those who shape decisions across various political arenas.

In recent decades the political system in most countries has come under pressure from its electorate demanding value for money as well as more efficient and better quality services. Governments have responded in a variety of ways. Many have, for example, introduced public sector reforms focused on setting targets and measuring outcomes. Some have introduced competition between service providers as a means to generating greater efficiency. This can be seen in the Swedish healthcare and education systems and in the healthcare reforms introduced in the Netherlands and Germany. There has been a huge growth in private provision of social care in many countries. On the other hand, there has been only modest growth in private education and healthcare in some countries while others have taken very few initiatives in this direction.

In arguing for private sector involvement and a greater role for the market in areas of welfare provision, governments tend to highlight the deficiencies of state provision which have led, in turn, to declining confidence in the state's capacity to improve the quality of the services provided or to get the best value for the money it spends in these areas. This obviously is an additional problem which forms part of the context to be addressed.

How successful these approaches have been is unclear. There are many reasons why markets have not worked well in many areas covered by the welfare state. However, there is little doubt that the demand for more efficiency and better quality in social services will persist. It is not clear how governments will respond to this demand. They may, for example, give service recipients a greater voice in the provision of the service they receive. Or they may have more competition. Or they may develop options that enable service recipients to exit state provision. Or they may adopt any combination of these responses. However, the resourcing of these options remains an unresolved issue. There are major questions concerning governments' approach. For example, if government provides a specific amount of money for a particular service provider to deliver a service how can the provider ensure that the funding is not reduced while the demands increase. This latter has been the experience of many service providers in the community and voluntary sector in Ireland during the current recession. The government washes its hands of any responsibility once a certain amount has been allocated. The service provider on the frontline is left facing those who need a service but without adequate funding.

This is obviously unacceptable. An even more unacceptable practice is the approach used by Ireland's Department of Health in allocating resources to fund a specific initiative in a particular budget and then agreeing to this money being reallocated to fund over-expenditure in other parts of the service while still claiming credit for the original allocation! Yet another danger in this context is the situation where government provides grants for additional service provision by the private or the community and voluntary sector and then lets the public sector's provision of the service lapse.

Obviously there are issues of efficiency and effectiveness involved in all of this. How can one be balanced against the other? How can decisions be made that produce a fair outcome given the various issues involved? There are tensions between legal entitlements, standards of provision and budget allocations. A comprehensive debate and a workable way of finding the appropriate balance between these various aspects and how they are to be provided and resourced at any particular moment in time are needed.

There is another challenge that the political system faces in the years ahead. For a century or more the issue of the services available for people has been at the core of the political agenda at national level across the world. Poverty was reduced. Social housing provision increased. Education and healthcare came to be seen as services to which all should have access. In the decades ahead there will be other issues that may well dominate political debate ranging from the world banking crisis to climate change to the situation of the Third World. In contrast to welfare state issues in the past century which were addressed for the most part at national and local levels, these issues require international action with countries working together to develop and deliver solutions. However, these developing arrangements do not necessarily have to reduce the interest in or support for welfare state issues. In fact, addressing these issues could lead to a more balanced approach to global and national development in which, for example, environmental, welfare and economic issues are seen as impacting on each other and consequently are addressed in a genuinely integrated manner.

The meaning (cultural) dimension: is the welfare state sustainable from a moral perspective?

Some have argued that the changing economic world and a growing focus on the individual rather than the social or the community will undermine the moral basis for the welfare state. They see this growing focus as leading to a lack of commitment to others which will erode their solidarity and commitment to support the welfare state. This view is being reinforced following the very angry reactions of many people to the decisions of government to rescue banks and other financial institutions with tax payers' money. These decisions have put huge pressure on national budgets. Some argue that people will conclude that they themselves do not carry any responsibility for others and consequently support the reduction of social expenditure.

Market optimists have always argued that the market has the capacity to ensure that all the services provided by the welfare state can, in fact, be made available by the market. They urge the state to introduce rules that ensure people provide for their needs through private provision for their health, long-term care and pension needs and to take the financing of their education and accommodation into their own hands (Thaler and Sunstein, 2008).

However, the record shows that there has been growing inequality in the gross incomes of people in many countries in recent years. If this inequality is to be reduced then the State must play a key role which in turn means that taxes and/or benefits have to be increased. The key question is how much of the inequality generated by the original market effect should be reduced or eliminated. Different countries have provided different answers. Sweden, for example, has reduced its original market-based inequality by much more than countries such as Ireland, the UK,

Canada, Finland or Germany. There have been substantial, but varied, levels of redistribution. When benefits-in-kind are included there is even more redistribution. This continued redistribution would suggest that the fears of losing moral support are unfounded.

There is growing support also for the argument that unequal societies are dysfunctional. A recently published book entitled *The Spirit Level: Why More Equal Societies Almost Always Do Better*, (Wilkinson and Pickett, 2009) has produced a great deal of evidence showing that inequality does matter. It shows that the dysfunctionality arising from inequality impacts on both the poor and the rich and affects areas from health, to happiness, from murder rates to teenage pregnancy, from social mobility to educational performance. It is clear that for a great many people inequality matters, why it occurs matters, the damage that it does matters, and so seeking greater equality matters.

Another aspect of concern for the sustainability of support for the welfare state at a moral level has been the understandable worry that social policy designed to create a more equal society might make the economy less efficient. However, a range of recent publications on social policy show that social protection measures don't necessarily make an economy less efficient. In fact, it is becoming clearer that economic efficiency is much more likely to be affected negatively by unrestrained capitalism. The recent banking crisis has undermined the belief that unrestrained individual greed can result in better welfare for all.

The social dimension: is the welfare state a place in which people wish to live in the years ahead?

There are many new challenges that could arise in the social context. For example, technological changes and the rewards of innovation may lead to even greater inequalities in income and in wealth. This situation could be exacerbated by the terms of trade in a world of growing international trade. At another level major climate change could well produce food shortages and rising sea levels. These would, in turn, produce large numbers of displaced people who would migrate. This in turn could have huge implications for better off countries that will be challenged to support poor people migrating to their countries. Paradoxically, this could generate support for the welfare state as well as working against it. People might well conclude that they would be far better off, on balance, working together to attain a future in which all could live with dignity.

There is another, quite different, issue that arises in the social context. This concerns the providers of social services whether they are teachers, nurses, doctors or community development workers and what is called 'provider capture'. 'Provider capture' refers to a situation where a service is developed primarily in the interests of the service provider rather than in the interests of the person receiving the service, whatever it may be. For example teachers are expected to provide a service that is primarily of benefit to the students, nurses and doctors are to provide a service focused primarily on improving the health status of people. Claims have been made that decisions are made in the education system, in the healthcare system and in many other areas that form part of the welfare state, in the interests of those who are employed to deliver the service rather than in the interests of those whom they are employed to serve.

This is a huge issue and would best be addressed in another chapter or book. It involves issues around the relationship of the state to various actors in the provision of welfare whether these work for the state, the community and voluntary sector or the private sector. It involves issues around roles and relationships and how these are perceived. It involves issues around partnership and mutuality and shared responsibility. It involves issues around support structures. Above all it involves recognition in both theory and practice that those receiving the service should be the primary focus at all times. This is assured by appropriate participation in decision-making regarding the service. However, in the context of this chapter it is important to recognise that ensuring 'provider capture' does not happen will be a necessary pre-requisite for the successful development of the welfare state in the years ahead.

In this struggle to develop a society where the well-being of all is the focus we should keep the following question in the spotlight: is this the kind society in which people want to live? If the welfare state is to have support and be a place that attracts people then it must seek to provide a core set of outcomes that would promote the well-being of all. We now identify some of the key components we believe should be at the heart of the welfare state in the twenty first century.

Key components of a 21st century welfare state[102]

1. An appropriate, secure income distribution system

The income distribution system that is seen as ideal at present involves all adults of working age having paid employment. This is supported by a welfare system that ensures people have a basic amount of money if they are unemployed, ill or otherwise unable to access income from having a job. This system has consistently failed to eliminate poverty. It has consistently failed to generate full employment on any kind of permanent basis. It needs to be radically overhauled to address the world of the 21st century.

The present authors have argued for a long time that the tax and social welfare systems should be integrated and reformed to make them more appropriate to the changing world of the twenty-first century. We suggest that the present system be replaced by a Basic Income system. A Basic Income is an income that is unconditionally granted to every person on an individual basis, without any means test or work requirement. In a Basic Income system every person receives a weekly tax-free payment from the Exchequer, and all other personal income is taxed, usually at a single rate.

For a person who is unemployed, the basic income payment would replace income from unemployment payments. For a person who is employed

---

[102] The ideas in this section have been developed at much greater length by the authors in Healy and Reynolds, 2008.

The Future of the Welfare State

the basic income payment would replace tax credits in the income-tax system. Basic income is a form of minimum income guarantee that avoids many of the negative side effects inherent in the current social welfare system. A basic income differs from other forms of income support in that

• it is paid to individuals rather than households;

• it is paid irrespective of any income from other sources;

• it is paid without conditions; it does not require the performance of any work or the willingness to accept a job if offered one;

• it is always tax free.

A Basic Income system would replace welfare payments. It could guarantee an income above the poverty line for everyone. It would not be means tested. There would be no "signing on" and no restrictions or conditions. In practice a basic income recognises the right of every person to a share of the resources of society.

The Basic Income system ensures that looking for a paid job and earning an income, or increasing one's income while in employment, is always worth pursuing, because for every euro earned the person will retain a large part. It thus removes the many poverty traps and unemployment traps that may be in the present system. Furthermore, women and men get equal payments in a basic income system. Consequently the basic income system promotes gender equality.

Ensuring people's well-being requires a secure income system. Basic Income is a system that is altogether more guaranteed, rewarding, simple and transparent than the present tax and welfare systems. It is far more employment friendly than the present system.

A new system is required to secure an adequate income for all in the twenty-first century. Basic Income is such a system.

2. Recognition of all meaningful work, not just paid employment

The importance of work for people's well-being is not disputed. However, the understanding of work has been narrowed in practice to paid employment. But paid employment is not available for many people at any particular time. Other kinds of work which are not remunerated such, as care work, are not seen as 'real' work. This situation raises serious questions about the meaning and perception of work. The authors believe that meaningful work is essential for people's well-being. The authors believe that every person has the right to meaningful work. The challenge faced by many societies today is to ensure that right is honoured for all even if paid jobs do not exist for all. We believe that it is possible to produce a situation where everyone has meaningful work even if full employment has not been achieved. It would involve the recognition of all forms of meaningful work, not just paid employment.

A major question raised by the current labour-market situation concerns assumptions underpinning culture and policy making in this area. One such assumption concerns paid employment which is assumed to be achievable in a relatively short time frame if only the correct policies were put in place. The reality raises serious questions concerning this assumption. There are hundreds of millions of people unemployed or underemployed across the world. Even in the most affluent countries there are many who are unemployed or under-employed. It is crucial that job-creation be promoted and that all that is possible be done to create well-paid jobs in which people do meaningful work. However, it is also crucial that societies face up to the fact that there will be many unemployed people for the foreseeable future. One possible pathway towards a solution might be to address a second assumption in the whole area of work.

This second assumption concerns the priority given to paid employment over other forms of work. Most people recognise that a person can work very hard even though they do not have a conventional job. Much of the work carried out in the community and in the voluntary sector fits under this heading. So too does much of the work done in the home. The authors' support for the introduction of a basic income system comes, in part, from a belief that all work should be recognised and supported.

There has been some progress on this issue particularly in the growing recognition of the value of voluntary work. The need to recognise voluntary work has been acknowledged in the Government White Paper, *Supporting Voluntary Activity* (Department of Social, Community and Family Affairs, 2000). The current national social partnership agreement *Towards 2016* also contains commitments in this area.

A report presented to the Joint Oireachtas Committee on Arts, Sport, Tourism, Community, Rural and Gaeltacht Affairs established that the cost to the state of replacing the 475,000 volunteers working for charitable organisations would be a minimum of €205 million and could cost up to €485 million per year.

Government should more formally recognise and acknowledge all forms of work. We believe that everybody has a right to work, understood as contributing to his or her own development and/or that of the community and/or the wider society. However, we believe that policy making in this area should not be exclusively focused on job creation. Policy should recognise that access to meaningful work is an important factor in human well-being. A Basic Income system would create a platform for meaningful work. It would benefit paid employment as well as other forms of work.

3. A strong focus on strengthening participation by all

The need to strengthen participation by all has two aspects. One concerns participation in development at an economic and/or social level. This has been addressed to some extent under the preceding item i.e. the need to value all work. The second aspect concerns participation at a political level. Participation in both of these ways is important for people's well-being.

Democracy means 'rule by the people'. This implies that people participate in shaping the decisions that affect them most closely. This is a significant feature of individual and societal well-being according to Amartya Sen (Sen, 1999). This includes people having the freedom and the processes to express themselves politically and creatively. While we live in a democracy and freedom of expression is accepted in theory at least, there are problems with the current model. What we have, in practice, is a highly centralised government in which we are 'represented' by professional politicians. The more powerful a political party becomes, the more distant it seems to become from the electorate. Party policies on a range of major issues are often difficult to discern. Backbenchers have little control over, or influence on, government ministers, opposition spokespersons or shadow cabinets. Even within the cabinet some ministers seem to be able to ignore their cabinet colleagues. This makes participation in real terms difficult.

The democratic process has certainly benefited from the participation of various sectors in other arenas such as social partnership. It would also benefit from the development of a new social contract against exclusion and a new forum for dialogue on civil society issues.[103] However there is also a need to move towards deliberative democracy and to develop structures where power differentials are neutralised. This would produce a situation where far more emphasis was given to the analysis of situations, to the alternatives proposed and to the implementation pathways being identified.

4. Sustainability (economic, environmental and social) is at the core of all policy-making

The search for a humane, sustainable model of development has gained momentum in recent times. After years of people believing that markets and market forces would produce a better life for everyone, major

---

[103] For a further discussion of these issues see Healy and Reynolds (2003: 191-197).

problems and unintended side effects have raised questions and doubts. There is a growing awareness that sustainability must be a constant factor in all development, whether social, economic or environmental.

This fact was reiterated by Kofi Annan, the then-Secretary-General of the United Nations, at the opening of the World Summit on Sustainable Development in Johannesburg, South Africa (September 2002). There he stated that the aim of the conference was to bring home the uncomfortable truth that the model of development that has prevailed for so long has been fruitful for the few, but flawed for the many. And he further added that the world today, facing the twin challenges of poverty and pollution, needs to usher in a season of transformation and stewardship – a season in which we make a long overdue investment in a secure future.

Sustainable development has been defined in many different ways. Perhaps the best- known definition is that contained in Our Common Future (World Commission on Environment and Development, 1987:43): development that meets the needs of the present without compromising the ability of future generations to meet their own needs.

It is crucial that the issues of environmental, economic and social sustainability be firmly at the core of the decision making process if the well-being of all, today and into the future, is to be realised. Principles to underpin sustainable development were suggested in a report for the European Commission prepared by James Robertson in May 1997. Entitled *The New Economics of Sustainable Development*, the report argues that these principles would include the following:

• systematic empowerment of people (as opposed to making and keeping them dependent) as the basis for people-centred development

• systematic conservation of resources and environment as the basis for environmentally sustainable development

• evolution from a "wealth of nations" model of economic life to a "one-world" economic system

- evolution from today's international economy to an ecologically sustainable, decentralising, multi-level one-world economic system

- restoration of political and ethical factors to a central place in economic life and thought

- respect for qualitative values, not just quantitative values

- respect for feminine values, not just masculine ones.

At first glance, these might not appear to be the concrete guidelines that policy-makers so often seek. Yet they are principles that are relevant to every area of economic life. They also apply to every level of life, ranging from personal and household to global issues. They impact on lifestyle choices and organisational goals. They are at least as relevant today as they were when first proposed in 1997. If these principles were applied to every area, level and feature of economic life they would provide a comprehensive checklist for a systematic policy review.

5. What matters is measured

A central initiative in putting sustainability at the core of development would be the development of "satellite" or "shadow" national accounts. Our present national accounts miss fundamentals such as environmental sustainability. Their emphasis is on GNP/GDP as scorecards of wealth and progress. These measures, which came into widespread use during World War II, more or less ignore the environment, and completely ignore unpaid work. Only money transactions are tracked. They fail to register the benefits of the welfare state. On the other hand they do count its failures. For example, when children are cared for in the home no monetary value is added to GNP/GDP. On the other hand if the child is cared for in a crèche the costs involved are added. Even more dramatic costs are added if the child has to be cared for by the state. Similarly, while environmental depletion is ignored, the environmental costs of dealing with the effects of economic growth, such as cleaning up pollution or coping with the felling of rain forests, are added to, rather than subtracted from, GNP/GDP. New scorecards are needed.

If well-being is the purpose of the welfare state then it is important that data is collected and analysed on the main indicators of well-being. The OECD has done a great deal of work on this issue in recent years and produces a regular publication on social indicators called *Society at a Glance*. The OECD global project on measuring progress and some of the challenges it faces were addressed at some length in a recent publication in this series (Morrone, 2009). The OECD states that "social indicators aim to provide information on well-being beyond that conveyed by conventional economic measures" (OECD, 2007, p.20). Such indicators matter in the assessment of well-being. Measuring what matters should be a key component of the future welfare state.

6. Complete health is promoted

Health is a major element of well-being. People's health is influenced by social conditions such as poverty, social exclusion, discrimination, inappropriate accommodation, a polluted environment and lack of community networks (World Health Organisation, 2004; Farrell et al., 2008). A few statistics on Ireland will serve to illustrate that this is so:

• Between 1989 and 1998 the rates for all causes of death in Ireland were over three times higher in the lowest occupational class than in the highest.

• The death rates for all cancers among the lowest occupational class is over twice as high as it is for the highest occupational class, it is nearly three times higher for strokes, four times higher for lung cancer, six times for accidents.

• Perinatal mortality is three times higher in poorer families than in richer families.

- The incidence of chronic physical illness has been found to be two and a half times higher for poor people than for the wealthy.

- The rate of hospitalisation for mental illness is more than 6 times higher for people in the lower socio-economic groups as compared with those in the higher groups.

- The incidence of male suicide is far higher in the lower socio-economic groups as compared with the higher groups.

- The 1998 and 2002 National Health and Lifestyle Surveys (SLAN) found that poorer people are more likely to smoke cigarettes, drink alcohol excessively, take less exercise, and eat less fruit and vegetables than richer people. Poorer people's lifestyle and behavioural choices are directly limited by their economic and social circumstances.

Promoting complete health would involve addressing issues such as life expectancy, healthy life years, access to healthcare services, chronic illness, mental illness and many related aspects of health. It would also involve addressing the fact that people with lower levels of education or low income, for example, face a higher risk to their well-being. Producing such an approach to health is more than challenging at the present time. A major re-structuring and huge increases in public expenditure in Ireland are not seen to have delivered a better system or improved people's overall health or well-being.

The health system should take a 'whole of health' approach and consider its purpose to be the promotion of complete health, defined by the World Health Organisation as "a state of complete physical, mental and social well-being and not merely the absence of disease or infirmity."[104] A substantial proportion of the expenditure on health goes on medical provision. Policy-makers recognise there is a need to move from a medical

---

[104] Preamble to the Constitution of the World Health Organisation as adopted by the International health Conference, New York, 19-22 June, 1946; signed on 22 July 1946 by the representatives of 61 states and entered into force on 7 April, 1948. This definition has not been amended since 1948.

model to become more prevention oriented. There is still a long way to go. Far higher priority should be given to prevention, primary, community and continuing care.

7. The focus of education is broadened to ensure it produces fully rounded human beings

Education is another essential part of people's well-being. It contributes to human flourishing by enabling people to acquire knowledge and develop their capabilities. It can promote well-being of the person by helping their own development and it can promote the well-being of society by engaging the person in development at that level. It is also closely linked to people's job opportunities. Education can be an agent for social transformation. It can be a powerful force in counteracting inequality and poverty. However, it needs to be acknowledged that, in many ways, the present education system has quite the opposite effect. Recent studies in Ireland confirm the persistence of social class inequalities which are seemingly ingrained in the system. Even in the context of increased participation and economic boom, the education system continues to mediate the vicious cycle of disadvantage and social exclusion between generations.

Early school leaving is a particularly serious manifestation of wider inequality in education, which is embedded in and caused by structures in the system itself. We believe that the core objective of education policy should be: to provide relevant education for all people throughout their lives, so that they can participate fully and meaningfully in developing themselves, their community and the wider society. Education should help to create capable and emotionally well-rounded people who are happy and motivated.

As in health, there should be a holistic approach to education. The curriculum should include the opportunity to cultivate the variety of 'intelligences' people have including musical, spatial, physical, interpersonal and intrapersonal.[105] The key should be the development of

---

[105] For further development of this issue see H. Gardner (1993).

an education system focused on producing fully rounded human beings who can live in solidarity with other human beings and the environment in which they live.

8. Adequate and appropriate accommodation is available for all

The availability of appropriate accommodation is essential in any model of a welfare state. A secure and pleasant place in which to live is a basic requirement for human flourishing. The official objective of Irish housing policy is "to enable every household to have available an affordable dwelling of good quality, suited to its needs, in a good environment, and as far as possible, at the tenure of its choice" (Department of Environment at www.environment.ie). Despite huge growth in the numbers of housing units built annually in Ireland in the period 1988-2006 (up from 14,204 dwellings to 82,979), Ireland failed to address its social housing needs problem. The number of households on local authority waiting lists more than doubled from 27,427 in 1996 to 56,249 in 2008. This failure was exacerbated by a housing price bubble which saw house prices rise dramatically.

Central to the welfare state in the coming years should be an approach that sees housing as a home rather than a market commodity (Drudy, 2005, 2006). Drudy points out that there is a fundamental philosophical question that should be addressed concerning the purpose of a housing system. Should it be a system to provide investment or capital gains for those with the necessary resources or should its critical aim be to provide a home as a right for all citizens? In his view Ireland should move away from seeing housing as a commodity to be traded on the market like any other tradable commodity; and to accept the latter opinion that views housing as a social requirement like health services or education. This is a view with which the authors agree.

9. All cultures are respected

Ensuring the welfare state is available to and benefits everyone is especially challenging in difficult economic times. This challenge can be even greater in a society with different cultures, different expectations and different understandings of well-being. Since the beginning of time people have been divided because of their different cultures, values and beliefs. Centuries have passed and societies still have problems with the acceptance of others. In the recent past Ireland experienced substantial immigration as tens of thousands of people from abroad were needed to meet the employment needs of, and sought to benefit from, the Celtic Tiger. A well functioning welfare state focusing on the well-being of all would structure itself so that all can contribute to the underpinning values and meaning of society and have their own culture respected and valued in the process.

10. Social capital, civil society, social well-being and active citizenship are strengthened.

Many of the aspects already outlined have implications for civil society, social well-being and active citizenship. Research produced in recent years shows the profound importance of communities and relationships in determining people's quality of life. Robert Putnam describes social capital as "features of social organisation, such as networks, norms and social trust that facilitate co-ordination and co-operation for mutual benefit". He argues that the major components of social capital are trust, norms, reciprocity and networks and connections. Social capital has been shown to have positive economic effects while also impacting on people's health and general well-being. It has also been shown that community engagement not only improves the well-being of those who are engaging in such activity but also improves the well-being of others.

In his perceptive analysis Tom Healy reminds us that David Myers defines well-being, at its simplest, as: 'the pervasive sense that life has been and is good. It is an ongoing perception that this time in one's life, or even life as a whole, is fulfilling, meaningful, and pleasant.' However, Tom Healy goes on to point out that well-being goes well beyond mental states of pleasure, happiness or satisfaction for individuals, important as these are. Social well-being concerns the match between our goals and the kind of life we experience. In other words it concerns what we value and seek and how we evaluate our lives in this light.[106] Drawing on reflections from Aristotle to latter-day philosophers like Amartya Sen we can say that well-being involves coherence between the moral ends and chosen values of an individual or society, and the objective circumstances of life as perceived by them. The welfare state has a huge role to play in delivering such an outcome.

Two key issues concerning pathways towards a 21ˢᵗ century welfare state

There are a wide range of issues that need to be addressed if pathways are to be found towards an appropriate welfare state in the twenty first century. We wish to raise two of these in the final section of this chapter i.e. the issue of financing and the issue of responsibility.

The issue of financing

Following on the understanding of the purpose of the welfare state, the issue of financing is of critical importance. Idealism, aspiration and expectation must be matched by resources. If the welfare state cannot be funded in the future then it will not survive. In fact the political acceptability of any developments in the welfare state is closely linked to economic sustainability. While the world continues to be organised economically as a capitalist market economy there will be pressure to ensure that the cost of the welfare state does not fall too heavily on market enterprises so as not to impede free competition in production and trade. Despite benefiting generously from the advantages of the welfare state,

---

[106] For further elaboration on this see Tom Healy (2005)

the middle classes are often reluctant to support a generous level of redistribution. The cost of financing the various components of the welfare state has, for the most part, been rising. Simultaneously, the fact that people live longer has also been increasing the costs. There may well be further pressure on funding as improving living standards may lead some to feel they don't need the welfare state. At the same time there may be a growing tendency to reduce the redistribution element by providing support only for the 'deserving' poor.

These developments suggest the welfare state needs to provide a comprehensive rationale to explain and justify demands. Firstly, there will be a growing demand for transparency. People will want to know precisely who is paying what for the welfare state and who is gaining what from it. This should be possible without too much difficulty given the world's improved technological capacity. However, the results will have to be reliable and verifiable. There have been some recent examples where the level of accuracy and of transparency left a great deal to be desired (cf. For example, Social Justice Ireland, 2010).

Secondly, there may be a demand to ensure social justice. This is not just an issue about adequacy, which of course is a critically important issue. There is also a need to ensure that the welfare state promotes the human dignity of participants and the common good as core values.

A third issue that has already arisen is the issue of people living longer. This would not be a problem for the welfare state as long as people extended their 'working' lives beyond the traditional retirement age. In the 1980s a century-long process of reduction in the working age in the US was reversed. The UK saw a similar reverse emerge about 1995. More recently other OECD countries have been following this trend. Another approach is the one adopted by Sweden and Germany where they reformed their pension systems and built in automatic reviews of the level of pension payments to ensure they remain in line with the increasing life expectancy. An interesting comparative statistic was produced by the UK's Pension Commission which showed that in 1950 the average male spent 17 per cent of his adult life in retirement. By 2000, it had risen to 31 per cent. The Commission argued that this could not continue to rise. They proposed that retirement be accepted as the norm for about 30 per cent of adult life and that the age when one becomes eligible for a state pension should be raised as required to meet this target.

A fourth aspect of the financing issue concerns its sustainability. For example, the EU countries will have to increase the percentage they spend on social welfare payments by about 4 per cent of GDP to meet the costs of current welfare payments and promises made for the future. When one extends the number of countries involved to include all OECD countries then the requirement rises to between 5 and 6 per cent. These increases are definitely feasible. Ireland is in a slightly different situation as its population is much younger and the aging of the population experienced by most EU countries is still a few decades away. However, Ireland's social expenditure is one of the lowest in the EU at 18.9 per cent compared to an EU-27 average of 26.2 per cent of GDP. Given that Ireland's pension provision is far less generous than most EU-15 countries it should be possible to meet the rising costs with something to spare and remain one of the low-spend countries in terms of social spending.

A fifth aspect of financing in the future concerns alternatives to raising taxes. Different approaches are emerging where people are encouraged or forced to support their own social provision. In Sweden, for example, 2.5% of workers earnings must be invested in privately-funded pensions. Private health insurance is now compulsory in the Netherlands. Compulsory health insurance is also imposed in some states in the USA and the US government is moving towards near-universal healthcare coverage. Various forms of graduate taxes have been introduced to fund third level education.

A sixth area of activity in addressing the issue of financing has been and will continue to be the move to reduce or eliminate disincentives to taking up paid employment. Maximising labour-force participation is seen as the key to providing the funding required for the welfare state. So we may well see increased subsidisation for low-paid jobs and increased funding for training programmes for those who are unemployed. Some may move towards a workfare approach to labour market activation even though the evidence suggests that this is a high-cost route to take. Another approach might be the development of voluntary programmes where those in receipt of unemployment payments could work in the public or the community and voluntary (non-profit) sector doing real jobs for the going hourly 'rate for the job.' They could work the required number of hours to receive their unemployment payment (up to a maximum of half the normal length of the working week) and then be free to take up any further employment that was available and pay tax in the normal way.

Failure to address the financing issue could lead to a situation where a large proportion of a society's population was unable to provide privately for its welfare while no alternative was available to them. Historically, such a problem has led to the elimination of the existing social order and its replacement with some form of totalitarian, collectivist regime which in turn failed. The twentieth century has made great progress in recognising and supporting human rights. But rights can become an illusion unless the financing to deliver these rights is secured and sustained.

The need for shared social responsibility

If a pathway is to be found to securing everyone's well-being through the welfare state or through any other means, the issue of responsibility must be addressed. If a democratic society is to function effectively then the exercise of responsibility is both a right and an obligation. Given the current situation of crisis across the world in so many contexts e.g. economic, political, cultural, environmental and social, and given the collapse of confidence in key institutions ranging from the economy to church, from banking to the legal to politics, the issue of responsibility needs to be highlighted.

Nation states and the world itself are facing huge challenges to rebuild confidence and to find credible responses to the challenges already identified in this chapter. To achieve this it is essential that the understanding of responsibility for the well-being of all be re-defined and broadened. It should be understood as meaning a responsibility that is shared by all, that is exercised by all in the context of their capacity and capability. It should also mean that this responsibility is shared by individuals, by institutions and by society generally, including governments. Given the inter-dependence of so much of modern life and the process of globalisation it is crucial that people and nation states recognise the global nature of many of the problems they face and recognise that addressing these effectively requires that all accept they have a shared responsibility for developing and implementing a viable alternative to the present system.

Sharing responsibility must be at the core of any credible pathway forward. We have argued already in this chapter that the economy should be at the service of people, of the present and future generations, rather than people being at the service of the economy. A viable future also requires conservation of the planet as the common home of humanity and of life in general. None of this will happen unless there is a new approach that recognises and acts on the need for an approach based on shared responsibility.

There are many rights that have been secured in the European Convention on Human Rights and Fundamental Freedoms, the revised European Social Charter and the European Union's Charter of Fundamental Rights; likewise, with the UN Declaration on Human Rights and other similar instruments. But actually having those rights vindicated and delivered in practice requires that responsibilities to others alive today and in the future be recognised and addressed pro-actively.

In finding a way out of the current series of crises it is crucial that the unequal impact of these crises on different groups be recognised. Poor and/or vulnerable people suffered most as a result of these crises. These are the same people who bear least responsibility for the mechanisms which produced these crises. In many cases they are the people who have to pay a lot more tax to rescue these mechanisms (such as the banking system) and who see the services provided by the welfare state eroded as governments' finances are re-directed to the rescue of these same banks.

In practice what this situation shows is that some people who have more power and information are able to minimise or eliminate their own responsibility for what happens while vulnerable people who have no say and did not cause the problems are left carrying much more of the responsibility.

If there is to be a viable, desirable future where everyone's well-being is secured and promoted then it is crucial that social responsibilities be shared more fairly between governments, citizens, business, civil society, faith communities and all others involved in any manner. All actors should be involved in developing a shared vision of the future based on some shared values and developing pathways towards that vision at a wide range of levels. For this to happen, a genuinely participatory process is required. As we have outlined already we favour a deliberative process in which power differentials are neutralised.

In arguing for shared social responsibility to be at the core of a new approach, we see social responsibility going far beyond the obligation to answer for ones actions; it also includes approaching issues with a perspective that includes promoting the well-being of others including future generations. We also realise that not everyone can be involved in shaping all decisions. However, we believe shared social responsibility involves a commitment to generating a consensus concerning both the vision and the pathways and then involving people in different situations in deciding how best to move forward within these parameters. In practice this requires major reorganising at the political, economic and social levels. In recent decades the demand for autonomy and for freedom of choice produced an approach that relied to a great extent on self-regulation of individuals and markets. That model has failed. We now require an approach that links autonomy, as the ability of each individual to manage his/her own existence in accordance with a freely chosen lifestyle, to social justice in which individual preferences are balanced against the group interest and each person's fundamental rights.

References

Adema, W. And M. Ladaique, (2009) *How Expensive is the Welfare State?* OECD, France

Bryson, L. (1992) *Welfare and the State: Who Benefits?* Basingstoke, Macmillan.

Department of Social, Community and Family Affairs (2000), *Supporting Voluntary Activity*, Dublin, Stationery Office.

Farrell, C, H. McAvoy and J. Wilde (2008) *Tackling Health Inequalities: An All-Ireland Approach to Social Determinants*, Dublin: Institute of Public Health and Combat Poverty Agency.

Gaudium et Spes, Pastoral Constitution on the Church in the Modern World, 1965 accessed at: http://www.vatican.va/archive/hist_councils/ii_vatican_council/documents/ vat-ii_cons_19651207_gaudium-et-spes_en.html

George, V. (2010) *Major Thinkers in Welfare: Contemporary Issues in Historical Perspective*, Bristol, The Policy Press.

Healy, S. and Reynolds, B. (2009), *Beyond GDP: What is progress and how should it be measured?* Dublin: Social Justice Ireland

Healy, S. and Reynolds, B. (2008), *Making Choices, Choosing Futures*, Dublin: CORI Justice Commission.

Healy, S. and Reynolds, B. (2005), *Securing Fairness and Wellbeing in a Land of Plenty*, Dublin: CORI Justice Commission.

Healy, S. and B. Reynolds (2003), "Ireland and the Future of Europe – a social perspective" in Reynolds B. and S. Healy (eds.) *Ireland and the Future of Europe: leading the way towards inclusion?* Dublin, CORI.

Healy, S. and Reynolds, B. (1996), "Progress, Values and Public Policy" in Reynolds, B. and Healy, S. (eds.), *Progress, Values and Public Policy*, Dublin, CORI, pp. 11-59.

Healy, S. and Reynolds, B. (1993), "Work, Jobs and Income: Towards a new Paradigm" in Reynolds, B. and Healy S. (eds.), *New Frontiers for Full Citizenship*, Dublin: CMRS.

Leonard, P. (1997) *Postmodern Welfare: Reconstructing an Emancipatory Project*,

Sage Publications, London.

Jamrozik, A. (2001) *Social Policy in the Post-Welfare State*, Longman, Sydney.

Mishra, R. (1990) *The Welfare State in Capitalist Society: Policies of Retrenchment and Maintenance in Europe, North America and Australia*, Harvester Wheatsheaf, Hemel Hempstead.

Morrone, A. (2009), The OECD Global Project on Measruing Progress and the challenge of assessing and measuring trust in B. Reynolds and S. Healy, *Beyond GDP: What is prosperity and how should it be measured?* Social Justice Ireland, Dublin.

National Economic and Social Council, (2009) Report 119 Vol. 1, *Well-being Matters: A Social Report for Ireland*, Dublin, NESC.

Orenstein, M.A. (2000) *How Politics and Institutions affect Pension Reform in Three Post-Communist Countries*, Policy Research Working Paper. Washington DC: World Bank.

Oyen, E. (1986) 'The Sociology of Social Security' Editorial introduction, *International Sociology*, vol 1, no 3, pp 21921.

Rawls, J. (1971) *A Theory of Justice*, Harvard University Press, Cambridge, Mass.

Rys, V. (2010) *Reinventing social security worldwide: Back to essentials*, Bristol: The Policy Press.

Pierson, P. (1994) *Dismantling the Welfare State? Reagan, Thatcher and the Politics of Retrenchment*, Cambridge University Press, Cambridge.

Sen, A. (1999) *Development as Freedom*. Oxford University Press, Oxford.

Social Justice Ireland, (2010) *Building a Fairer Tax System: The working poor and the cost of refundable tax credits*, Dublin, Social Justice Ireland: Policy Research Series.

Thaler, R. H. And C. R. Sunstein, (2008) *Nudge: Improving Decisions About Health, Wealth, and Happiness*. Yale University Press: New Haven & London

Timonen, V. (2003) *Restructuring the Welfare State: Globalization and Social Policy Reform in Finland and Sweden*, Edward Elgar, Cheltenham.

Wilkinson, R. and K. Pickett, (2009) *The Spirit Level: Why More Equal Societies Almost Always Do Better*, Penguin, London.

World Commission on Environment and Development, (1987) *Our Common Future*, Oxford University Press, Oxford.

World Health Organisation, (2004) *Commission on the Social Determinants of Health (CSDH): Notes b the Secretariat, Document number EB115/35*. WHO: Geneva.

THE RACE
OF THE
CENTURY

Grundy and Bustino
at Ascot

Christopher Hawkins

London
George Allen & Unwin Ltd
Ruskin House   Museum Street

First published 1976

ISBN 0 04 796046 9

George Allen & Unwin (Publishers) Ltd
Ruskin House, 40 Museum Street
London WC1A 1LU

Printed in Great Britain
in 11 point Baskerville type
by Butler & Tanner Ltd
Frome and London

Author's Preface

Grundy and Bustino, two outstanding racehorses, staged what for many was the race of the century in the King George VI and Queen Elizabeth Diamond Stakes at Ascot in July 1975. Great races which are won by inches after a prolonged duel have a profound emotional effect on those lucky enough to see them. Physically the effect can also be shattering – it can be fatal. But, as they say, what a way to go!

I have tried in this book to recreate Diamond Day at Ascot. I have traced the paths which led Grundy and Bustino to meet that afternoon, from the time their sires Busted and Great Nephew met in the Eclipse Stakes at Sandown Park eight years before. Thoroughbreds are in existence to race but they spend only a small proportion of their lives on the racecourse. Most of their time is spent at home where they are looked after with affection by lads whose lives demand great dedication. I have tried to give a glimpse of life in a stable and an insight into the meticulous preparation which goes into training the racehorse. Without the help of the lads connected with Bustino and Grundy at West Ilsley and Seven Barrows, this would not have been possible. And, of course, without the help of Dick Hern and Peter Walwyn, the trainers, the book would never have got off the ground. I would like to thank all of them for their co-operation and hope the end-product has made their efforts worthwhile.

Thanks are also due to Lady Beaverbrook for her willingness to talk of her racing career and her racing philosophy; Edgar Cooper Bland, who bred Bustino, and Tim Holland Martin, the breeder of Grundy, have also given assistance; while Keith Freeman, the bloodstock agent, has been wonderfully frank.

Racehorses have given enormous pleasure for centuries now

and have reached perfection through selective breeding. The principal intention of this book, therefore, is to be a tribute to the magnificence of the thoroughbred and, more particularly, Grundy and Bustino, who together embodied all the most admirable qualities of a noble animal.

Contents

Illustrations

ACKNOWLEDGEMENTS

Acknowledgements and thanks for permission to reproduce the photographs are due to E. G. Byrne, with the exception of No. 11 (Fiona Vigors), and No. 19 (De Beers Consolidated Mines Ltd).

Acknowledgements are also due to the Clerk of the Course, Ascot Racecourse, for permission to reproduce the race card for the King George VI and the Queen Elizabeth Diamond Stakes.

I've heard them speak with bated breath
  Of the heroes of the past
Of how the giants of yesterday
  In sterner moulds were cast.

SUSAN COLLING
Bustino v. Grundy

Chapter 1

'Well I'm busted that eclipses everything'

Bill Rickaby, a veteran of over 10,000 rides and 1,320 winners, mounted the four-year-old racehorse Busted with eager expectation. It was a glorious July afternoon, his wife Bridget's birthday and the occasion of the 1967 Eclipse Stakes over a mile and a quarter at Sandown Park. Among the opposition in a good-class field for this race, worth £22,677 to the winner, was the French-trained but English-owned Great Nephew, on whom Rickaby had finished second, beaten by a short-head, in the previous year's 2,000 Guineas. To those without the possession of some very special knowledge, it seemed that the jockey now on Great Nephew, Jean Duforge, was the more likely to win this time. But that knowledge was the reason for Rickaby's elation.

Throughout the spring and summer of 1967, Rickaby had been Busted's regular work rider, since, in fact, the colt had joined Noel Murless's stable from Brud Featherstonhaugh in Ireland. When Busted arrived he had been headstrong and very hard to settle both in work and in his races. Some thought he would never fulfil his potential, citing the Irish Derby as typical of his nature. In that race at The Curragh in June 1966 he had led the field for ten furlongs but utterly sapped himself of energy and dropped out to finish a long way behind the winner, Sodium. Even a reduction of distance to nine furlongs and to a mile, in his last two races that season, failed to prevent him squandering his strength and running out of steam in the vital final stages. It was clear that he would have to be taught to relax and this was Rickaby's job.

Rickaby's biceps were subjected to plenty of punishment in the spring of the year, as he fought Busted into submission, but the lessons were gradually learned until the colt began to gallop within himself, conjuring visions among the work watchers of what a good horse he might be. Noel Murless was well aware of Busted's potential and began to mark him down as a suitable galloping companion for Royal Palace, the stable's classic hope of that season. Three weeks before the 2,000 Guineas, Royal Palace, Sucaryl, Busted and the lead horse Minera took part in a serious gallop. The instructions were to come at a good pace and allow the three colts to improve together in the last furlong. Busted settled in last place but when brought out took hold of his bit and in Rickaby's words 'went like a bomb'. It was a sight that must have left Murless with mixed feelings: did he have two world beaters or was Royal Palace not so good after all? The answer would not be found at home anyway and Busted was never worked seriously again with Royal Palace since Murless feared overtaxing the three-year-old. As events on the racecourse subsequently proved, there was certainly no three-year-old in the country capable of beating Royal Palace at this time and he went on to win the 2,000 Guineas and the Derby, the latter in easy fashion from Ribocco.

Busted had his first race of the season in the Coronation Stakes over a mile and a quarter at Sandown on 29 April. On home form he looked a certainty to beat the opposition which amounted to second class. There was no catastrophe. Busted was backed from 9–2 to 3–1 and landed a useful gamble for the stable, beating Haymaking by a comfortable three lengths coming from behind just as he had been taught. George Moore, the stylish Australian, was the man in the saddle on this occasion, being the jockey retained by Noel Murless.

Busted moved rather stiffly in subsequent work and a muscular strain was diagnosed which required a month's rest. The Eclipse Stakes was drawing close but Busted's principal objective was the King George VI and Queen Elizabeth Stakes

at Ascot at the end of July. In spite of the strain, his preparation was not interfered with seriously and in his first strong
work since the lay-off he revealed all his power, prompting
Murless to let him meet the Eclipse engagement. The ride was
offered to Bill Rickaby. So that day, as the runners wound
their way down through the rhododendron walk at Sandown,
Rickaby felt full of confidence. He would not have swopped
rides with anyone, not even to take the mount on an old friend
like Great Nephew.

Bill Rickaby's association with Great Nephew went back to
the previous season, 1966, when Sir Jack Jarvis had charge of
him and he was thought good enough to be worth running in
the 2,000 Guineas at Newmarket. A preparatory run at
Kempton Park had been designed to bring Great Nephew to
peak fitness but he fell after three furlongs and the race gave
him no benefit at all. As a result Paul Cook, first jockey to the
stable, had no hesitation in passing him over in favour of
Pretendre, who had the Epsom Derby as his main target but
was well fancied for the 2,000 Guineas. Bill Rickaby had been
associated with the Jarvis stable for years and was married to
Sir Jack's niece. He thus came in for the ride on Great Nephew.

Rickaby's instructions were to let the horse take his time and
run his own race in order to restore any confidence that might
have been lost by the fall at Kempton. Accordingly Rickaby
was disinclined to push him in the early stages of the contest
and at half-way Great Nephew had plenty of ground to make
up on the leaders. Pretendre was prominent at The Bushes
but was unable to quicken, something that Rickaby found
Great Nephew could do when asked two furlongs out. Making
ground fast he caught the leader, Kashmir II, ridden by Jimmy
Lindley, and in the final strides it was a desperate affair. The
verdict went to Kashmir II by a short-head but Great Nephew
looked very unlucky. Rickaby thought he would definitely have
won had he not been told to ride a quiet race.

Great Nephew was not favoured with much luck in his remaining races in 1966. Immediately after the 2,000 Guineas

he was again involved in a photo-finish for the Lockinge Stakes at Newbury. Paul Cook had taken over the ride by now and dismounted in the unsaddling enclosure telling the owner Jim Philipps: 'I don't know why they've called for a photo – I've won half a length.' In fact Silly Season had won and Cook had mistaken the winning post. When the season closed, Great Nephew had managed only a single victory and Jim Philipps felt frustrated. He decided that if the horse was not to miss his potential completely, he had better compete for the bigger prize-money in France.

To find a trainer was the first step, therefore, and Philipps made a diffident approach to Etienne Pollet, who always restricted the number of horses in his stable to forty-eight. That was the rule – no more, no less and no exceptions. Not surprisingly Pollet was full but out of politeness to the enquiring owner he asked the name of the horse concerned. 'Great Nephew', came the reply. 'I'll take him', said Pollet. Explaining the reason for his abrupt change of mind, he recalled that he had been at Newmarket for the 2,000 Guineas and, after surveying the runners beforehand, had scribbled on his race-card: 'The best horse is Great Nephew but he's not fit.'

Great Nephew prospered with Pollet and matured into a strong, good-looking colt. He quickly won two races without ever being headed, and became a confirmed front runner. A horse has to possess more than an average amount of courage to be a successful front runner and it was this quality that characterised Great Nephew. He won the Prix Dollar by a short-head and in the Prix Ganay went down by half a length to Behistoun after a prolonged duel. Behistoun had won the Washington International the previous year and so, in view of Great Nephew's high-class French form, it was no surprise to see him well backed when Pollet decided to send him over for the Eclipse Stakes.

Sandown Park is not an ideal course for a front runner since it has a long testing uphill run to the finishing post, but Great Nephew's quality could not be denied and he was consequently third favourite at 5–1. The favourite at 15–8 was Sodium, who had won the Irish Sweeps Derby and the Doncaster St Leger the previous year. Next in the betting came Fleet. This filly was a stable companion of Busted and was to be ridden by George Moore who had triumphed on her in the 1,000 Guineas. She appeared to be better fancied than Busted and was priced at 9–2. Busted was at 8–1, having opened at 10–1.

Great Nephew showed a marked reluctance to enter the stalls but had no such reservations about leaving them. Encouraged by Duforge he raced into a clear lead, going a terrific gallop. The pundits in the stands shook their heads at such folly and put it down to the flamboyant French temperament. But Great Nephew kept going. A furlong from home he was still in front and those know-alls who had criticised Duforge for his seemingly break-neck pace were beginning to squirm. Looking back through the field they saw that Sodium was beaten and that Fleet was floundering under severe pressure. Surely the Frenchman was not going to win? Resting their binoculars on the pink and green stripes of Bill Rickaby, however, they saw with relief that Busted was still on the bit.

Duforge had unknowingly played into Rickaby's hands by setting such a strong pace and Busted had been easy to settle at the rear of the field until being asked to improve on the inside of the field three furlongs out. He made ground easily and Rickaby sat against him, dreading to come too soon and scarcely able to restrain the impatient power. With two hundred yards to run the moment arrived. Rickaby switched Busted to the outside, relaxed his grip and was amazed to find himself two lengths clear in a matter of strides. It was a performance that etched a memory of brilliant acceleration. Busted was running away at the finish and Rickaby had to struggle to pull him up.

A great reception greeted the pair in the winner's enclosure. The gallant Great Nephew drew respectful applause in the runner-up berth but Busted's appearance brought concerted cheering. It was a popular victory, mainly because Bill Rickaby had earned great affection over the years as a man of integrity. He was regarded as deserving of better opportunities in the saddle and now, for the first time since his 2,000 Guineas success on Privy Councillor in 1962, he had won a major race. His brother Fred was not present to witness the triumph, being one of the top trainers in South Africa, but he sent a telegram which read: WELL I'M BUSTED THAT ECLIPSES EVERYTHING.

Eclipse Stakes   1m 2f; Sandown Park 1967

1	BUSTED,	4–9–5	W. Rickaby
2	GREAT NEPHEW,	4–9–5	J. Duforge
3	APPIANI II,	4–9–5	C. Ferrari
4	Fleet,	3–8–4	G. Moore
5	Jolly Jet,	4–9–5	L. Piggott
6	Chinwag,	3–8–7	A. Barclay
7	Sodium,	4–9–5	A. Breasley
8	Kedge,	3–8–7	G. Starkey
9	Blue Rullah,	4–9–5	W. Williamson

Distances: $2\frac{1}{2}$ l, $1\frac{1}{2}$ l, hd, 4 l, 4 l.

Betting: 15–8 Sodium, 9–2 Fleet, 5 Great Nephew, 8 Busted, 100–9 Jolly Jet, Chinwag, 100–7 Appiani II, 25 Blue Rullah, 50 Kedge.

At the end of the season Bill Rickaby retired. His career had lasted thirty-seven years and after such a spell it was hardly surprising that he could not forsake racing. He went abroad to act as a stipendiary steward to the Hong Kong Jockey Club but three years later was involved in a horrific car accident which ended his activities and left him very deaf. He still takes great pleasure from his association with Busted and Great Nephew, however, and regards Busted as the best horse he ever rode.

After the Eclipse Stakes, Busted won the King George VI and Queen Elizabeth Stakes at Ascot and the Prix Henri Foy in France, on both occasions being ridden by George Moore. Noel Murless's plan was to run him in the Prix de l'Arc de

Triomphe in October but he damaged a tendon ten days beforehand and had to be retired. Busted had been ante-post favourite at 5–2 and looked well nigh unbeatable. He was voted 'Racehorse of the Year' by a panel of racing journalists and hailed as the best English-trained colt since his sire Crepello had won the 2,000 Guineas and the Derby in 1957.

Busted had been bred at the Snailwell Stud by Stanhope Joel and in retirement he returned there as a stallion at a covering fee of 1,500 guineas. At the same time Great Nephew stood at the Derisely Stud. He had returned to France after the Eclipse Stakes and managed one more victory – in the one-mile Prix du Moulin – from three races. In three seasons he had won five times from six furlongs to a mile and a quarter and on all types of going. He was consistent, courageous and good-looking. Jim Philipps had turned down an offer of $300,000 from America for him and this steadfastness was ultimately to bring great rewards.

Chapter 2

Stud

Breeding racehorses is an inexact science and in every mating there are imponderable factors that can upset the best-laid plans. Even when a successful mating produces a classic winner there is no guarantee that a repetition of the same mating will not produce a selling plater: Brigadier Gerard's full sister Lady Dacre, for example, failed to win even once. Breeders can strive for perfection and eradicate faults by trial and error, but in the final analysis the process is in the lap of the gods. This is what adds the excitement of uncertainty which besets racing and bestows its special appeal.

Most breeders attempt to select a stallion for their mare on the basis of compatibility. This encompasses the racing ability, physical and temperamental characteristics of the animals concerned, their parents, close ancestors and any previous offspring. The covering season begins on 15 February and mares are often sent to visit a stallion when still in foal from the previous year, the gestation period being eleven months. Nine days after foaling the mare will come into season and thereafter on a three-weekly cycle. On the 38th, 39th, 40th, 41st and 42nd day after being covered, the mare will be 'teased' by an old horse not suitable for stallion duties. If there is no sign of the mare coming into season she will be tested, usually by the manual method, to ascertain whether in fact she is in foal.

Genetics is a vast and complicated subject of which the prospective breeder attempts to acquire as much knowledge as possible. Brigadier Gerard's dam La Paiva, for instance, was inclined to throw curbs, a malformation of the hock, but a corrective mating produced a perfect result. Peter Willett describes the corrective theory in his book *An Introduction to the Thoroughbred*: 'It is important that the animal showing the fault should be mated with an individual who is flawless in that respect. Thus an animal with upright pasterns should be mated with one possessing pasterns of perfect slope and length, not with one possessing horizontal pasterns.'

Faults are not necessarily evident in an animal, but can be carried as a recessive, hence the importance of knowing fully the characteristics of parents and close ancestors. Even when pedigrees have been researched at great length and all factors have seemingly been taken into account, results can be very disappointing from the point of view of racecourse performance. The element of chance always exists and is relevant to the achievement of all stallions at stud.

Busted was by Crepello out of Sans le Sou – a mediocre immediate female line. Crepello traces to Blandford who suffered from leg trouble and has had a tendency to pass on this weakness. Crepello had his career curtailed because of this and of course Busted suffered similarly, although this may only have been coincidence. Busted had his first covering season in 1968 and his first runners in 1971, when he produced at least two promising two-year-olds in Bog Road and Redundant. He was also responsible for Work and Play, a colt out of Ship Yard. Work and Play was trained in France without achieving anything of note and the next progeny of Ship Yard, a filly called Salami, died before she ever saw a racecourse. Ship Yard's first two visits to Busted were not a great success, therefore, but the element of chance had still to step in, for this union was eventually to produce a champion.

Edgar Cooper Bland, who owns the Rutland Stud at Newmarket, had bred Ship Yard in 1963. She was by Doutelle out of Paving Stone and her granddam was Rosetta, who proved a prolific source of winners and was a half-sister to Alycidon and Acropolis. Thus Ship Yard was a member of the famous Marchetta family which has been represented by a succession of top-class horses like My Babu, Larkspur, Altesse

Royale and English Prince. Ship Yard was sent into training with Sam Armstrong at Newmarket and proved to be a useful two-year-old, winning three times, once over seven furlongs and twice over a mile. As a three-year-old she ran only once, without winning.

Busted's second crop – this was the one that included the ill-fated Salami – had established him as a high-quality sire, for among his sixteen winners in 1973 was Weavers Hall, winner of the Irish Sweeps Derby, and Cheveley Princess, who won the Sun Chariot Stakes, beating the 1,000 Guineas and Oaks winner Mysterious. But these successes came after Edgar Cooper Bland had decided to send Ship Yard to Busted for a third successive season when he had no proof either of Busted's ability or the quality of this particular union. Cooper Bland must be given credit for his perseverence, therefore, and ultimately it was rewarded. After the third mating Ship Yard foaled a bay colt. The colt grew into a handsome yearling and fetched 21,000 guineas at the Newmarket Yearling Sales of 1972. His purchaser was Lady Beaverbrook, who was to name him Bustino.

While Busted stood at the Snailwell Stud, Newmarket, Great Nephew began his career at the Derisley Stud, now renamed the Dalham Hall Stud, only a short distance away. Great Nephew sired twenty-one winners with his first two crops but did not make quite the same impact as Busted. Maybe the quality of the mares he covered was inferior, but he performed well as a stallion and had 89 per cent fertility in his first season. His third crop included his first two-year-old of merit in Red Berry, who was second in the Cheveley Park Stakes of 1973, but it was in his fourth covering season, when visited by Word From Lundy, that the genes combined to produce a colt of real significance.

Word From Lundy was the property of the Overbury Stud in Gloucestershire owned by the Holland Martin family. She was a bay and had been foaled in 1966 and sent into training with Fulke Johnson Houghton at Blewbury. After winning over 7 furlongs in her first season she developed into a useful stayer the next, winning over 11.7 furlongs and 12 furlongs. In her only race over two miles she finished fourth and appeared to stay the distance. Her stamina was inherited from her sire Worden II, a chestnut with an unusual flaxen mane and tail. Worden II won the Washington International at Laurel Park, USA, and five other races. He died in 1969, but not before siring some notable stayers including Bon Mot, who won the Prix de l'Arc de Triomphe, and Golden Fire, winner of the Cesarewitch, the Chester Cup and the Goodwood Stakes (twice).

Word From Lundy had an excellent temperament and, like many lop-eared animals, was particularly honest and genuine. She was out of Lundy Princess by Princely Gift by Nasrullah by Nearco who had four crosses of St Simon in his first five generations. St Simon was one of the greatest racehorses in the history of the Turf and a great sire – in 1900 he sired the winners of all the five classics. He appears on both sides of Great Nephew's pedigree, Great Nephew being by Honeyway out of Sybil's Niece. This is the Pretty Polly family which was represented by successive Derby winners in St Paddy and Psidium in 1960 and 1961, and more recently by Brigadier Gerard.

Honeyway, Great Nephew's sire, had been trained by Sir Jack Jarvis and raced during the Second World War, winning sixteen times. He won the Victoria Cup, the July Cup, Cork and Orrery Stakes and King George Stakes, which suggested he was a sprinter pure and simple, but he had stamina as well as speed which he proved by winning the Champion Stakes over ten furlongs. Eventually he did well as a sire but not before certain complications had been ironed out. He was sent to stud at the end of his five-year-old season but it was found that neither of his testicles had dropped – he was a double rig. He was consequently unable to get mares in foal and was sent back into training for another season after which he was tried again as a stallion. After treatment he was able to do his job and proved a successful sire, among his many winners, besides Great Nephew, being Honeylight (1,000 Guineas), Dictaway (French 1,000 Guineas) and Donald (Ebor Handicap and Jockey Club Cup).

The mating of Word From Lundy to Great Nephew combined speed with stamina, a courageous nature being uppermost in both animals. After the covering Word From Lundy went back to Overbury and in the spring of the following year went to the Woodpark Stud in Ireland to visit Tower Walk. She was still in foal to Great Nephew when making the passage to Ireland and in April gave birth to a chestnut colt.

Peter Diamond, the stud groom at Overbury, remembers the foal that came back from Ireland in July as being small but lively and full of character. So full of life was he, in fact, that after being back home only a few days he almost killed himself. He had to be placed in quarantine on returning from Ireland and, resenting the restriction on his freedom, he somehow managed to escape. But jumping through a paddock rail he became enmeshed in barbed wire. The more panic-stricken he became the more he cut himself and he was rescued only in the nick of time. The damage was extensive to his quarters and hind legs, and 150 stitches were required, but showing the toughness that was also to salvage his three-year-old career, he recovered quickly.

He spent the rest of that summer in the company of other colt foals, roaming the paddocks at night, being brought in at 11 a.m. to prevent a pestering from flies and being let out again at 4 p.m. Then only in the event of a thunderstorm would he be returned to his box. Life on a stud farm is good for the young foal but in October the routine changes with a hint of the disciplined life that lies ahead. The foals are weaned then and are tied up at night, being let out during the day.

On 1 January all foals become yearlings, but life is still carefree and in the summer the routine of night-time roaming is reintroduced. Suddenly, however, in August the freedom ends.

The yearling is brought in, he is tied up and dressed over. For an hour and a half every morning except Sunday he is exercised, which involves essential education in walking on main roads. Then three days a week – usually Monday, Wednesday and Saturday – he has half an hour's lunging, the

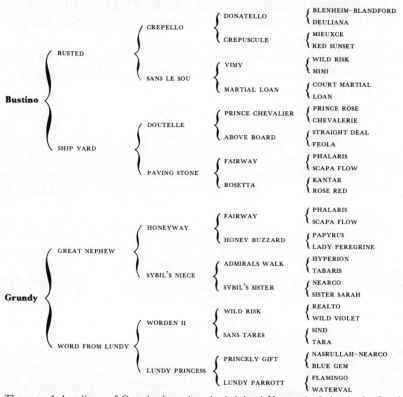

The extended pedigree of Grundy shows how he is inbred Nearco 4 × 5, i.e. in the fourth and fifth generations. The extended pedigree of Bustino shows how he traces from Blandford in the fifth generation. Blandford was unsound and has had a tendency to pass this on.

first stage of horse-breaking, being sent round on a single rein, attached to a bitless bridle, in left-hand and right-hand circles. The yearling will naturally go left-handed and to make him move in the opposite direction sometimes causes problems. For eight to ten weeks, less for fillies, this routine is followed strictly until he goes to the autumn sales recognisable as a young racehorse.

Word From Lundy's foal grew into a tough yearling, was a good walker and appeared very proud of himself. He was sent to the Newmarket Tattersalls Sales and bought for 11,000 guineas by the Italian industrial chemist, Dr Carlo Vittadini. Dr Vittadini always likes to incorporate in a new horse's name part of the name of both the sire and the dam. This originated with his first racehorse in this country, Exar, who was by Arctic Prince out of Excelsa; so now Great Nephew and Word From Lundy produced Grundy.

Chapter 3

West Ilsley

Sir Gordon Richards, at 68 still wrapped up in the romance of racing and actively involved as racing manager to Lady Beaverbrook, went through the catalogue for the Newmarket Yearling Sales in October 1972 with his usual interest. He was looking for probable purchases, a task made easier by the generous funds available, but one which required careful study and knowledge of breeding. On turning to the page giving details of a bay colt by Busted out of Ship Yard, Sir Gordon's interest quickened. He had trained Ship Yard's first progeny some years earlier, a colt by Aureole called Oarsman who had finished second in the French St Leger. Sir Gordon had liked Oarsman's looks and temperament and, knowing the fine winning record of Ship Yard's family, it seemed to him that the colt was worth prior examination. So, with Major Dick Hern, Lady Beaverbrook's trainer, he drove to Newmarket two days before the sales to look over the yearling.

What was he looking for? Soundness is the first requirement in a horse for no matter how well bred an animal is, if he has bad legs he is unlikely ever to see a racecourse let alone prove successful. The forelegs in particular are, therefore, studied for any signs of splints, growths on the side of the cannon bones, and a condition called 'back at the knee', which means concave joints unlikely to stand strain. A horse that is back at the knee is prone to suffer jarring on firm ground. There is also the opposite condition 'over at the knee', but this is not regarded as a serious malformation and indeed this sort of knee joint helps to absorb shock. Horses that are over at the knee are usually tough and stand plenty of racing.

Straight pasterns on the other hand are regarded as a definite hindrance and Levanter, trained by Ryan Price, is a recent example of a horse with classic pretensions unable to fulfil his potential because he was 'straight in front'. The existence of any one of these faults does not necessarily mean that a horse will be useless, however, as illustrated by Colorado, who was said to be back at the knee but won the 1926 2,000 Guineas and Eclipse Stakes before making a success of an all too short stud career – he died after two years.

Besides good legs, Sir Gordon and Dick Hern were looking for a yearling with clean, well-shaped shoulders, a strong neck, a full, intelligent eye, a deep girth and loins, a good length of quarters and a good length from shoulder to buttocks enabling the horse to stand over plenty of ground. The yearling they saw was a bright bay colt of near perfect conformation and as a result they decided to bid at the auction. An offer of 21,000 guineas secured the colt and Sir Gordon felt they had possibly bought a bargain.

As yet the colt was unnamed and to fit the Beaverbrook tradition his appellation had not to exceed seven letters. Seven is regarded by Lady Beaverbook as her lucky number – coincidentally there are seven letters in the word *Express*, Lord Beaverbrook's newspaper. So in this case the letters INO were added to the first four letters of the sire to make Bustino, a name with a pleasant ring. A good name, it is believed, is the first step to owning a good racehorse.

Lady Beaverbrook takes a very real interest in her horses and was present when the decision was taken to buy Bustino; also before a race she likes to cast her experienced eye over the runners in the paddock. And it is an experienced eye. All her life Lady Beaverbrook has been interested in horses and she used to ride regularly to hounds. Her two husbands, Sir James Dunn and Lord Beaverbrook, had both owned racehorses although a classic victory eluded them. Lord Beaverbrook, however, bred one or two useful horses including Miracle, who was bought by Lord Rosebery as a yearling for only 170 guineas. Miracle proved a bargain, winning the Gimcrack

Stakes and the Eclipse Stakes, and finishing third to April the Fifth in the 1932 Derby.

After the death of Lord Beaverbrook in 1964, Lady Beaverbrook was in mourning, but one of the friends who helped her was Lord Rosebery. 'He thought I should not sit around and mope but have a go with racehorses,' she says. So that was what she did – adopting racing colours of beaver brown, maple leaf green cross belts and cap – and it was Lord Rosebery who bid 4,800 guineas to buy her first yearling in 1965. This was a chestnut filly, appropriately named Rosebid, who was sent to be trained at Epsom by Walter Nightingall. Rosebid was Lady Beaverbrook's first winner, scoring first time out at Epsom in the Banstead Stakes. Rosebid subsequently proved disappointing and Lady Beaverbrook quickly became familiar with the frustrations of racing. As a broodmare, however, Rosebid was more of a success and, when sent to Aggressor, foaled a filly called Magical, who coincidentally won the Banstead Stakes first time out and later won the Cucumber Stakes at Goodwood.

Walter Nightingall died in 1968 after a career as a trainer lasting forty-two years. During that time he won the 1943 Derby for Dorothy Paget with Straight Deal and the 2,000 Guineas in 1965 with Niksar. He also had some successes with horses owned by Sir Winston Churchill, notably Colonist II, Vienna and High Hat: High Hat sired winners at stud and Lady Beaverbrook was particularly interested in a chestnut colt by him at the yearling sales of 1968. She paid 6,300 guineas for the colt whom she named Miracle, after Lord Rosebery's horse bred by Lord Beaverbrook. As a two-year-old Miracle won the Solario Stakes at Sandown Park. He also won once as a three-year-old and, when Sir Gordon Richards retired from training at the end of 1970, he was transferred to Dick Hern's stable. Hern and Scobie Breasley now became Lady Beaverbrook's trainers.

Lady Beaverbrook spent a lot of money at the sales in search of a top-class performer but got little return. To begin with, she placed a great deal of faith in the progeny of Sea Bird II, but after several costly failures lost her enthusiasm for the sire whose stock tended to be temperamental and to have an aversion to racing. In 1971, however, Lady Beaverbrook bought Royalty, who won six races out of seven as a three-year-old, but not a classic. His only defeat came in the Prix de l'Arc de Triomphe which was won in record time by Mill Reef – Royalty finished sixth.

All Lady Beaverbrook's purchases have been characterised by their good looks and rarely can an owner have had a string of such consistently handsome horses. One of the best looking was Biskrah, who developed into a good-class stayer and won £13,327 before retiring to stud in 1973. Boldboy, Richboy, Kinglet, Bigribo and Riboson in recent seasons have also ensured that Lady Beaverbrook has seen at least an acceptable return on an outlay of well over £1 million.

'I may be regarded as crazy to have paid such high prices for some of my yearlings who alas have not turned out well, but my sole aim was to try and prevent at least a few well-bred lines leaving England. It upsets me when this is considered ostentatious,' she says.

True to her word she paid the record price for a yearling in this country, when going to 202,000 guineas for a colt by Mill Reef out of Lalibela. The underbidder was Ravi Tikkoo whose horses are trained in France. The colt, called Million, has yet to run but one thing seems certain, he will never be as good a buy as Bustino, who at 21,000 guineas, was to prove the bargain Sir Gordon Richards imagined he might be.

Bustino was indeed a fortunate animal. He was now bound for the Elysian fields of racing stables – West Ilsley, in the heart of the Berkshire downs midway between Newbury and Oxford. The stables represent a community set aside from the village itself. To reach them one turns right, after passing the thirteenth-century church in the village, up a tarmacadam road liberally dotted with signs reminding one that this is private property until, turning a corner, one finds a dignified manor house with a duck pond in front and several cedar-wood bungalows. It is a small hamlet clustered round a formidable brick-built stable block. This is the secluded community which prompted Lord Wigg on a visit to tell Dick Hern: 'You're not the trainer here, you're the mayor.'

Bustino was an unbroken yearling when he first turned that corner and passed the duck pond in mid-October 1972, but within five weeks he could be ridden, thanks to the attentions of Jim Foggerty, Bob Turner and a band of lads assigned to breaking the yearlings. Bustino was put in the care of a young apprentice, Pat Scallan, who had been with Dick Hern for eighteen months and whose father was stud groom at the Sandringham Stud. Scallan fed Bustino plenty of hay in those early days, a feeding plan with a high calcium content designed to strengthen bone.

Tom Barnes, the man in charge of feeding the horses at West Ilsley, allocates to all the yearlings 7 lb of corn a day, as well as hay, while they are being broken. The main feed comes in the evening when they have 4 lb of corn plus a big spoonful of honey which is smeared around the manger to encourage them. Gradually the feed is increased in step with the amount of exercise each horse is getting and, by the end of January, 9 lb of corn is the daily quota plus occasional carrots, apples and vitamin additives.

By mid-December Bustino was being ridden in three-furlong canters with a bunch of other yearlings, and being made used to the company of other horses – but at this stage he was not being taught to stretch out in racing style. Everyday, however, he was ridden through starting stalls. The self-contained West Ilsley complex has a mile circuit of roads, and for a month until the end of January, Bustino's exercise was restricted to walking and trotting on these roads, unmolested by the hazards of traffic. This trotting on a hard surface is designed to strengthen joints. Towards the end of January, Bustino, now a two-year-old of course, began cantering again but although the work was not yet in earnest he was being sent over four furlongs.

Dick Hern's training theory is to keep the horse enthusiastic above all else: 'A horse must always feel like doing it. You must never overdo the homework. Once they get sick of it they are finished. Let them go at their own pace, never push them.'

Hern is an upright man of military bearing, automatically commanding respect. Taciturn and bluff, he is a formidable character to meet for the first time but there is a warmth beneath the exterior and a concern for other people. He began as assistant trainer to Major Michael Pope in 1952 and became private trainer to Major Lionel Holliday five years later, before taking over West Ilsley from Jack Colling in 1962. Since then his conscientious approach, coupled with considerable flair, has brought consistent success. He has won virtually all the major events but in English classic races only the 2,000 Guineas and the St Leger have fallen to him. Hethersett in 1962 and Provoke in 1965 were his St Leger winners, while Brigadier Gerard took the 2,000 Guineas in 1971 without a prior race as a three-year-old.

Practising what he preaches, Hern did not start any serious work with Bustino until April, although the first entry concerning the colt in the work book is in the last week of March when he went four furlongs on the shavings gallop with another two-year-old, Taunted. At this stage Taunted was regarded as a suitable working companion, being bred for stamina like Bustino and unlikely, therefore, to possess precocious speed. In April, Bustino took part in his first proper gallop, going four furlongs with Taunted, Final Chord, Pop Song and Mons Madness. He continued to work with this bunch of youngsters, gradually putting on muscle and learning, from Mons Madness particularly, to stretch out in good style.

Some trainers like to gallop a two-year-old with a good-actioned older horse. The two-year-old will instinctively imitate the older animal but the danger is that the youngster may overstrain himself in trying to keep up. For this reason work is usually restricted to a couple of furlongs. Dick Hern does not follow this school of thought, however, and relies on

1 Bustino's great depth of shoulder and power is evident as he goes down for the Great Voltigeur Stakes at York.

2 Bustino keeps on to beat Snow Knight and Understudy to win the Sandown Classic Trial in only the second race of his career.

3 Bustino beats Sin Y Sin and Snow Knight (sheepskin nose band) in the Lingfield Derby Trial.

a two-year-old that has raced to take along the others. Mons Madness had his first race in May when he was unplaced at Newbury but he made all the running to win next time out at Bath in June and again at Windsor the following month over six furlongs. These victories were not in good company and of no great significance, except that Bustino went at least as well as Mons Madness at home and for a horse bred for stamina, therefore, he was showing real signs of ability.

Hern decided to prepare Bustino for the six furlongs Acomb Stakes at York in August, a suitable race in which to introduce the colt as it was restricted to horses sired by stallions that had won over a mile and a half or more. Bustino would be meeting others like himself, therefore, and not any sprinters likely to run him off his feet. Joe Mercer, first jockey at West Ilsley since Dick Hern took over, rode Bustino in the race. The colt was not strongly fancied and started at 11–1. The run was primarily meant to be educational although this did not preclude the possibility of winning. In fact, Bustino finished third behind Consolatrix and Radical, beaten two and a half lengths in all. Consolatrix was blinkered for the first time in this race, being one of the Irish trainer, Paddy Prendergast's famous 'York specials', and she made virtually all the running. Bustino managed to keep in touch and ran on strongly in the final furlong to put up a very satisfactory and promising first appearance.

His trainer was pleased and decided to pursue the programme he had pencilled in for Bustino, which meant a trip to Doncaster a month later for the Feversham Maiden Stakes over an additional furlong. This extra distance was expected to suit Bustino and the colt left West Ilsley the day before the race, under the care of the travelling head lad Buster Haslam, as a likely winner. But, on the morning of the race, Haslam found Bustino had a runny nose and possible influenza symptoms and as a result it was felt best to withdraw him. A number of the stable's two-year-olds ran temperatures that autumn, Bustino among them. He recovered slowly and plans to run him in the Dewhurst Stakes at Newmarket in October had to be scrapped. It was decided instead to put Bustino away for the following season, and so 1973 ended with his having had just the one run in public.

Chapter 4

Derby preparation

Bustino had shown promise and ability, but his comparative lack of experience put him at a disadvantage for the 1974 classics, so an early preparation was essential to give him more racing before his first big objective, the Epsom Derby. He was being taught to come from behind and work up to his lead horse and in early spring he began to show impressive form. He was improving quickly, so much so that his work-rider, Brian Procter, was amazed by the response he got during a six-furlongs gallop with Pop Song, Final Chord and Royal Quarter: 'I got hold of him, cracked him down the shoulder and he shot through to get the better of the others.'

By April Bustino was in steady work with Riboson, a familiar galloping companion. On Saturday 6 April he went a mile and a half for the first time on the summer downs, a left-hand undulating gallop similar to Epsom. The first three furlongs were only cantered and at no time was Bustino allowed to come off the bit. That same Saturday, Pop Song went to Ascot for his first-ever race, the Humber Maiden Stakes over a mile, and beat a field of thirty-two horses with ease. This result pointed to the class of Bustino which was emphasised further two weeks later when Royal Quarter won first time out at Newbury, followed the next day by Final Chord and another of the stable's three-year-olds, Hector.

Virtually all Bustino's working companions had won within two weeks and it was becoming ever more clear that he was high-class, perhaps even top-class. He was to make his re-appearance at Sandown on 27 April in the Classic Trial Stakes over a mile and a quarter, and on the Tuesday beforehand he galloped a mile at even weights with the four-year-old Kinglet and Riboson. Joe Mercer rode Bustino and Brian Procter was on Kinglet, who led by some six or seven lengths entering the final two furlongs only to be cut down in no time at all by Bustino. This was an impressive piece of work and there was abundant confidence behind the horse when he set out on the Saturday morning for Sandown, to run over the same mile and a quarter where his sire Busted had beaten Great Nephew seven years earlier.

There was a field of nine for a prize of £2,910 but only one horse apart from Bustino was strongly fancied. This was Snow Knight, trained at Lambourn by Peter Nelson, a colt who had won two of his five races as a two-year-old but had apparently had his limitations exposed when unplaced and a long way behind Apalachee in the Observer Gold Cup at Doncaster in October. Peter Nelson thought Snow Knight had been past his best then, however, and believed the colt capable of much better things. Like Bustino, he had done plenty of work at home and was certainly considered fit enough to do himself justice. Accordingly he started favourite at 7–4 but Bustino was backed to beat him and started at 5–2.

Joe Mercer was content to let Brian Taylor, a tall jockey who most of all resembles Lester Piggott in the saddle, make the pace on Snow Knight, who was conceding 5 lb, and tucked Bustino into fourth place. Approaching the furlong from home marker, Bustino pulled out to challenge and got to Snow Knight with two hundred yards to run. He could not shake off his rival, however, and in the final one hundred yards had to be driven right out by Mercer to win by half a length. It was a satisfactory effort and there could be no complaints. Bustino was running for only the second time of his life in public and was inexperienced compared to Snow Knight. He certainly fulfilled the promise he had been showing at home.

After the Sandown race, Bustino returned to West Ilsley and the linseed mash prepared for all home-coming runners by Tom Barnes. By now Bustino was eating 14 lb of corn a day. Not all horses sleep lying down but Bustino preferred to do

things properly and by eight o'clock he was stretched out asleep
as usual. The head lad, Geordie Campbell, visited him at 6.15
in the morning to run hands over his legs, feeling for any heat,
but Bustino showed no ill effects from his race. Evidence that
he had not had a hard time was that he lost only 6 lb in weight.
On the Sunday morning he was led out for a pick of grass and
for the next three days was ridden for an hour and a half at a
walk and a trot out on the downs. On the Thursday he did two
quiet canters. This is the routine followed by all horses at West
Ilsley after racing, provided they have stood up to their exertions satisfactorily.

Dick Hern expected Bustino to take his race well for he was
a fit horse and the next stage of the programme could, therefore, be proceeded with. This was the Lingfield Derby Trial,
two weeks after the Sandown event. On the Tuesday before
this next race, Bustino worked a mile on the peat moss gallop,
giving the maiden, Straight Flight, 21 lb. He moved nicely and
was now nearing peak form. Once again the stable was confident of victory.

The Lingfield Derby Trial is over a mile and a half and is
generally regarded as a good guide to the Epsom classic. Lingfield is similar to Epsom in that it is a left-handed course with
a sharp descent on the turn into the straight. To run Bustino
here would tell whether he would come down Tattenham Hill
without becoming unbalanced, but Hern had few doubts,
having worked him on the undulating summer downs. Bustino
was meeting Snow Knight on 5 lb worse terms at Lingfield
compared to their Sandown running, but opinion was solidly
behind Bustino who started favourite for the first time in his
career. In all there were seven runners in the field, including
Meon Hill, who had been fourth in the Sandown contest, and
Sin Y Sin, a colt who had a consistent two-year-old record in
second-rate company. This time Bustino was not to be held up
for quite such a late burst, but the tactics were also changed
for Snow Knight on whom Brian Taylor was told to wait instead of setting the pace. Thus, although the ingredients

were the same as at Sandown, the race was to be entirely different.

Hard Choice, a 50–1 chance ridden by Ernie Johnson, made the running for a mile with Bustino close up in fourth and Snow Knight in the rear. Sin Y Sin, ridden by Geoff Lewis, went to the front soon after turning into the straight but Joe Mercer tracked him on Bustino who was sent to the front, exactly as planned, a furlong and a half out. Mercer settled into his familiar rhythmical style, pushing out Bustino with hands and heels. The encouragement had the desired effect and Bustino kept going to beat Sin Y Sin by a length with Snow Knight making steady headway to finish third, beaten a further length and a half.

This victory, although not a scintillating one, put Bustino in the forefront of the 1974 Derby picture. The ante-post betting on the race had for a long time been dominated by Vincent O'Brien's Apalachee and Cellini; but that had changed dramatically since the defeat of Apalachee by Nonoalco and Giacometti in the 2,000 Guineas. Apalachee was unlikely to run again, and his stable companion Cellini had also been scratched from the Derby after being beaten in the Irish 2,000 Guineas. The French-trained Nonoalco was Derby favourite now, followed by Giacometti, trained by the super-confident Ryan Price. Of the two, Giacometti was the more likely to stay the distance, but many believed that Nonoalco's brilliant speed might prevail provided he could be held for a late run. Bustino was advertised at 10–1 in the betting. He had plenty of supporters and Brian Procter thought he was a certainty to win.

Bustino had lost only 2 lb after the Lingfield race and was very fit. Dick Hern had to be careful not to overdo the work at home. A week after the Lingfield race he sent the colt over a mile at what is termed 'half speed' with Bobby Elliott in the saddle. At racing pace it takes about 1 minute 40 seconds to cover a mile, at 'half speed' it should take two minutes. The following Tuesday, Brian Procter rode Bustino another half-speed mile gallop with the Queen's Rekindle as company, but on Saturday 25 May Hern decided it was time for a serious workout. He arranged a mile and a quarter gallop with the four-year-olds, Sunyboy, and Buoy, who was himself being tuned up for the Coronation Cup at Epsom which he won. Buoy was giving Bustino 4 lb but Sunyboy was at level weights with the three-year-old. Sunyboy led, followed by Buoy and Bustino, until the three were upsides with three and a half furlongs to run. Buoy and Bustino were then allowed to quicken in the hands of their jockeys and finished together on the bridle.

With ten days to go, Hern thus had Bustino entirely to his satisfaction and just two more half-speeds over six furlongs on Thursday and Saturday were required to keep him on the boil. The ground everywhere was firm, but although Bustino did not mind such conditions he was worked on the peat moss gallop just in case he jarred himself.

Some horses are sent to Epsom several days before the Derby, mainly foreign challengers, and are allowed to canter round the course on the morning before the race. This year Nonoalco and Northern Taste from France, Mistigri from Ireland and the Epsom-trained Sin Y Sin and Snow Knight were sent out for a Tuesday morning canter. Peter Nelson, the trainer of Snow Knight, was present to see Nonoalco exercised and re-marked that the colt looked a typical miler. While Nonoalco attracted most of the attention of the film camera crews, Snow Knight was virtually ignored and Brian Taylor's real optimism as he dismounted sounded like wishful thinking. After all, was he not a 50–1 shot?

Bustino set off for Epsom on the morning of the race, Dick Hern seeking to involve him in the occasion as little as possible. Joe Mercer was soon in the midst of the action, however, and won the opening Great Surrey Stakes on The Gubba, a two-year-old trained by Ron Smyth. The weather was brilliantly sunny and the going firm – an ideal surface to help the favourite Nonoalco stay the distance, but considering the doubt about his stamina his price of 9–4 was not attractive. The two horses wanted in the market were Giacometti, who closed at 5–2, and Bustino who was backed from 11–1 to 8–1.

The race plan discussed between Hern and Mercer was simple enough. Bustino was to be handily placed, ideally in the first four at Tattenham Corner and brought to challenge two furlongs from home.

The rank outsider, Grand Orient, led until Grey Thunder took over a mile out closely tracked by Brian Taylor on Snow Knight. Bustino was in the middle of the field when Snow Knight took up the running with six furlongs to go, being pushed clear by Taylor who had reverted to the tactics used in the Sandown race. Snow Knight stretched out going down Tattenham Hill, hugging the rail and rounding the corner with a two-lengths advantage over Imperial Prince, who was a length ahead of Giacometti. Bustino was back in eighth place. Taylor now asked Snow Knight for maximum effort and the pair quickly opened up a decisive advantage. It was clear that, unless the colt ran out of stamina, he was not going to be caught. In fact, the first three round the corner were the first three past the post and in the same order – Snow Knight, Imperial Prince and Giacometti. Bustino finished strongest of all up the centre of the track and came to within a neck of Giacometti to be placed fourth, but he had come on the scene too late.

For the eventual winner to lead fully six furlongs out was most unusual and Snow Knight's victory must go down as a brilliant tactical triumph for Brian Taylor. It was an inspired performance, sparked by the tense, exciting atmosphere of Epsom which affected not only Taylor but Snow Knight as well, for before the race, the horse had been particularly fractious and had thrown his rider in a frenzy of nervous tension during the parade down the course.

After the Derby Bustino lost only 4 lb and he recovered marvellously. Dick Hern cannot remember another of his runners to come back from this race in such fine shape, for there was no sign or soreness or jarring. This discounted any theories that Bustino either could not act on the track or found the going too firm. Dick Hern never tried to put defeat down to these reasons. It was simply that in the hurly burly of the race, Bustino had been unable to take up the position Mercer wanted, something which might not have counted against him so drastically had the race been run in more orthodox fashion.

Bustino's defeat was of value, however, in that it confirmed Dick Hern's view that here was a horse of undoubted stamina. His three-year-old career, therefore, was now to be planned to exploit this strength and sights were set high, at the toughest and richest staying event for three-year-olds in Europe – the Grand Prix de Paris over a mile and seven and a half furlongs at Longchamp. The race was on Sunday 30 June. Three weeks was not much time for a horse to recover who might have had a hard race, but Bustino was proving himself to be a tough animal with a strong constitution.

Chapter 5

Seven Barrows

At the end of the 1973 flat season, when Bustino had been put away for the winter after having had just one run, Great Nephew's colt out of Word From Lundy first came to public notice. Immaculately turned out by the Overbury Stud, he was led round the Tattersalls sales ring at Newmarket, eliciting comments about a certain charismatic appeal. He was a flashy fellow all right and it was this striking appearance that had caught the eye of a bloodstock agent, Keith Freeman, on a visit to Overbury some weeks before. Freeman had been acting as agent for Dr Carlo Vittadini since 1959, when he had bought him Exar, and over the years he had formed some definite opinions about thoroughbreds. One of these was that he did not like chestnuts; another, that he did not like animals out of dams who had run over two miles or more. This particular colt failed on two counts, therefore, and there was yet a third count which seemed to damn him totally – Freeman's aversion to the progeny of Great Nephew, whom he regarded as a moderate sire.

Why then did Freeman find himself bidding in that Newmarket sales ring? The answer was simply that he had fallen in love with a dazzling, well-balanced little colt blessed with a superbly handsome head. Nonetheless, his business sense told him not to get carried away and when the bidding reached 10,500 guineas he turned to Dr Vittadini saying it was time to stop; but the Italian too had become captivated and replied: 'Let's have one more go.' And at 11,000 guineas they found they had silenced the opposition.

For the time being the colt went back to Overbury until word went out to Peter Walwyn, the Lambourn trainer, to come and look at three yearlings either home-bred or bought at the recent sales by Dr Vittadini. Walwyn had been training for Vittadini since 1970 when he had taken charge of Ortis, who was to finish second to Mill Reef in the 1971 King George VI and Queen Elizabeth Stakes. Since then Habat had been their most successful horse and had just won £42,295 as a two-year-old. The three yearlings awaiting Walwyn's approval this time were a bay colt by Crepello called Krios, another home-bred bay by Petingo, and the flaxen chestnut to be named Grundy. Walwyn was not attracted by the Petingo colt, who in the end went to be trained in Italy; but he was pleased to take charge of Krios and Grundy, the latter striking him as 'a bit flash, impetuous but with something you couldn't help liking'.

Peter Walwyn had recently passed into statistical middle age and acknowledged it by 'taking a pull' and giving up sugar! A tall man, given to wearing a cap and carrying a cane, he bestrides Seven Barrows stables on friendly, approachable terms with all his staff. His finger is always on the pulse. He is interested in all that goes on and this, combined with his accessibility, is one of the key factors in a success story which began with his taking up training in modest quarters in Lambourn High Street in 1960, after an education at Charterhouse and a spell as assistant trainer to Geoffrey Brooke at Newmarket. He also held the licence for his cousin Helen Johnson Houghton at Blewbury for a time. Now he trains at Seven Barrows, about three miles outside the village, living in a large house over a hundred years old, amid the expansive sweeps of the Lambourn downs with coppice clumps guarding ancient burial grounds – mysteries left by stone-age man. Racehorses have been trained here for over a century. There is history in the air and ghosts of a thousand horses that strode the roads and downland turf, but none so famous as the colt who came in November 1973.

Like all the newly arrived yearlings, Grundy had to be broken, a process that normally takes about four weeks but in Grundy's case a little longer. From the start he was a boisterous colt and it was because of this that the stable lad, Jimmy Brownlie, chose to look after Krios rather than Grundy, who was put in the charge of Charlie Johnson, a lad of twenty.

Ray Laing, the head lad and feeder at Seven Barrows, who has been with Peter Walwyn since the start, gives all the horses a dose of physic at Christmas. A week of preparation is necessary. Feed is gradually reduced until all corn is stopped and thirty-six hours before the dose is administered, even hay is cut out. It takes a week for the horse to recover from having his system drastically purged but he starts the New Year clean and ready to accept an expensive diet of Australian corn, the best available. Ray Laing started Grundy on 10 lb of corn a day, with a linseed mash twice a week, but by the middle of the colt's two-year-old days he was such a prodigious 'doer' that 18 lb of corn was his normal daily consumption. He would eat this in four separate meals. At 6 a.m. Laing goes round all the horses with a barrow of oats, giving a level bowlful to all who want it. Grundy never said no to this early morning snack and would feed again after exercise at 9.15 a.m. He would have another level bowlful at noon and was always more than ready for his main feed at evening stables. In between, of course, he could crop at a hay net and run his tongue around a salt lick placed on the wall of his box.

Developing the muscles of a young horse is of paramount importance. At Lambourn the terrain is hilly and there is a particularly stiff climb to the Faringdon Road gallops where the Walwyn string does most of its work, so the animals 'use' themselves quite naturally. Even so if a horse continually leads with his near fore – the leg automatically favoured – the muscle development will not be the same all round. There is a large muscle, the latissimus dorsi, which runs from the left shoulder to the right hip and similarly from the other shoulder. Thus, continual trotting with, say, the near fore leading means that there will be inconsistent muscle development, which in time may result in the horse going much better on a left-handed racecourse than a right-handed track. That, at least, is the theory and to ensure consistent muscle development the Seven Barrows yearlings use a figure-of-eight exercise pattern, when the leading leg should change naturally.

In the early spring of 1974 Grundy was galloped with the other two-year-olds in bunches, but he was a real handful for his rider and pulled hard for his head. He was not a popular ride with the lads, and it was not until Matt McCormack got on him in March that he began to settle. But even with McCormack he would jump off very fast until assenting to lob along with his companions after fifty yards or so. Matt McCormack had been with Noel Murless at Newmarket in his previous job when he had ridden the likes of Lorenzaccio, Welsh Pageant and Mysterious. From the moment he first cantered Grundy, however, he was sure the colt was superior to any animal he had ever mounted. He told this immediately to Peter Walwyn, who could see for himself what a superbly fluent mover the horse was. Grundy had an effortless low action, the same 'floating' style as Mill Reef.

By the end of March the two-year-olds had sorted themselves out and Grundy's regular working companions were Red Regent, No Alimony, Consol and Corby. None of them had been 'tried', in the old-fashioned sense, but had merely emerged as a superior group in various mixed gallops. Peter Walwyn never tries to find out exactly how good his horses are at home and has never used a weight cloth in his life, but in July he galloped Grundy over four and a half furlongs with the three-year-old sprinter Cawdor, who possessed plenty of pace and had been second to Boldboy in the Abernant Stakes at Newmarket in the spring. Matt McCormack rode Grundy in this gallop and remembers the experience well: 'We shot off in front and I never saw the other one the whole way.' There was no doubt Grundy was special.

Walwyn planned his first appearance for the Granville Stakes at Ascot on Friday 26 July, a race in which he had also entered No Alimony. On the Tuesday before the race, the stable jockey, Pat Eddery, who at the age of twenty-one was to become champion that season, motored down from his Cheltenham home to work both horses and decide which he would ride at Ascot. With no hesitation he plumped for Grundy, who prompted the time-honoured phrase: 'He gave me a great feel.' Frank Morby is second jockey at Seven Barrows but on this particular Friday he had been booked by the Blewbury trainer, Fulke Johnson Houghton, to ride at Carlisle. This meant Walwyn had to find a jockey for No Alimony and he went for the best available – Willie Carson, of the famous punching style.

The Granville Stakes is a race restricted to unraced two-year-olds and on this occasion had attracted a field of seventeen horses. The favourite was Amerrico, trained at Newmarket by Neville Callaghan and ridden by Lester Piggott, but there was no real confidence behind this colt and he drifted from 5–4 to 7–4 in the betting. Grundy was second best at 5–1, having opened at 6–1, and news of his gallop with Cawdor was obviously not common knowledge. Conditions were ideal for racing. The going was good, the weather was fine and there was only a slight head wind. Pat Eddery got the leg up from his trainer with the usual instructions on a two-year-old first time out: 'Get as close as you can but don't give him any sort of a hard race.'

Willie Carson was told the same on No Alimony and nearly pulled off a shock 25–1 victory. Carson roused his mount to dispute the lead with Amerrico two furlongs out and got in front with a furlong to run. Meanwhile Grundy had been restrained by Eddery and it looked as if the colt might have difficulty in getting a clear run. To find space, Eddery switched him to the stands rails hoping maybe that Amerrico, who was racing on the rails, might hang away into the centre of the track and allow some daylight. That was exactly what happened. A gap appeared and Grundy quickened to go through in a trice. He caught No Alimony inside the final furlong and ran on to win by two lengths from his stable companion.

The significance of the performance lay in the acceleration

shown by Grundy. Here was a horse with the most sought-after quality of instant speed; it remained to be seen whether he possessed the other great quality, courage. A combination of both makes a champion racehorse.

It was early days yet, however, to be thinking, let alone talking in such terms and Peter Walwyn was experienced enough to keep quiet about his hopes at this stage. His belief was that Grundy already wanted seven furlongs and an ideal race seemed to present itself at Newmarket on 10 August. This was the Child Stakes sponsored by Walwyn's bankers Child and Co. To take over £3,000 from his bankers rather appealed to Walwyn, but the plan was thwarted when Grundy contracted a slight cough and runny nose. He missed the race and in consequence went instead to Kempton on 30 August for the Sirenia Plate over six furlongs. The object of running here was to give him more experience before tackling high-class opposition in the Champagne Stakes at Doncaster. The field for the Sirenia, a minor event worth only £621 to the winner, included four previous winners, but Grundy dominated them totally and, leading at half way, cantered home at odds-on. He merely confirmed here that he was above average and no greater conclusions could be drawn from a race primarily meant to educate.

After this race Ray Laing noticed a difference in Grundy's behaviour at home. Until now the colt had been rather too full of vitality for comfort, 'a bit hot' in Laing's own words, but increasing exercise and two races had a calming effect and Grundy was less of a handful. He was magnificently muscled for a two-year-old with strong quarters indicative of a sprinter rather than a stayer. But he was still on the small side overall, being 15.2 hands high.

Just before Grundy's Kempton success, No Alimony had been sent to Haydock Park to win a small race over seven furlongs and he was shaping like a useful stayer in the making. Peter Walwyn began to think in terms of the Observer Gold Cup at Doncaster in October as the main end-of-season objective for this horse, but he was not contemplating running Grundy over further than seven furlongs. The Champagne Stakes and the Dewhurst Stakes were to be his final two races of the year. There was a good-quality field for the Champagne run at the Doncaster St Leger meeting, when Bustino was to take the glory. It comprised ten runners, all but two having won. Anne's Pretender, trained by Ryan Price, looked the principal threat to Grundy and had made a tremendous impression on his début at Goodwood when making all the running to win in a canter from a decent Henry Cecil-trained two-year-old, Gaelic. In consequence there was little to choose between the two in the betting but Grundy was just favourite at 13–8.

As events proved, Anne's Pretender was no threat at all and indeed he was the first horse beaten, coming under pressure after little more than a quarter of a mile. He clearly had not produced his proper form. With him out of the way, Grundy's supporters were full of optimism but with a furlong to run their horse appeared to be pocketed on the rails, with Whip It Quick being driven all out in the lead by Lester Piggott. Once again, however, that Ascot acceleration was evident as Eddery pulled Grundy out for a spectacular spurt which brought a clever half-length victory.

This success marked the beginning of the hero-worship of Grundy as he became recognised for what he was – an embryonic champion. There were other horses active, however, who had stirred the public imagination and that of the Press, principal among them being Steel Heart, trained in Ireland by Dermot Weld and owned by the shipping millionaire Ravi Tikkoo. Steel Heart had won the Gimcrack Stakes at York in August and captured the Group I Middle Park Stakes at Newmarket at the beginning of October. An aura of invincibility was being built around the colt, aided by the fact that he was ridden by Lester Piggott, still apparently regarded as possessing some mystical power when he mounted a racehorse. When Tikkoo announced, therefore, that Steel Heart would

4 Dick Hern is dressed to keep out the cold on a sharp morning on the gallops. His hack is Hardbake, a useful racehorse in his time.

5 Two-year-olds working on the shavings gallop at West Ilsley.

6 Bustino strides home alone to defeat Giacometti and give Lady Beaverbrook a first classic success in the Doncaster St Leger.

7 Joe Mercer is hard at work as Bustino breaks the course record when winning the Coronation Cup at Epsom. Note Bustino's tongue, a sign that he is at full stretch.

take on Grundy in the Dewhurst Stakes there was considerable excitement and it looked as if the 2,000 Guineas picture for next season would become clear. Not since Lemberg in 1909 had a horse won the Middle Park Stakes and Dewhurst Stakes, so Steel Heart was attempting an unusual feat. The reason so few had done it, was that few had tried. The two races are designed for different types of animals, with sprinters normally running in the Middle Park and potential stayers in the Dewhurst. In view of this there were plenty of people who had definite ideas about the outcome, one of them being Peter Walwyn.

He had not been too impressed by Steel Heart in the Middle Park Stakes when the colt had come home by a neck from Royal Manacle, who had won four races but in moderate company at such tracks as Pontefract and Folkestone. But by now of course Grundy was revealing his full repertoire and this, rather than any possible weakness in Steel Heart, prompted Walwyn's great confidence. A weakness could exist in Steel Heart, however, and it concerned his stamina. He was by Habitat, a miler, out of A.1 who was by Abernant, a sprinter. There appeared at first glance to be a preponderance of speed in his pedigree but the dam was related to some fair middle distance performers and there was a chance at any rate that Steel Heart might stay up to a mile. There was one sure way to find out and, sensibly, his connections had decided to try it.

Their cause was not helped by the weather and for several days before the big race on 18 October, it rained and rained heavily. The going became soft and the seven furlongs of the Dewhurst Stakes would demand a lot of stamina. For this reason the punters declared strongly for Grundy on the day, making him a 6–5 favourite with Steel Heart at 2–1. There were six others in the race but they were ignored. Tactics looked as if they would be important. Grundy possessed brilliant acceleration and the question was whether this would be used to cut down Steel Heart or whether, in view of his better stamina pretensions, he would be sent on to force the pace and run his opponent ragged. Walwyn decided on the latter course and still appeared optimistic, despite the fact that the soft ground would not suit Grundy's low action.

Depending on one's loyalties the race was either a total anti-climax or a colossal triumph. There was a strong cross wind, it was raining and the ground was cloying; a thoroughly wretched afternoon when a racehorse's dream of heaven is a warm box and a hay net. But that day Grundy showed his tremendous enthusiasm for racing. In spite of such unpleasant conditions, he stretched out in devastating and remorseless style, taking the lead two furlongs from home and drawing clear for a six-lengths victory.

Peter Walwyn never weighs his horses and it was hard to measure the amount of strain imposed on Grundy by racing, but judging from his appetite and general demeanour, it was not great. With the Dewhurst Stakes behind him, Grundy was retired for the season – unbeaten in four races. Ray Laing gradually cut down his consumption of corn by feeding a linseed mash, two-thirds bran to one-third oats, more frequently. Exercise was reduced in intensity to walking and trotting; and the unwinding process was nearly complete by the end of October.

Chapter 6

St Leger

The Grand Prix de Paris, coming as it does only nine days after Royal Ascot, is not a popular race among English owners and trainers. Another factor that dissuades English representation is the distance of the race, one mile and seven and a half furlongs, since it is thought to be a severe test of stamina for a three-year-old still far from physically mature. If a three-year-old is bred to need a test of stamina, however, there is no reason to think the race can inflict harm, although Bustino in fact lost more weight – 34 lb – after this contest than any other during his career. Travelling was primarily the cause of this and Dick Hern, who weighs all his horses before and after racing, has ample evidence to show that weight loss is related to the distance travelled and the time spent away from home, rather than to any experience on the racetrack.

Before the Grand Prix on Sunday 30 June, Bustino did little serious work but, on the Friday nine days before the race, he was galloped a mile and a half with the nine-year-old Crucible and Appleby Fair, who at one time looked the stable's main classic hope for 1974 but who failed to fulfil his promise. The following Tuesday, Bustino did a half-speed gallop with Crucible and that was his final piece of preparation. He left for Longchamp on Friday, being flown from Southampton with Boldboy, also due to run on the Sunday. Bustino had never seen an aircraft before, let alone flown in one, but in the familiar company of his lad and Buster Haslam, he saw no reason to be alarmed and quietly picked at a hay net during the flight of just over one hour.

Buster Haslam, the travelling head lad at West Ilsley, is responsible for the safe keeping of runners virtually every day during the summer, one of the most arduous and time-consuming jobs in racing. He is away from home four nights a week on average and in the height of the season goes to France almost every weekend. Like so many key background men, he came into racing hoping to be a jockey and was apprenticed to Jack Colling at Newmarket in 1937. He had over a hundred rides but was not successful in making the grade. Racing was in his blood, however, and he continued to work in stables, becoming second head lad to Colling and eventually travelling head lad when the trainer moved to West Ilsley. He has been trekking round racecourses most of his life, therefore, and there are few people in a better position to comment on the respective standards of accommodation and treatment in France and England. His compliments are reserved for the tracetracks abroad where everything is laid on for the lads. In England only Newmarket, in his opinion, can begin to compare.

The flight to France may have taken little more than an hour but the total journey time for Bustino was eight hours and it was 3 p.m. before he and Boldboy were installed in the security block at Longchamp. Due to the strangeness of the surroundings, horses do not usually eat up as well as at home, and to encourage them to feed, their own corn and hay is taken on journeys with them. Bustino settled down satisfactorily and on Saturday morning Haslam cantered him on the racecourse. At 8 a.m. on Sunday, the day of the race, Haslam gave him damp bran and a water bucket, leaving him to eat at his leisure for three hours. But at 11 a.m. the water bucket was taken out and Bustino was muzzled up – routine practice for runners prior to a race.

Both Bustino and Boldboy ran well, but Boldboy was beaten a length into fourth place behind El Rastro in the Prix de la Porte Maillot over seven furlongs on soft ground. For the Grand Prix too the going was soft and Bustino had not met such conditions before, which prompted a rather pessimistic forecast from Joe Mercer. However, the colt was not troubled and after turning into the straight close behind Sagaro, ridden by Lester

Piggott, it looked as if he had a great chance. Sagaro ran on with real enthusiasm to spike Bustino's guns, however, and won by two lengths. Bustino finished half a length in front of Kamaraan, who had been third in the French Derby, and thereby confirmed himself a top-class performer.

Although Bustino had run four times in two months now, the Doncaster St Leger in September was an obvious objective. It was clear that, all being well, he would have an outstanding chance of giving Lady Beaverbrook a first classic success but he had merited a rest and was given an easy time throughout July before beginning a preparation for the traditional St Leger trial, the Great Voltigeur Stakes over a mile and a half at York on 21 August. This gave Bustino seven weeks to recover from his gruelling trip to France.

In the Voltigeur he had only two opponents, the Irish Derby winner English Prince, and Straight As A Die, a moderate three-year-old who could have no hope of winning. Such a small field was hardly ideal and with English Prince being a resolute galloper, somewhat in the same mould as Bustino, there was the possibility of a slogging match. English Prince was the pick of the paddock and a strong favourite at 7–4 on. Bustino opened at 13–8 and drifted to 15–8.

Straight As A Die, ridden by Lester Piggott, led for over a mile tracked by English Prince with Bustino close behind. With two and a half furlongs to go Pat Eddery went to the front on English Prince. Bustino was right on his heels, however, and responded in magnificent style to Joe Mercer's driving rhythm. He headed English Prince a furlong and a half out and quickened to go clear. English Prince was eased by Eddery when defeat was certain and Bustino's winning margin was four lengths.

On paper it looked a tremendous victory and the colt's finest performance so far. As a result it was no surprise to see him immediately made a hot favourite for the St Leger, the final classic looking absolutely at his mercy. This dominant position was strengthened further with the news from Lambourn that

English Prince would not challenge and had been retired. Persistent soreness in the colt's off-fore had forced this decision by Peter Walwyn and the injury gave rise to doubt that English Prince may not have been at his best at York.

West Ilsley to York is a round journey of some 500 miles and Bustino once again showed the effect of the travelling by losing 13 lb in weight. This was by no means excessive, however, and Dick Hern was able to give him a swinging canter over seven furlongs six days after the Voltigeur. Bustino was proving a wonderful horse to train. He was sound, resilient, he never fretted and always ate up with gusto, in fact he was a thoroughly contented thoroughbred. Two weeks before the St Leger he galloped a mile and a quarter with Kinglet and Zab, the latter ridden by Bobby Elliott, who was soon due to return to Hong Kong where he was a leading jockey. Elliott had been champion apprentice in England in 1959 and 1960 but had been lured away by a lucrative offer at a time when he was not exactly inundated with riding opportunities at home. He rode Bustino in a mile and a quarter gallop on Tuesday 3 September and was most impressed, telling the trainer that this was the best horse he would ride for a very long time.

Bustino was certainly going from strength to strength. A week before the St Leger he gave Kinglet 17 lb and Riboson 4 lb in a mile and a half gallop on the summer downs and finished with great zest. Everything seemed set fair and he looked one of the biggest classic certainties of all time. No one was more aware of this than Brian Procter as he mounted Bustino on Thursday morning, two days before the race, to give the horse a sharp five-furlongs pipe-opener. But as they walked peacefully down to the start there was suddenly a moment of high drama. Bustino shied at a gallops harrow, whipped round and threw his rider. Procter had the presence of mind to keep hold of the reins and was dragged some thirty yards. 'Knowing the Leger was so close, I hung on for dear life,' Procter says. Thankfully, no harm came to horse or rider.

The reason Bustino was regarded as such a certainty for the St Leger, apart from his own ability, was that his opponents looked either non-stayers or sub-standard. Giacometti, who had finished just ahead of Bustino in the Derby, was not bred to last a mile and three-quarters, although the booking of Lester Piggott maximised his chances. No man was better at nursing a horse of doubtful stamina and it must have been because of Piggott's presence that a few days before the race Giacometti became the subject of heavy ante-post support. Imperial Prince was another runner to have beaten Bustino in the Derby but unlikely to stay the St Leger distance. Geoff Lewis, his jockey, had been reported in the press as saying Imperial Prince hardly stayed beyond a mile and a quarter. The rest of the field was composed of handicappers and Riboson, who was cleverly put in by Dick Hern to act as pacemaker for Bustino enabling him to utilise his stamina to the full, thereby turning the screw even more tightly on the non-stayers in the field.

Riboson was owned by Lady Beaverbrook as indeed he had to be. A pacemaker must always be in the same ownership as the stable's principal hope because his task is purely sacrificial. No other owner would willingly see his horse run into the ground for the benefit of another. Pacemaking is not the simple job that it may appear, for there must always be control over the speed set and thus an experienced jockey, who knows exactly how fast he is going, is essential. Dick Hern secured the ideal man in Jimmy Lindley. Riboson too seemed an ideal horse. He was a decent-class three-year-old, having run a close sixth to Take A Reef in the Extel Stakes at Goodwood, and an enthusiastic galloper.

The Doncaster St Leger, first run in 1776, is the only classic race run in the north of England but, of course, there are several important training centres in Yorkshire and the locals grasp their only opportunity to enjoy fully a great racing occasion. There is always a vast crowd crammed into the course where an additional attraction is a fair of Epsom proportions in the middle of Town Moor. This particular afternoon was warm and sunny and it seemed that even more people than usual had come to back and cheer home what appeared to be a 'good thing'.

Curiously, in the pre-race preliminaries, the 'good thing' drifted in the betting for, after opening at odds-on, Bustino went to 11–10 against. Those who foresaw some evil influences at work, however, were happily proved wrong. As Hern had planned, Riboson went to the front straight away and set a pace strong enough to stretch the field but not so strong as to become detached and, therefore, ignored by the other runners. Riboson led into the straight, which at Doncaster is half a mile long, but Mercer was full of confidence on Bustino and wrested the initiative with nearly three furlongs to run. Bustino was kicked on and set sail in imperious style.

A quarter of a mile from home Bustino looked likely to win without being tackled but a roar of warning went up from his supporters as Piggott brought Giacometti out of the chasing pack to deliver a challenge. It was merely a flickering effort, however, and quickly fizzled out as Giacometti reached the bottom of his stamina reserves. Imperial Prince had been struggling all the way up the straight and, like the remainder of the runners, was never a threat. Bustino strode on alone to win by three lengths from Giacometti with the gallant Riboson plugging on to take third.

There had been no finer moment on an English racecourse for Lady Beaverbrook. It was a fitting triumph – indeed one might say, with Riboson gaining a place at 100–1, almost an annihilation – for someone who had supported racing with such obvious enthusiasm and dedication for many years. Lady Beaverbrook now lists Doncaster as among her favourite racecourses which is perhaps not surprising since Bustino had finally achieved for her there the long sought-after classic breakthrough.

At the same time Bustino had earned for himself a special place in Lady Beaverbrook's affections. 'I love Bustino,' she

said after the race. 'He's so gallant, kind and lion-hearted.'
It was a fair character portrait, for these same qualities
Bustino was to show in even greater measure as a four-year-
old. His finest hour was yet to come.

Chapter 7

Injury

Meanwhile, by the end of October of 1974, Grundy's standing as the season's top two-year-old had been challenged by the French-trained colt Green Dancer who had come over to win the Observer Gold Cup at Doncaster over a mile. In this race No Alimony had run well to finish third, beaten one and a half lengths and three-quarters of a length respectively by Green Dancer and Sea Break. At one point No Alimony had looked capable of winning but had not been able to accelerate after leading with a quarter of a mile to run. He had, however, finished six lengths in front of Whip It Quick, who had been only half a length behind Grundy in the Dewhurst Stakes.

Thus a literal interpretation of the form made No Alimony considerably superior to Grundy, a view given credence by the well-publicised stable confidence behind Whip It Quick before the 'Observer'. Bill Marshall, the colt's trainer, had thought his horse a near certainty and on the day of the race there had been a flood of money forcing Whip It Quick's price from 7–1 to 4–1. It must have been a nasty blow to Marshall's morale when the colt was shown to be so far from the top class.

There was room for difference of opinion about the respective merits of Grundy and Green Dancer, but the official view was that Grundy was the better and he was allotted top weight of 9 st 7 lb in the Free Handicap, a list of the top 101 two-year-olds to run in this country in 1974. Green Dancer was given 9 st 6 lb, No Alimony 9 st 1 lb and Whip It Quick, eighth in the list, 8 st 9 lb. The handicapper had taken the view that Whip It Quick ran below form in the Observer Gold Cup, for Green Dancer had in fact given him a 24 lb beating – if a length is taken to represent 3 lb – and that Grundy had beaten the same horse with plenty to spare in the Dewhurst Stakes. Subsequent events proved this opinion correct and at Seven Barrows there was not much doubt that the handicapper had calculated it right, the impression there being that Grundy was something like 12 lb to 14 lb superior to No Alimony.

Over Christmas Grundy had the usual dose of physic and in January was given an anti-flu vaccine. That month he started cantering in the covered ride, six times round being the prescribed amount of exercise. At this time the winter gallops can be hazardous with the frost causing ruts, and it is far safer to keep the horses on the move by trotting and cantering on the sand of the indoor area. To keep them and their riders happy, they trot round to the accompaniment of popular music, broadcast through a tannoy system.

At the end of January, Peter Walwyn and his wife Virginia, the sister of Nick Gaselee, an amateur rider of some prowess but at this time assistant trainer to Peter's cousin Fulke Walwyn, flew off for a holiday in the Far East. Their first stop was Hong Kong, where they joined Pat Eddery who was keeping his hand in riding a few winners at the local racetrack. After going on to Singapore, they returned home in mid-February, fully aware that they could be on the threshold of a fantastic season. There were over a hundred horses in the yard and one of the strongest collections of three-year-olds ever assembled in a single establishment. There were twenty-seven English classic entries and five French classic entries.

Certainly the season would make great physical and mental demands. During the next nine months Walwyn would be out of telephone or conversation range only when driving to race meetings. Those hours in the car would represent welcome respite and for this reason Virginia ('Bonk' to her friends) would do the driving.

Walwyn was greeted on return from holiday by an advance copy of *Racehorses of 1974*, published by the Timeform Organisation. Turning to the appropriate section, he quaked inwardly to read the providence-provoking phrase: 'For the life of us we cannot see what is likely to beat Grundy in the 2,000 Guineas.'

Since Grundy's training programme was geared to the 2,000 Guineas on 3 May, it was planned to give him a preparatory run in the Ascot 2,000 Guineas Trial on 12 April. Habat had followed a similar programme the year before but, after winning at Ascot, he had been beaten into sixth place behind Nonoalco in the classic. Habat had not been a big horse and neither was Grundy, who stood now at 15–2½ hands. He was a powerful individual, thick in the neck, deep through the shoulders and particularly well muscled around the quarters. He was in strong work by the beginning of March and on 4 March went well in a gallop with No Alimony and Consol. Three days later he worked with Corby, a big, long-striding horse, who was about to play a significant and dramatic role in the story.

St Patrick's Day, 17 March, started in the usual routine way at Seven Barrows with Ray Laing making his early morning round, feeling legs, gauging well-being and giving a small feed to those who wanted it. Grundy was made ready to go out with the 'first lot' which was to loosen up in the covered ride, and Matt McCormack mounted with no particular apprehension seeing Grundy in his usual fresh, early morning mood. The string of thirty or so horses assembled and Grundy dropped in behind Corby. It was only a short walk to the covered ride but long enough for Grundy to make his impatience felt. Just before the entrance to the track he bounded forward, at the same time putting his head down. Corby, frightened by this sudden rumpus, lashed out with a hind leg, which smashed into Grundy's face.

'Grundy didn't flinch,' says McCormack. 'I thought Corby had just caught Grundy's martingale but suddenly blood began to pour from his nose. I jumped off and led him back to his box while somebody went to tell the guv'nor.' Peter Walwyn took one look and rang for his vet, Charles Frank, who lived in the nearby village of Childrey. When Frank arrived, Grundy was standing quietly and the flow of blood had been staunched, but there was a three-inch square indent below his near eye. It was soft to the touch and the bone had clearly been shattered. The first thing was to inject antibiotics to prevent infection. Then an X-ray was taken to determine the extent of the damage and this revealed a fracture and splintering of the nasal bone. The big worry was whether the passage of the nose and sinus had been penetrated, for this could seriously impair the horse's breathing. If the sinuses were damaged, an operation would be necessary, meaning a two-months lay-off. It was decided to wait and see how Grundy fared in the next few days before contemplating surgery.

Within twenty-four hours, however, Grundy was eating up with his customary gusto and it began to look as if, miraculously, the damage had not affected his breathing. Mucus continued to drain from the nose and Charles Frank saw him every day for the first week. 'I thought he must go off his food but his speed of recovery was beyond anything I'd known in thirty years with racehorses. It was quite remarkable. He must have had a tremendously strong constitution.'

On the day of the accident Peter Walwyn had informed the Press Association, and through them the news reached the BBC who recorded a telephone conversation with the trainer. In a radio broadcast, he said that it was now unlikely that Grundy could be made fit enough to run in the 2,000 Guineas.

But so sensible was Grundy's behaviour – he was content to stay quietly in his box – and so swift his progress, that five days after the accident he was being walked out, and after a further five days he was trotting. After two weeks he did his first canter. This was on 1 April when he covered six furlongs led by another three-year-old, Hard Day. From then on he worked on a regular basis and despite sleet and snow on 4 April, he galloped with No Alimony. Five days later he went with Corby, Consol and Patch and on Saturday 12 April Pat Eddery came down to ride him in a serious work-out with the four-year-olds Charlie Bubbles and Acquaint, and the three-year-old Record

Token. This was over six furlongs on the Faringdon Road gallop which is against the collar all the way. Grundy pleased Eddery, who found that the old 'feel' was still there.

By now the 2,000 Guineas had become a real possibility again but the Ascot Trial had been missed – the meeting was abandoned anyway because of waterlogging – and the only race which was suitable was the Greenham Stakes at Newbury, two weeks before the Newmarket classic. The Greenham was a straight seven-furlongs race, but, curiously, to win it seemed to be the kiss of death for a prospective 2,000 Guineas candidate. Not since Orwell in 1932 had a horse won both races.

Walwyn was determined to give Grundy a preliminary outing, however, and decided that, come hell or high water, the colt would run at Newbury. High water in fact nearly put paid to the plan, and for most of the week preceding the meeting it rained heavily. Walwyn was at the Newmarket Craven fixture on Tuesday, Wednesday and Thursday and, driving home, he called in at Newbury to see the state of the going. He found that from four furlongs out there was a strip of ground, on the stands side, about four yards wide which was 'superb considering the weather'.

Provided there was no more rain, therefore, there was a chance the going might be reasonable. But although the rain relented a little on Friday it deluged down during the night and there was no prospect of the ground being anything but heavy. Peter Walwyn was in a quandary now. He knew Grundy was short of work and desperately in need of a race, and so he telephoned Dr Vittadini in London: 'I told the Doctor what the ground would be like. I told him about Mark Anthony who was reported to be very fit and a big danger to us, but I also told him that I would not be worried if Grundy were beaten. After that we decided to run.'

Mark Anthony was an ex-Irish colt bought for 52,000 guineas by Captain Marcos Lemos, a Greek shipping millionaire, and trained at Newmarket by Clive Brittain who was making a great success of training on his own after being head lad to

Noel Murless for twenty-three years. Mark Anthony had shown form on soft ground in Ireland as a two-year-old but he had been rated 13 lb behind Steel Heart in the Irish Free Handicap. On paper he was no threat to Grundy but in these peculiar circumstances he could beat him and Lester Piggott had been engaged to maximise the chances. Mark Anthony looked almost as lean as his famous jockey in the parade ring and it was plain that, although this was his first outing of the season, he was very fit.

Besides Mark Anthony there were seven other runners, only one of whom, Hillandale, trained by Duncan Keith, seemed worth serious consideration, for he had won the Kempton 2,000 Guineas Trial on heavy ground on Easter Monday. Victory over Grundy would be particularly satisfying for Keith, who three years earlier had been stable jockey at Seven Barrows and at the peak of his career when thyroid trouble, linked with weight problems, had forced his retirement. He was now ensconced in training quarters at Littleton near Winchester.

The rain had stopped by the time the horses were being led round the parade ring, but a miserable, cold afternoon had not deterred a large crowd who came to see if Grundy could keep his unbeaten record. Grundy looked well, but after what he had been through it was imperative he should not be subjected to a punishing contest. Pat Eddery was well aware of this, but at the same time thought he might still win. Despite the lack of confidence in Grundy, he hardened in the betting to start at 6–4 on, with Mark Anthony second favourite at 11–2 and Hillandale at 15–2.

In the early stages of the race Jumping Hill, ridden by Geoff Lewis, made the running. Lewis may have been re-living the day three years earlier when he had made all the running to win this race on Mill Reef, but he knew Jumping Hill was a vastly inferior animal and the colt was passed by Town Farm after a quarter of a mile. Town Farm, trained by Reg Akehurst at Lambourn, kept up a steady gallop in the atrocious conditions but Eddery found Grundy rather keen to start racing in earnest. It was clear from the stands that Grundy was running too free and two and a half furlongs out he took the lead.

Hillandale was another who wanted to hurry, but he pulled hard only to produce little when the time came to give chase to Grundy. Eddery had the favourite on the stretch of ground, near the stand rails, that had looked decent on Thursday but was now, like the rest of the course, a morass. A furlong from home Grundy began to show signs of flagging, a sight made worse for his supporters when they glimpsed the cocky angle of Lester Piggott's behind on Mark Anthony, who was moving up to challenge and was still on the bit. He simply cruised up and, unless Grundy was to show incredible fight, the race was lost. For a few strides Mark Anthony was held, but Eddery knew the writing was on the wall and he was not severe on Grundy. In the end Mark Anthony drew away to win by two lengths.

There was a certain amount of consternation around the unsaddling enclosure and the opinion was being voiced by some that Grundy's Guineas chance had gone. Peter Walwyn was first and foremost relieved that Grundy had come through without showing any signs of distress. The colt did not blow excessively, which showed his basic condition was good, and there was every prospect, so his trainer thought, of his improving enough during the next two weeks to reverse the running with Mark Anthony. The bookmakers were not reacting in a rash manner and most merely pushed Grundy out a point to 7–2 favourite in their ante-post lists. Mark Anthony varied between 6–1 and 10–1, the more cautious firms anticipating a favourable reply from Piggott who was deliberating an offer to ride at Newmarket.

During the next fortnight the discussions and arguments raged about how much improvement Grundy was capable of making. Leading racing journalists took up interestingly different standpoints. Richard Baerlein of *The Guardian* was definitely not impressed: 'Grundy may have been short of work

8. No wonder Keith Freeman fell in love with him. Grundy looking superb as he goes to post for the Irish 2,000 Guineas.

9 Mark Anthony throws up the mud as he beats Grundy in the Greenham Stakes at Newbury. Pat Eddery can be seen riding almost as short as Lester Piggott.

10 Bolkonski beats Grundy by half a length in the 2,000 Guineas at Newmarket. Mark Anthony, the grey, is well behind this time while No Alimony struggles in at the rear to settle the argument about which of the two Seven Burrows horses was the better.

owing to his temporary setback and the Greenham is a notoriously deceptive race especially when it was run, as was the case on Saturday, in 16 seconds over average time. But in my opinion Grundy's was not the performance of a possible 2,000 Guineas winner. Grundy is a rather flashy individual with a decisively formed crest on his neck, which I do not like to see in a possible classic colt. Peter Walwyn and Pat Eddery are still not really willing to place Grundy and No Alimony in the same category, for at home Grundy has always shown himself to be the better horse. I believe the 2,000 Guineas will prove otherwise.'

Michael Phillips, *The Times* Racing Correspondent, was not willing to accept what he had seen at face value: 'Disappointment was the first reaction on seeing Grundy beaten, but when trying to analyse his performance, it is only fair to realise that he was two weeks behind the likes of No Alimony going into fast work because of an accident and that Saturday was the earliest moment that he could have had a race. Furthermore both his trainer and rider were adamant that Grundy was a much better horse on better ground even though it was soft when he beat Steel Heart so decisively at Newmarket in the autumn. Although Mark Anthony coped admirably with the terrible conditions, many must have left the course wondering whether this particular page should be torn from the form book.'

The difference of opinion and the uncertainty that makes racing so special and fascinating was never better illustrated, but it is fair to say that generally during this period, the severity of Grundy's injury was underestimated. The horse had undergone a nasty and debilitating experience, one which would, in the experience of the veterinary surgeon Charles Frank, have laid most horses low for at least a month. Yet here was Grundy actually racing within that period.

Chapter 8

Lucky defeat?

Close examination of the Greenham Stakes result suggested that Grundy had run a long way below his two-year-old form. Besides the line through Mark Anthony to Steel Heart, which made the discrepancy 21 lb, there was further evidence from the proximity of the third horse, Great Ball, four lengths behind Grundy who was conceding 5 lb. Great Ball, trained by Dave Hanley at Lambourn, had been little out of the ordinary as a two-year-old winning once at Leicester and being trounced by over a dozen lengths by Anne's Pretender at Goodwood. Anne's Pretender had been rated 22 lb inferior to Grundy in the Free Handicap for which Great Ball had failed to gain a rating. Working to figures, this meant that Grundy had run 41 lb below his two-year-old mark.

When one discusses form an important proviso is 'all things being equal'. In this case things were certainly not equal. Grundy had met with a serious training setback and made his reappearance on very heavy ground. Anyone who believed Grundy was inferior to Mark Anthony on the evidence of this one run, therefore, was adopting far too naive an approach. Even so, any horse better than Mark Anthony now had a chance of beating Grundy in the 2,000 Guineas; and in Ireland there were two such challengers – Sea Break and It's Freezing. Thus the season's first classic had taken on an intriguing appearance; but Peter Walwyn had just two weeks to get Grundy fit enough to do himself justice.

While the immediate problem of Grundy's fitness concerned all at Seven Barrows, the spring of 1975 was a time of unrest on the shop floor of the racing industry. Disagreement between stable lads and their employers reached a head during the

Guineas meeting at Newmarket, culminating in strike action and the picketing of stables and the racecourse. An attempt was made to prevent the running of the 1,000 Guineas on the Thursday but, although it failed, the strikers were saving their main effort for the Saturday and the 2,000 Guineas; and they received support from the television technicians who refused to cross picket lines and thus ensured there would be no screening of the race.

The striking lads numbered little more than 200 of the 700 employed in the 38 Newmarket stables. Reports had pictured the dispute as the landed gentry, upper lips at their stiffest, arrogantly refusing to increase the abysmal pay of a small but dignified country band that Wat Tyler might have been pleased to have led. But it was not quite like that. The cap-doffing days were past and in any case the strikers were not from the cap-pulling generation, being mostly teenagers whose heart was not in racing, seeing it merely as an alternative to the factory bench. At the behest of the TGWU they had struck for an increase of £4.75 a week, being promised higher pay as an immediate benefit of membership of a union anxious to obtain a foothold in an industry relatively free of worker representation.

The older working lads were not so sure that they welcomed this intervention, their view being summed up by one who said: 'There are twelve lads in our yard, six are in and six are out, and we don't want anything to do with those who are out. We happen to have a job we like doing and there's an end to it. You will get nothing by sitting on a rail jeering at your boss. Over fifty of the lads have torn up their union cards since this dispute started. They don't want to be involved. We like working with horses and that's it. It's no cap-pulling job. If you can do it well, you'll be respected for it.'

For the opposition a spokesman said: 'We don't care about upsetting the trainers. We think we are in a dead end job with no place to go. We think racing is in a bad state and owners are going to pull out some of their horses and then we will have to go too. Pulling your weight gets you no more pay and we are fed up with being kicked around for damn all. If you try to ask for a rise they look at you as if you had just shot their favourite horse.'

One of the yards affected by the strike was Marriott Stables where Henry Cecil had successfully established himself since the retirement in 1968 of his step-father Sir Cecil Boyd-Rochfort. Henry Cecil had charge of a strong, good-looking chestnut called Bolkonski of whom he had classic aspirations, despite the fact that the colt had been well beaten by No Alimony in the Craven Stakes at the April meeting at Newmarket. Bolkonski was having his first run in this country on that occasion, having been trained in Italy in 1974 when he was rated second in the Italian two-year-old handicap. In the 2,000 Guineas he would be ridden by the Italian champion Gianfranco Dettori, and news began to filter from Newmarket about some spectacular work-outs by the horse, whose lad incidentally was on strike.

It was at this time that Len Dawson, an experienced sub-editor on the *Sporting Chronicle* in London, received a strange, anonymous telephone call one afternoon. The caller came on with a simple question: 'Who trains Bolkonski?' On being told, he said just two words, 'Help yourself', and rang off. Backing Bolkonski, as the caller advised, seemed tantamount to throwing money down the drain for he stood at 40–1 in the ante-post lists, and to those outside the stable, who thought they knew something about racing, he appeared a forlorn hope. Inside the stable, however, they knew rather different for Bolkonski had given 14 lb to the four-year-old Deerslayer in his final gallop and beaten the older horse easily.

Meanwhile Grundy had recovered from his run in the Greenham Stakes with characteristic speed and the following Friday worked well with Red Regent and Acquaint. He had learned thoroughly by now to gallop within himself, tucked in behind his lead horse until pulled out and asked to quicken. He had matured mentally and was developing into a steady worker rather than a spectacular one—an attitude which suggested that he knew the job of a racehorse was to save his best for the track. As the Guineas drew closer Ray Laing increased Grundy's feed to 20 lb of corn a day until, on the Friday, the time came for the journey to Newmarket.

Peter Walwyn had been engaged all week in security discussions with Brigadier Henry Green about the stabling arrangements at Newmarket, both men being worried in case strikers attempted to interfere with the favourite. Stabling Grundy in a private training establishment was discussed but discarded as almost certainly this would have meant crossing picket lines. It was decided, therefore, to put Grundy in the ordinary racecourse stables and shelter behind the normal but tighter security network. Thankfully there were no untoward incidents and Grundy, who was a fidget when travelling, bounded out of his box with usual enthusiasm and was led straight inside. Guards patrolled at night and on the morning of the race Grundy was ridden out and trotted on the links by Charlie Johnson.

There was only a handful of demonstrating strikers outside the racecourse as the crowds began to arrive, but a big body of men could be seen assembling about six furlongs down the straight Rowley Mile. The first race on the card, an apprentice event, was run without interference but the gathering of a hundred or so lads down the course was clearly intent on disrupting the 2,000 Guineas and no sooner had the twenty-four runners reached the start than the demonstrators moved en masse to sit on the track, forming a human barrier three or four deep across its width. A concerted carrying and dragging effort by police managed to move the demonstrators, and the horses, who had been dismounted now for about ten minutes, made their way behind the starting stalls. When half of them had been loaded into the stalls, the demonstrators moved back to occupy the course. It seemed like stalemate. Again the police started clearing operations and had partially succeeded when the starter decided to dispense with the stalls and shouted to the jockeys: 'Line up in front of the stalls in a good line and I'll let you go.'

Grundy was drawn 19 towards the outside of the field between Bolkonski (20) and No Alimony (18). In the betting he had drifted to 9–2 at one stage but had returned to 7–2 favourite just before the off. Mark Anthony and Sea Break shared second favouritism at 9–2, Mark Anthony, with Piggott riding, having been backed from 6–1. It's Freezing was at 10–1 and the 'phone call horse' Bolkonski 33–1.

A few lingering demonstrators were still on the course when the race started and one ran across the track only 100 yards or so in front of the field. Pat Eddery was finding it difficult to cover up Grundy with the runners spread wide, but Grundy was not fighting for his head despite the amount of daylight he was seeing. It's Freezing led on the stands rails for half a mile, tracked by Dominion, who then took over. Grundy was ploughing almost a lone furrow in the middle of the course although Bolkonski was racing just behind him. At The Bushes, two and a half furlongs from home, Eddery found Grundy was only cantering and decided to kick on. It looked as if Grundy would win now for he quickly headed Dominion and there appeared to be no horse going as well in the stands side group. But behind him in the centre, Gianfranco Dettori was travelling smoothly on Bolkonski who challenged with a furlong and a half to run. He passed Grundy with incredible ease, but perhaps Dettori found himself in front sooner than he expected or wanted. Certainly in the final half furlong Bolkonski lost his rhythm and Grundy began to come again. Throughout the final hundred yards Grundy was inching his way back. He got to within half a length at the line and in another half furlong it seemed he might have reasserted himself. It was a performance not unlike that of Mill Reef when he stayed on to deprive My Swallow of second place in the 1971 Guineas won by Brigadier Gerard.

There was disappointment, naturally, in the Grundy camp but the horse had run a courageous race. His stable companion No Alimony had never been seen with a chance and finished in the rear to settle the argument finally about which of the two was better. Mark Anthony had finished sixth, beaten just over five lengths by Grundy, who had thus shown 21 lb improvement on his Greenham Stakes form. Incredibly this 21 lb was exactly the amount one calculation had shown the deterioration in Grundy to be compared with his two-year-old rating. Who says horses never run to figures?

It is debatable whether Grundy's Guineas defeat was caused by lack of fitness, by a tactical error on Eddery's part or simply because, over the course run at a distance 32 yards short of a mile, Bolkonski was superior. In view of the emphatic reversal of form with Mark Anthony, it is clear that Grundy was far fitter than he had been at Newbury and indeed the figures show he ran very close to his two-year-old rating. It seems unlikely, therefore, he could have produced a significantly better performance, although had he been held up longer he might have been able to match Bolkonski's speed and run him desperately close. In view of Bolkonski's subsequent victories at Royal Ascot and Goodwood, however, he was clearly a high-class miler and for Grundy to fail by half a length was no disgrace for an animal who was to prove that he needed a mile and a half to be seen at his best.

On reflection Peter Walwyn believes it was lucky that Grundy did not win the Guineas. The colt had shown so much speed, and resembled a sprinter so much in looks, that the policy had been to keep him to one mile and one mile and a quarter races and follow a similar programme to Brigadier Gerard as a three-year-old. This would have meant the end of any further classic attempts, and no Derby challenge – a different route indeed to the one Grundy was now about to take. For, with nothing to lose, it was decided to send him for the Irish 2,000 Guineas, a race over the stiff Curragh mile exactly two weeks after the English Guineas. If he proved successful there it would suggest that he had a real chance of staying a mile and a half.

Grundy did virtually no serious work between the two races and the only entry in the Seven Barrows work book worth mentioning was for 13 May, when he went seven furlongs with the four-year-old Understudy, Record Token, Consol and No Alimony. The object was to keep him on the move without allowing any dissipation of energy, an art known as keeping a horse at concert pitch. Intuitive knowledge is required to gauge just the right amount of work to give a horse and it is here that Walwyn excels. Noel Murless once said: 'Training racehorses is four-fifths knowledge and one-fifth intuition. The only fifth that really matters is the last.'

Matt McCormack and Eddie Towell, assistant travelling head lad, accompanied Grundy on the hour and a quarter flight to Ireland, leaving Southampton on Wednesday afternoon. McCormack cantered Grundy on Thusday morning and on the Friday rode him in a sharp four-furlongs gallop with Consol, who was due to run that evening in the Royal Whip Stakes over a mile and a half.

Peter Walwyn, his wife and Pat Eddery planned to fly from Heathrow to Dublin on Friday lunchtime. Their Aer Lingus jet was due to leave at one o'clock and the plane taxied from the terminal ready for take off. Everything went normally and the plane halted at the beginning of the runway with the pilot awaiting final clearance from air traffic control. The passengers had secured their seat belts and the engines began to build up thrust. Suddenly there was a violent jolt and a noise of tearing metal. Anxious passengers peered out of their windows to be confronted by a towering Jumbo, which on turning at the dispersal point had crashed a wing into the Aer Lingus jet's tail plane.

For Pat Eddery in particular, the delay was serious and when he eventually touched down three hours late in Dublin, he had precious little time to get to The Curragh to ride Silky for Harry Wragg in the Irish 1,000 Guineas – the first classic in the British Isles to be run in the evening. Jonathan Powell, racing correspondent of *The People*, was also on the Dublin plane and had a self-drive hire car laid on for the twenty-mile drive to the racecourse. Eddery and press photographer Ed Byrne jumped into the car with Powell, who predicted with typical confidence: 'I'll get you there in time.' This he proceeded to do by breaking virtually all the rules of the road but the Irish police obligingly turned a blind eye to the car that overtook queues of race traffic by driving down grass verges. The dash achieved its objective but Silky was beaten into second place by Miralla in the fillies' classic. In the next race Eddery won on Consol from Hurry Harriet, the mare who had become famous after defeating Allez France in the 1973 Champion Stakes. Consol's victory augured well for the morrow.

Among those awaiting to do battle with Grundy was his old rival Mark Anthony and another horse beaten by him at Newmarket, It's Freezing. There seemed no obvious reason why either should do better this time and the most interesting and possibly dangerous opponent was the French-trained Monsanto, to be ridden by Yves Saint-Martin. Monsanto had finished fourth to Green Dancer, beaten three and three-quarter lengths, in the Poule d'Essai des Poulains, the French 2,000 Guineas, and so his performance at The Curragh would be a good yardstick to the respective abilities of Grundy and Green Dancer. He started second favourite at 6–1 with Grundy fractionally odds-on at 10–11.

The mile course at The Curragh is totally unlike the Rowley Mile at Newmarket. It has a right-hand bend which swings into a five-furlongs straight, being uphill all the way. The rising terrain makes it a stiff, galloping track and it is reckless optimism to run doubtful stayers. There was no doubt that Grundy stayed a mile but the manner in which he finished here would give a valuable indication about his prospects of staying further.

Grundy cantered to post in the collected and fluent manner that was becoming his hallmark. There was a slight trace of sweat around his loins but otherwise he was cool and beautifully behaved on a fine, sunny afternoon. His example was not being followed by Gay Fandango, a colt trained by Vincent O'Brien, who was having his first-ever race. Gay Fandango proved troublesome at the start and gave his rider, Thomas Murphy, anxious moments when refusing to enter the stalls. The remainder of the runners had to wait in their compartments while Gay Fandango was prised into his place but when that was achieved and the stalls suddenly sprang open, Golden Aim, another English challenger, was caught flat footed and lost several lengths.

Grundy got away on terms and settled easily in the middle of the field, Eddery being pleased to allow Monsanto to dispute the lead in the early stages. Saint-Martin was certainly making a lot of use of Monsanto, too much it seemed, and as the field swung into the straight, Mark Anthony and Grundy began to improve their positions. Grundy appeared to be off the bit with Eddery's arms far from still but the resolution of the response, when it was called for, left no doubt about who was going to win. With two and a half furlongs to run, Grundy struck the front and, keeping up a strong gallop, came away on his own. Eddery eased him in the final hundred yards, allowing Monsanto to close to within a length and a half at the post. Mark Anthony was a further length away third and Gay Fandango, who had run a most encouraging race for a newcomer, fourth.

Before offering Eddery any congratulations Peter Walwyn blurted out: 'Well, what do you think?' 'He'll stay all right,' came the emphatic reply, for Grundy had triumphed with authority. In the space of 1 minute and 47 seconds, the Epsom Derby had ceased to be just a possibility and now seemed the logical next objective. Grundy had not beaten Monsanto by as far as Green Dancer, but he had won with plenty in reserve.

The final piece in the Derby jigsaw was the performance of Green Dancer in the Prix Lupin, to be run at Longchamp the day after the Irish Guineas. Green Dancer was meeting the unbeaten Mariacci and victory for him would almost certainly ensure that he came to Epsom as Derby favourite. If Green Dancer won comfortably, then Grundy might be confronting a world-beater. Or was Grundy himself perhaps a world-beater, capable of producing a performance that would put him among the immortals of the Turf?

Chapter 9

'This is the life'

Geordie Campbell, his craggy features beaming from under a bright orange helmet, looked more like a speedway rider than a stableman as he strode up the yard at West Ilsley to collect his mount for 'second lot'. It was 10.30 on a bitter morning with a cutting north wind blowing, but Dick Hern's head lad hardly felt it. After 25 years, and like most countrymen, his flesh had become tough and leathery through exposure to the elements. In any case, he had been busy for five hours already and having nearly a hundred horses to look after kept him warm.

He and Tom Barnes, the feeder, had been the first men to attend the horses just before 6 a.m. when Geordie, who conveniently lived in a bungalow only yards from the main stable block, had run his hands over the horses' legs to feel for any heat. This took him well over an hour, by which time all the lads had arrived to get the horses in the first lot ready to pull out at 7.30. Geordie Campbell had ridden out Crucible as usual, an old horse who had seen plenty of activity on racecourses throughout Europe, having enjoyed one particularly successful spell in France. The string first of all assembled in the covered ride where they trotted for ten minutes or so to see if they were sound, and all being well they then made their way through the estate, across the main road and up on to the downs.

This is the part of the life that all stablemen like the best, no matter how long they have been in the game. One of them summed up his feeling: 'When I get up on those gallops with a good horse under me and hear the skylarks singing in the sunshine, I look across to Harwell in the distance and feel real sorry for all those poor beggars working away in the factories. This is the life and there's nothing to beat it.'

Geordie had realised it was the life for him in 1950 when he left his Northumberland home and came south to be apprenticed to Jack Colling. He rode two winners before being called up for National Service and, although he enjoyed his two years in the army, the break did his career little good and he returned to stables too heavy to have any prospects of becoming a jockey. Colling had offered him the position of second travelling head lad, however, and he happily accepted, staying in the job for nine years. He became head lad under Dick Hern in 1968 and remembered the year well as it was the time he looked after Remand who finished fourth in the Derby, being rated 'a certain winner if he had been a healthy horse and not plagued by the virus'. The horse for whom Geordie had most affection, however, was Grey of Falloden, winner of the Cesarewitch in 1964 under the record weight of 9 st 6 lb.

When the second lot, mainly two-year-olds, had returned to the yard after working on the shavings gallop there was plenty of activity and Geordie had to organise a few horses for the third lot before going to his pharmacy to dispense and apply various ointments for horses requiring attention. A general discussion with Dick Hern then followed and it was around one o'clock before he went home for his lunch, passing on his way two young lads on hands and knees in one of the paddocks, tearing up handfuls of grass to be given to the horses later on.

For three hours after lunch an air of tranquillity overcame the yard, the majority of lads having a snooze before evening stables started at 4.15, when Geordie and assistant trainer Stan Clayton had the task yet again of checking legs. By six o'clock the rounds had been completed and a satisfied Geordie closed up for the night.

This had been a typical day in his life, the routine followed for fifty weeks of the year. He is entitled to three weeks holiday but only takes two in March when he goes home to Northumberland. Holidays and time off do not bother him, testimony to the fact that he loves the work, so typical of the dedicated men one finds in racing stables.

Curiously West Ilsley seems almost to have cornered the market in lads from the north-east and maybe their soft accents were responsible for the lulling of Bustino into the good-humoured, amenable mood that characterised him. Besides Geordie Campbell there is Brian Procter, Bustino's principal work rider, from West Hartlepool and David Blythe, the black-smith – from Blythe, where else? Brian Procter, born in 1939, joined Sir Gordon Richards' stable at Ogbourne as an appren-tice and moved to Whitsbury with Sir Gordon, staying until he retired in 1970. Procter was spare rides jockey to the stable and has continued to get the occasional opportunity since joining Dick Hern. Altogether he has ridden thirty winners and came closest to a big success when fourth in the Middle Park Stakes of 1972 on Lady Beaverbrook's Boldboy.

David Blythe's day starts at 7 a.m. when he looks round the horses due to go out second lot. He plates any that need doing, then has his breakfast, after which the horses who went out first lot have returned and are ready for inspection and plating. In the afternoon he makes shoes in his forge which is opposite the stable office. He is on call seven days a week and lives in one of the tied bungalows behind the stables. He corresponds exactly to the jolly, jowled image of a blacksmith with powerful forearms, a long leather apron and cap pushed back on his head. Before coming to West Ilsley he was at Newmarket for twelve years, when among the good horses he shod were Crepello, Twilight Alley, Hotfoot and Super Sam. He seldom goes racing except to Newbury, does not bet and although a great admirer of Bustino never saw him run.

Another key figure in the stable is Buster Haslam, travelling head lad since 1957. He is a hard-bitten, shrewd judge of a horse who needs convincing that an animal is out of the ordinary. 'One of the best jockeys for weighing up something he had ridden was Bill Williamson,' he says. 'Bill took a long time to get excited about anything and so many hopeful owners have approached him after a race to be told "He's only a horse, no more". That was Bill's favourite answer and when he said anything more you knew you had something special. I suppose I'm a bit like that and it takes time for me to get enthusiastic. Bustino didn't look outstanding as a two-year-old and what made him was the time we gave him. Only having that one race as a two-year-old did him a lot of good and it was a blessing he got that dirty nose before he was due to run at Doncaster. That meant we had to retire him for the season.'

During the winter Buster Haslam looks after the newly arrived horses, pulls their manes and clips them. He gets the young horses accustomed to the starting stalls and leads them through a simulated set every day, and of course he rides out two lots. At the same time that he is in the saddle his wife, Valerie, is riding out for the jumping trainer, Roddy Armytage, at East Ilsley. She has even been known to pay 100 guineas for a foal and put it into training with Armytage. Its name was Criticism, after the way Buster reacted when he heard what his wife had done!

Tom Barnes feeds all the horses at West Ilsley and is one of few Irishmen on the staff. He served with Cecil Brabazon for five years before coming to England to work for Tom Rimell at Windsor House, Lambourn – the yard where Peter Walwyn first set up as trainer. Barnes dropped out of racing for two years but horses were in his blood – his brother is stud groom at Eyrefield Lodge Stud – and he returned to work for Dick Hern. He believes 'competence, confidence and dedication' make a good stableman and he personifies this. He has found over the years that the good horses are generally the least trouble: 'Bustino was a very easy horse to feed and a lovely placid character. He was a pleasure to look after.'

Altogether there is a staff of over fifty people at West Ilsley where one gets the impression of a happy, cheerful group of men and women working for a common cause. There is no clock

watching and few complaints about pay and conditions. 'If we
do have a grouse, we have a meeting in the tack-room and
thrash it all out. Then we send someone in to state our case to
the guv'nor and he always listens and does his best to iron things
out. There's never any real trouble. We're paid over the odds
and pleased to be here,' said one man who has been in racing
all his life and was apprenticed to Major Fred Sneyd at the
same time as Joe Mercer.

There is similar contentment at Seven Barrows only a few
miles as the crow flies across the Downs from West Ilsley. Here
again there is a spirit of involvement that means every lad is
important. There are no girls in the yard, as Peter Walwyn
believes they could have an unsettling influence although he is
aware that they are conscientious and play a vital role in
racing these days. Most of the staff are experienced stablemen
but there are five younger lads who share a whitewashed cot-
tage in the village. Among them is Charlie Johnson, who must
be one of the luckiest lads in racing or at least one of the
greatest influences for good fortune. After being brought up
near Gloucester he applied to join Colin Davies's stable at
Chepstow but had to go further afield before finding an opening
– with Freddie Maxwell at Lambourn. He was taught to ride,
only he grew too big and heavy ever to have any chance of
becoming a jockey but the disappointment was forgotten when
he was given charge of a highly-strung filly called Cawston's
Pride, the same that ran eight times as a two-year-old without
being beaten and broke the course record at Ascot. She was
exceptionally talented but also an exceptional handful, and
Johnson thought that if this was a top-class racehorse he would
settle for a moderate one.

When he moved to Seven Barrows his wish was granted at
first when he looked after two ordinary horses, Sovereign Count
and Paper Palace, both of whom won but neither of whom had
any pretensions to breaking a record – not even at Hamilton
Park. When Jimmy Brownlie turned down the chance of 'doing'
Grundy as a yearling, however, it was Johnson who volunteered

to take charge of what he thought was a rather 'wishy-washy chestnut'. So the Johnson luck struck again. He is a pleasant, modest personality with an unruly mop of blond hair and he speaks with that rich Gloucestershire burr about his affection for Grundy: 'You couldn't help getting attached to him as he was such a grand looker when he grew up. He was no trouble in his box but more of a worry outside. I feel really proud to have been part of him.'

Matt McCormack must also feel proud of his contribution towards making Grundy what he was. It was McCormack who in the early days managed to settle Grundy on the gallops. He is a neat, stocky Irishman with the typical sparkling eyes. His official capacity at Seven Barrows is assistant head lad, a position he has earned after being in racing for over twenty years. He left home as a fifteen-year-old to live with relations near Leeds and was apprenticed to Bill Newton at Wetherby in a mixed-stable. After four years he moved to Tommy Dent at York and went to Newmarket later where he spent ten years in three of the country's finest stables – those of Cecil Boyd-Rochfort, Bernard van Cutsem and Noel Murless. He prefers living in Lambourn, however, where he has been for five years, finding the closer knit community far more friendly than Newmarket. 'You could walk down the High Street there and be ignored but here it takes you a quarter of an hour to do a hundred yards, unlike Grundy who, if you weren't careful, would cart you to Wantage in five minutes. In the early days he was certainly a bit of a tearaway.'

Another fast mover is Tony Driscoll, the travelling head lad, who when driving his Saab treats the Lambourn lanes like Nurburgring. He has one of the most demanding jobs, for Peter Walwyn sends out more runners than any other trainer and will send them to the extremities of the country if it helps them to win a race. This means that, for Driscoll, the months from April to November stretch ahead like one continuous road and he estimates he travels something like 30,000 miles in a season and spends on average three nights a week away from home.

11 The team behind Grundy. From left to right: travelling head lad Tony Driscoll, work rider Matt McCormack, Pat Eddery, Grundy, his lad Charlie Johnson, Peter Walwyn and head lad Ray Laing.

12 Grundy cruises home ahead of Nobiliary to win the Epsom Derby.

13 Pat Eddery gives Grundy a slap of delight after a scintillating performance in the Irish Derby. King Pellinore is second, Anne's Pretender (behind Grundy) third and Sea Anchor (on the wide outside) fourth.

14 Pat Eddery explains just how it was done to Peter Walwyn and his wife Virginia, after winning the Irish Derby.

What makes it all worthwhile? 'I like the racing and being there when we win. It's a great moment when those horses go past the post and come back to the winners' enclosure. I've been travelling for fifteen years and in racing for twenty-five but the excitement is still there.'

Driscoll was born in Liverpool. He started with Jack Colling at West Ilsley in 1951 at the same time as Geordie Campbell was an apprentice there. When he came back from National Service there was no job for him but he gained employment with David Hastings who was then running Seven Barrows. He worked for Keith Piggott for a spell, then joined Peter Walwyn at the start of his training career and has been with him ever since.

He is known to be a clever punter, but he bets only when the bookmakers are offering value for money. Since he backed a filly of Louis Freedman's called Guillotina at Longchamp several years ago and received 66–1 to his money, he has had a soft spot for both the filly and the pari-mutuel – unfortunately he finds the Walwyn horses always well-backed on the Tote in England.

On a Friday night during the winter Tony Driscoll may meet Ray Laing, head lad at Seven Barrows, for a drink in the British Legion Club at Lambourn where the price of a pint is amazingly low. Laing is a respected figure in the village where he has been since 1959, starting with Syd Mercer, 'the man who can charm warts off a horse,' at Windsor House. Thus Laing was already there when Peter Walwyn moved in. There is a touch of cynicism about Laing, no doubt partially brought about by the responsibilities of his job: 'It's a hell of a thing being head lad in such a big stable, but the winners make it worthwhile, not that I back any of them as I don't see that it should be necessary.' He is an uncompromising character, straightforward, blunt, a disciplinarian in the yard but with a sense of loyalty which evokes similar response from the lads under him. He is held in great esteem by Walwyn who regards him as the professional's professional – hardly surprising since

Laing is steeped in racing, coming from a long line of horsemen. He rode his one and only winner on the flat at Chepstow as long ago as 1939 when he was sixteen and Peter Walwyn five!

Chapter 10

Derby Day

The result of the Prix Lupin was a three-quarters of a length victory for Green Dancer over Mariacci, and when his trainer, Alec Head, confirmed that Green Dancer's next race would be the Epsom classic, the bookmakers were sure that all along they had had the right horse favourite. Green Dancer was at the short price of 6–4 but he was not absolutely certain to stay. He was among the first crop of Nijinsky out of the mare Green Valley by the French Derby-winner Val de Loir. He was a first foal and as such his stamina capabilities were unknown. The signs were that he would manage to last out a mile and a half for he had run on determinedly over a mile and two and a half furlongs to win the Lupin, although Mariacci had stuck to him like a leech through the final quarter-mile and the race was every bit as tough as had been expected. The first two had finished six lengths clear of the third horse, Matahawk, and the form looked top class. The Lupin is a Group I race with a first prize of £68,167 so it could hardly be described as a classic trial; but coming just over two weeks before Epsom it is not an ideal preparatory experience for a colt with the classic as his main objective. Some voiced fears that Green Dancer might have left the Derby at Longchamp.

By contrast Grundy had been given an easy time in the Irish Guineas and although that had been his third race of the season – one more than Green Dancer – he had not been subjected to any punishment. After returning from The Curragh, he was not worked strongly for a week and was still a relatively fresh horse. 'Fresh' was the right word, for he was becoming a boisterous individual outside his box again although perfectly amenable inside, giving no trouble to Charlie Johnson.

His Epsom build-up began with a gallop on 27 May with Corby and Patch, who had entered the Derby picture himself after winning the Lingfield Derby Trial at the beginning of the month. He too was owned by Carlo Vittadini and had run in Italy as a two-year-old. It was unlikely, however, he would run at Epsom but he would be left in the race until the last moment in case any accident happened to Grundy. Three days later, on the Friday before the Derby, Walwyn took four horses to Moss Hill to gallop over a mile and a quarter on what is regarded as the old Derby trial ground. The gallop has a left-hand turn into a straight which is against the collar. The horses in the work-out were Corby, ridden by Frank Morby, Red Regent, with Brian Taylor up, No Alimony, ridden by Joe Mercer who did not have a ride in the Derby for Dick Hern, and of course Grundy with Eddery riding.

Corby made the running followed by No Alimony and Red Regent with Grundy bringing up the rear. This order was maintained until, swinging into the straight, No Alimony and Red Regent went to join Corby with Grundy still tucked in last. In the final quarter of a mile, Eddery allowed Grundy to quicken on the bridle and finished alongside No Alimony and Red Regent, both of whom were to be in the Epsom line-up. This was the first time Grundy had ever gone more than a mile and there was no sign of him flagging. Eddery was extremely pleased by the way he had finished after what had been a good demanding gallop, and again was in no doubt that he possessed abundant stamina.

At lunchtime on Tuesday all three Derby runners were boxed-up for the journey to Epsom, travelling at this early stage being thought by Walwyn preferable to waiting until the morning of the race and risking traffic delays. Grundy was his usual lively self but he settled without fretting in the Epsom security block which is close to Dermot 'Boggy' Whelan's stable. Whelan is an appealing Irishman, not perhaps very likely to set the racing world alight with his training successes but willing to help any who might, and he allowed the Walwyn horses to trot on his small private gallop on the morning of the race.

It was on the Tuesday morning that Green Dancer had been exercised on the Epsom course, emerging from the stables to a sound of whirring cameras as television news crews filmed the hottest Derby favourite since Nijinsky. Green Dancer, not being a particularly robust or well-made animal, did not have great physical presence. It was hard to say whether he was trained to the minute or just a fraction over-trained, certainly there was no spare flesh on him. He was ridden in his exercise by the French champion Freddie Head, his Derby jockey, who had recently been married and was now returning to the scene of some hair-raising experiences in past Derbies.

Head was regarded by many as a 7 lb penalty for a horse at Epsom and, although this was overstating the case against him, it was true that he had not excelled in previous rides on the track. His effort on the well-fancied Lyphard in 1972 had sparked derisive laughter from uncommitted observers and unprintable utterances from those with a financial interest, when he had run very wide at Tattenham Corner, thereby for-feiting all chance. Those 'riders in the stands' may or may not have appreciated the hazards of Epsom with the first half-mile uphill, the sharp descent on the turn and the changing camber in the straight. This is a course where the well-balanced, smooth-actioned horse is favoured. Big horses have won the Derby like Windsor Lad, Coronach, Captain Cuttle, Pinza and Nijinsky but a smaller animal is far easier to keep balanced. Freddie Head rode very short indeed, however, which impaired his ability to correct a rolling, unbalanced mount. It was these short irons which caused the criticism.

On this particular morning, Head was not prepared either to practise his own approach to Tattenham Corner or find out Green Dancer's suitability to the track, for after setting off at the seven-furlong pole he eased the colt to a slow canter coming down the hill. The prime object, of course, was to allow Green Dancer to stretch his legs along with his compatriot Fidion and the Irish challengers Sea Break and Nuthatch, both of whom looked as if they would have liked more give in the ground. Another horse to be exercised on the track that morning was Royal Manacle ridden by his trainer Barry Hills who, after years as head lad to John Oxley at Newmarket, was now established as a leading trainer at Lambourn. Royal Manacle was one of the most interesting runners in the Derby field, being by the five-furlongs specialist Manacle, but apparently possessing enough stamina to stay at least a mile.

Unless there was a deluge on the morning of Derby Day, the going would be good to firm which would suit Grundy with his low, flicking action. Green Dancer had coped with similar fast ground well enough when winning the French 2,000 Guineas but it had been soft – the prevailing surface in France where courses are well watered – for the Prix Lupin. Epsom's unyielding surface often comes as a shock to the pampered feet of French challengers.

A field of eighteen runners looked likely and among them were the usual no-hopers, running mainly to satisfy the vanity of owners; although whether any satisfaction or prestige can be gained from seeing one's horse finish tailed off is a moot point. This year there appeared to be a particularly moderate horse, Tanzor, among the runners whom the bookmakers had 5–1 favourite to finish last. This sort of bet leaves the bookmakers wide open to exploitation and it is surprising they allow it.

A more likely contender to win, on the other hand, but one with history against her, was the filly Nobiliary, attempting to become the first of her sex to win the race since Fifinella in 1916 when the contest was staged at Newmarket. Nobiliary was by Vaguely Noble, and she came to Epsom having won the Prix Saint Alary from Lighted Glory, who had finished fifth in the English 1,000 Guineas. The form did not look outstanding but the filly came from the same stable as Dahlia and was reputed to be in the same mould. Yves Saint-Martin had decided to ride Nobiliary rather than Sea Break, who had been such a disappointing ride for him in the 2,000 Guineas at Newmarket.

Lester Piggott, with six Derby victories behind him, found himself left out in the cold this year, as can happen to a freelance jockey no matter how good, and only a few days before the race he had fixed his mount on Bruni, who had been beaten a short-head by No Alimony in the Predominate Stakes at Goodwood in May. Bruni was one of three horses in the race trained by Ryan Price – the others being Anne's Pretender and Whip It Quick.

To all intents and purposes it looked a two-horse race, however, and to some at Seven Barrows it looked a one-horse race. Charlie Johnson had no doubts and had backed his horse some weeks before, getting 8–1 about his money. On the day, Grundy started second best at 5–1 with Green Dancer the favourite at 6–4. The reason why Grundy was not more popular was that, in many people's minds, he was not certain to stay. His sire Great Nephew had never run beyond a mile and a quarter and his sire in turn had been the very fast Honeyway. Although Grundy's dam, Word From Lundy, had stayed two miles, her first foal by Crocket, called Whirlow Green, never managed more than nine furlongs. There was no concrete evidence either way but it was fair to say that Grundy had prospects of staying a mile and a half, that his manner of racing would help him, and fast ground was also in his favour. In sum, he looked a better value bet than the favourite about whom there was a similar slight doubt about his stamina.

For once, after a succession of brilliantly sunny Derby Days, the weather was overcast, but the atmosphere generated on the downs by a seething three-quarters of a million people was the same mixture of gaiety, expectation and tension as always. During the disciplined pre-race parade from the paddock to the furlong marker, that tension often permeates the minds of the runners; and of course Snow Knight had thrown Brian Taylor last year before winning Bustino's Derby. The unfortunate Freddie Head had been given a torrid time by Bourbon before

Derby Day

the 1971 race but on this occasion Green Dancer was behaving impeccably. Grundy threw his head around a few times but the air of restlessness about him evaporated immediately he turned and broke into that flowing stride. One sensed, then, that he was going to do the job for which he had been prepared.

This race represents the ultimate for a trainer and Peter Walwyn, after thirteen years, was just beginning to get the 'Gordon Richards feeling' that he might never win it. Twice he had saddled the second horse in Shoemaker and Linden Tree, the latter having been unlucky to run up against Mill Reef. In terms of class, however, Grundy was vastly superior.

A Derby start looks unreal. Viewed from the stands and rails the horses look insignificant, as if on film, although it must be a blessed relief for them to be back in a quiet country environment, away from the babbling, agitated masses. It is hard to believe that all this is happening now and that in a little over two and a half minutes those distant specks will come thundering past amidst a furore of passion. The finish of the Derby leaves no one indifferent.

Grundy's stable companion Red Regent was the first to show at the head of the field; yet even at the sedate pace that was being set Tanzor contrived to be a hundred yards behind the bunch after only a quarter of a mile. At this point Edward Hide, on Carolus, quickened the gallop and Grundy increased his speed easily to hold fifth place approaching the mile post. Anne's Pretender, ridden by Tony Murray, was stretching out with zest on the fast ground and at the top of the hill, beginning the run down to Tattenham Corner, he made a significant move, surging into a lead of two lengths to recall Snow Knight's effort the previous year. Grundy was sixth starting the run down to Tattenham, but he came down the hill with such grace and speed that at the entrance to the straight he was poised in the perfect position – fourth on the rails. This was in contrast to Green Dancer who had lost ground. Lavandin had come from far back to win in the hands of Rae Johnson in 1956, but Green

Dancer appeared hopelessly placed at least a dozen lengths off the leader.

Murray asked for full power from Anne's Pretender on entering the straight and forged three lengths clear of Red Regent and Nuthatch, who was on the bit and looking sure to be involved in the finish. With three furlongs to run Anne's Pretender's lead was a long one and Grundy's supporters had moments of doubt. These were not shared by Pat Eddery, however, as he pulled to the outside, feeling under him the strong rhythm of a horse still full of running. Grundy changed his legs when asked to quicken as if moving into overdrive. He reached his rival's quarters with an amazing economy of effort. Two furlongs from home the pair were level, but in another hundred yards Grundy had stormed two lengths clear. Eddery neither saw nor heard any other runner now, but kept Grundy going until well inside the final furlong when he eased right up to finish with his hands still and his bottom at the cocky Piggott angle.

Nobiliary came with a sustained run to finish second, beaten three lengths, after being sixth at the corner, but Hunza Dancer had finished in almost incredible style to take third place after having only two horses behind him coming down the hill. Anne's Pretender ran a gallant race to finish fourth – maybe not quite getting the distance – but Green Dancer could manage no better than sixth, some ten lengths behind Grundy. This did not look Green Dancer's proper form for he had been unable to beat Whip It Quick, so soundly trounced by him in the Observer Gold Cup. Nuthatch, who had looked so promising at Tattenham Corner, failed to quicken and finished tenth. Neither of Grundy's stable companions, No Alimony nor Red Regent, finished in the first ten, while bringing up the rear were Carolus and Tanzor, who was tailed off. The stewards asked for an explanation of Tanzor's running and heard from the jockey, Greville Starkey, that the horse had slipped a stifle.

Pat Eddery took his success with comparative calm, confessing that he had never been worried. Grundy had hung into the centre of the course in the final stages, which earned Eddery a wigging from the photographers who told him to keep closer to the rails next time so as not to spoil their pictures!

Peter Walwyn's post-race reaction, in contrast, was of over-whelming joy. As the Press crowded round in the unsaddling enclosure, he could not refrain from reminding some of them how they had belittled Grundy: 'I always said he was a star. You wouldn't believe me but I kept telling you.' In reply to a question about future plans for the horse, he said: 'I don't know about his plans but I know mine. He could go for the Irish Derby or the Eclipse, but I don't really care. I don't care if he never runs again.' This he did not mean literally, his mood reflecting the elation of the moment; for when the euphoria had passed he would care, and care very much, about Grundy running and winning other races.

For Dr Vittadini the occasion was momentous. It was 'the greatest thrill of my life' but he had not had a penny on Grundy. 'I never bet and though I knew we would win I could not change the habit of a life-time.' With a first prize of £106,465, the richest-ever Derby, who needed to bet? Victory had coincided with the Vittadini's 28th wedding anniversary and in the excitement of the day, he had forgotten to give his wife Henrietta an anniversary present. Happily she settled for the Derby.

Dr Vittadini's family – he has two sons and a daughter – mean a great deal to him and perhaps surprisingly, in view of his wealth and success, there remains more than a touch of humility about him. He is not a brash extrovert, rather the opposite, and in his quietly spoken manner he expresses amazement that such good fortune could have come to him. When one realises the extent of his success in racing it is not hard to see why he is so incredulous. His first horse Exar was bought for 1,900 guineas and won over £25,000. Then followed bargains like Accrale, purchased for 3,600 guineas – won £22,500; Equestrienne, purchased for 400 guineas – sold for £20,000;

No Mercy, purchased for 5,000 guineas – syndicated for 70,000 guineas; Habat, purchased for 14,500 guineas – won £43,000. Now Grundy was about to be syndicated.

The day after the Derby negotiations began between the Horserace Betting Levy Board and Keith Freeman, representing Dr Vittadini, about the possible syndication of Grundy to stand at the National Stud. Keith Freeman took the initiative over the matter, having some months before sounded out the National Stud about their attitude towards the horse if he turned out to be as good as was hoped. Discussions now took place between Sir Desmond Plummer, Lord Porchester, Colonel Grey, Peter Willett, Lady Halifax and Keith Freeman, the result of which was the purchase by the Board of a three-quarter share in Grundy for £750,000.

Certain conditions were imposed and originally it was decided that Grundy should run only three more times, finishing in the Champion Stakes at Newmarket in October. This meant, however, that there would be a long gap after his proposed participation in the King George VI and Queen Elizabeth Stakes at Ascot in July, and so an extra contest was allowed, intended as a preparation for the Champion Stakes. There was also discussion about whether Grundy should go for the Irish Derby or the Eclipse Stakes at Sandown Park and this was not immediately resolved. When the syndication agreement was announced it was stated publicly that Grundy would be allowed four more races in England and Ireland. There were no hard and fast rules, but the races were the Irish Derby or Eclipse Stakes, the King George VI and Queen Elizabeth Stakes, the Valdoe Stakes at Goodwood and the Champion Stakes. The Prix de l'Arc de Triomphe was not on the list, however, at the request of Freeman and Vittadini, neither of whom was enamoured of the race after past experiences.

Chapter 11

Coronation Cup

While Grundy had run four times in establishing himself an outstanding three-year-old, Bustino had not raced since his St Leger triumph. He had been kept in training with three races principally in mind – the Coronation Cup at Epsom, three days after the Derby; the King George VI and Queen Elizabeth Diamond Stakes at Ascot; and the Prix de l'Arc de Triomphe at Longchamp. During the eight months since his last public appearance he had let down into an imposing, powerful four-year-old, weighing nearly $9\frac{1}{2}$ cwt and standing $16-1\frac{1}{4}$ hands high.

Dick Hern had not needed to hurry his preparation and the colt was enjoying life rather as might a senior boy at school. He had been through the mill, knew the routine thoroughly and was a revered member of the community. It was plain to the head lad, Geordie Campbell, that Bustino was much more relaxed now and less perturbed when coming into contact with unfamiliar people like the vet, Charles Frank. Frank always found Bustino most unco-operative when it came to anti-flu vaccinations, and on one occasion the horse had nearly jumped out of his box with fright.

In February, Bustino was cantering regularly with the rest of the string going up the five-furlongs 'starting gate' gallop. There were no plans to run him until May and nothing serious was required of him until April when he began to be readied for the Yorkshire Cup over one mile and three-quarters at York. The race, on 15 May, was ideal as preparation for the Coronation Cup as Bustino had shown himself admirably suited by the galloping York track when winning the Great Voltigeur and indeed when making his satisfactory début in the Acomb Stakes in 1973.

Riboson had also been entered for the Yorkshire Cup, primarily to act as pacemaker. The three-day York meeting began on Tuesday when the going was good to soft. The Cup was not until Thursday, so there was a chance of the ground drying out to suit Bustino. But Tuesday night was wet, continuous rain on Wednesday morning changed the going to soft, and so Dick Hern decided not to run Bustino and rely solely on Riboson. The latter showed what an admirable type he was by winning; making all the running and holding off Kalpour by a neck.

Bustino had been spared the worry of travelling to York. He needed some strong work now, however, to compensate and on Tuesday 20 May he galloped a mile and a half with Kinglet. The following Saturday he gave his fellow four-year-old Attalus two stone and worked impressively over a mile and a quarter. On the Monday he was taken to Sandown Park, not to compete but to gallop on the course after racing. Attalus, ridden by Geoff Lewis, and Kinglet, with Tommy Carter up, were his working companions and Joe Mercer had no trouble in coming to beat this pair up the final hill, after a mile and a quarter at a good pace. Hern was delighted and was sure that Bustino had improved considerably since his three-year-old days. But the Coronation Cup was still twelve days away and Bustino could be made fitter yet. Two more pieces of work over a mile with Kinglet, put an edge on him, the last good gallop being on Tuesday, the day before the Derby.

There was no rain at Epsom in the intervening time and the ground that had been good to firm for the Derby, was decidedly firm by Saturday. This did not bother Dick Hern, but Ryan Price, who had intended to challenge Bustino with Giacometti, withdrew his horse on the Friday evening. This left only six runners, including Bustino's faithful pacemaker Riboson. The others were Ashmore and Comtesse de Loir from France, Mil's Bomb from the Noel Murless stable and another Newmarket-trained horse, Arthurian, whose 40–1 quote summed up his chance. It was unlikely that the French horses would relish the firm ground and Comtesse de Loir, second to Allez France in the Arc the previous season, drifted ominously in the betting from 5–2 to 4–1. Ashmore looked the main threat to Bustino, having won the Prix Jean de Chaudenay at Saint Cloud three weeks before with Dahlia well behind. The failure of Dahlia was not surprising – her record showed that she needed time before finding the scintillating form that had won her the King George VI and Queen Elizabeth Stakes twice at Ascot.

Joe Mercer had won the Coronation Cup the previous year on Buoy, a tall horse, who had negotiated the course with surprising alacrity. Bustino's ability to act on the track was not a source of worry and, with Giacometti a non-runner, the prospects of the stable landing the event for a second successive year looked good, provided Riboson could set a strong enough pace to run the speed out of the opposition.

Since the Derby the weather had turned warm and sunny, and considering the temperature was bordering on 80°F., Bustino looked remarkably cool in the parade ring as he walked round behind Riboson, who was to be ridden this time by Eric Eldin. Jimmy Lindley, who had done such an efficient job on the horse in the St Leger, had retired from the saddle and was now a television commentator. As the runners cantered to post after parading they made a resounding drumming noise on the hard ground, a noise which emphasised the power and weight of a mature thoroughbred. Bustino was as fine a specimen as one could wish to see.

The six runners were quickly installed and Riboson, as planned, jumped out to set a strong pace with Bustino tracking him. At the bottom of Tattenham Hill rounding the corner into the straight, the distinguishing red cap of Eric Eldin on Riboson began to nod vigorously as the horse came off the bit and was ridden along to stay in front for as long as possible. Riboson courageously kept up the gallop until two and a half furlongs from home when Joe Mercer made his move on Bustino. There was no other way to ride now except flat out and Bustino was a magnificent sight on that shimmering afternoon as he lengthened his stride and streaked for the line.

Although Yves Saint-Martin had been aware of the tactical plan he was unable to keep Ashmore close enough to go with Bustino at the crucial stage, and although Ashmore gave chase and was closing at the finish, he still had a length to make up at the post. The race had been won and lost a quarter of a mile out. Mil's Bomb, who had never got into the race, finished six lengths away third, holding off Comtesse de Loir by a short-head.

When the commentator announced a course record it came as no surprise. The time of 2 minutes 33.31 seconds had knocked 0.18 seconds off the previous best time put up by Knockroe in 1973. Bustino had bettered Grundy's time in the Derby by 2.04 seconds, both horses having carried the same weight of 9 stone. Too much could not be read into that, however, as the going on the Saturday was definitely faster, officially estimated at 0.20 seconds per furlong. If this allowance is taken into account, Grundy had achieved a relatively better performance.

Bustino's victory in the Coronation Cup was worth £14,465, which took his total prize-money earnings in this country to £92,334, and his performance at Epsom gained him new friends and admirers. There had been a general assumption after his St Leger success that he would make up into a top-class stayer as a four-year-old, but here he was proving himself an outstanding middle-distance horse. Like his sire Busted, who matured late, there was no doubt that he was only just beginning to attain the height of his powers. Despite his fast time at Epsom he lost only 10 lb in weight and the race had not been a punishing experience. He ate up with undiminished enthusiasm and was clearly thriving.

Dick Hern announced Bustino's next race as the King George VI and Queen Elizabeth Diamond Stakes at Ascot on 26 July and, for the first time, there was an inkling of a possible clash between Bustino and Grundy. But while Bustino was to have six weeks in which to recharge his batteries, Grundy was about to take the field again.

Chapter 12

Irish Derby

Peter Walwyn had been horrified to learn there was vacillation among Grundy's owners about whether the horse should run in the Irish Derby. The Eclipse Stakes at Sandown was regarded as perhaps the more suitable race as it would be less difficult to win. Grundy must be protected if possible, so it was thought, from defeat, as the loss of prestige would adversely affect his chances of being sent the best mares when taking up stallion duties at the National Stud. But while Walwyn was prepared to go along with the restriction regarding the Arc, he was certainly not going to allow the Irish Derby to take place without Grundy in the line-up. It was lunacy to stop the horse running; Grundy was certain to win. These were Walwyn's views and he expounded them with such conviction and perseverance that the opposition was crushed.

Prejudice against the Irish Derby was founded on the fact that the average Epsom Derby winner is not good enough to win both races. In the last eleven years, six horses had attempted the double and only two – Nijinsky and Santa Claus – had succeeded. The failures were Charlottown, Sir Ivor, Blakeney and Roberto. Sir Ivor has been singled out by Lester Piggott as the greatest horse he has ever ridden, but the colt failed at The Curragh because his stamina ran out. Roberto probably failed for the same reason although he had been subjected to a particularly hard race at Epsom.

Charlottown and Blakeney had possessed sufficient stamina but were simply not good enough and have since been rated rather moderate Derby winners. There was little doubt that Grundy was superior to Charlottown and Blakeney, and indeed, the clock suggested that of the horses under discussion he

15–16 Going to Post. Bustino before the Coronation cup at Epsom and Grundy on Diamond Day at Ascot.

17 A head-on view of Grundy and Bustino battling up the Ascot straight. Note the difference in the style of the jockeys.

was second only to Nijinsky. Grundy's Epsom time was 0.67 seconds slower than Nijinsky's and beat Sir Ivor's time, rather surprisingly, by over three seconds.

There was reason to believe, therefore, that Grundy would be good enough to do the double, but the same clock that gave him such a fine chance also pointed to a live danger in King Pellinore, trained by Vincent O'Brien. On the same day that Grundy took the Irish Guineas, King Pellinore had won the Lumville Stakes over the same mile in nearly three seconds faster time. Of course, Grundy had not been pushed right out to win but King Pellinore had also hacked up and beaten Polar Jinks by three lengths.

Piggott was said to have 'talked' O'Brien into running King Pellinore in the Irish Derby, although it seemed a perfectly reasonable, even obvious course of action. But there was one doubt and that concerned stamina. King Pellinore was a half-brother, by Round Table, to the brilliant miler Thatch. Round Table was the sire of Apalachee and had himself stayed thirteen furlongs when racing. If his influence was greater than the dam, Thong, then King Pellinore could be expected to stay a mile and a half. He had already won over a mile and a quarter at The Curragh when beating Phoenix Hall by six lengths on 7 June, and the conclusion to be drawn was that he was a high-class performer.

Grundy's class was now a proven fact but while his race-course performances had reached the realms of excellence, his home form was deteriorating. Walwyn was not worried by this. It was quite common for a talented horse to become lazy at home and it at least ensured that energy was not being wasted. Grundy had nothing to prove on the gallops any longer and, in consequence, when he was disinclined to exert himself, neither Matt McCormack nor Eddery was interested in rousing him for more effort.

An example of this laziness was given eight days before the Irish Derby when Grundy was taken to White Horse Hill for a change of scenery and to work on Derryck Candy's gallops. The four-year-olds, Understudy and Our Nicholas, took part in the mile and a quarter work-out along with Corby and Patch. All the horses carried the weight of their riders or, in other words, no weight cloths were used. Understudy set off in front and stayed there. He won the gallop hands down with Our Nicholas second and Grundy third, some five lengths off the winner.

This was Grundy's final serious work before leaving for Dublin on the Thursday – two days before the race. He flew from Southampton, as he had on his previous trip to Ireland, having for equine company this time his old rival Anne's Pretender, and a promising three-year-old trained by Dick Hern called Sea Anchor. All three horses were to run in the Irish Derby.

The flight was uneventful and Grundy behaved himself beautifully, not needing to be tied up, and standing quietly with Charlie Johnson and Tony Driscoll taking it in turns to hold his head. He continued in amiable mood when transferred from the plane to a horsebox at the airport, but when he arrived at the racecourse stables his mood changed. After anxious moments Driscoll and Johnson managed to get him safely into his stable when, true to form, he quietened down almost immediately.

Neither of the lads responsible for him were looking forward to the morning with much relish, however, and their fears were realised when Grundy came out of his box like a broncho. 'If the guv'nor had been there he would have had a heart attack', says Driscoll. 'I thought Grundy was going to injure himself. He was rearing up to the point where he was almost falling over backwards. Charlie got on him and he quietened down a bit and eventually we managed to get him out on the racecourse for a bit of a canter. Willie Robinson sent his sprinter Bold Tack over and they went six furlongs.' With some exercise Grundy became less boisterous but by the next morning his high spirits had returned and, after being led round for twenty minutes with some difficulty by Tony Driscoll, he was put back in his box on the advice of Peter Walwyn, who had flown in the previous evening.

Grundy's antics were not a real source of concern and there was nothing vicious or savage about his demeanour. It was only outside his box that he became excitable and even that excitement was under control by the time he was required to be saddled and paraded. He never behaved badly in the paddock before a race.

Bold Tack, who had led Grundy at exercise on the previous morning, won the opening race of the Derby programme, ridden by Pat Eddery. This was the Scurry Handicap over six furlongs and Bold Tack bolted in under top weight of 9 st 5 lb. The portents were good. Grundy was fractionally odds-on for the Derby at 9–10 while King Pellinore had predictably attracted heavy local support and started second favourite at 7–2 having been 7–1 four days earlier. The only other runners in a field of thirteen worth consideration were Maitland, a French challenger rated a 6–1 chance after three successive victories in minor events, and Dick Hern's Sea Anchor, a big chestnut by Alcide out of the famous female line of his owner Dick Hollingsworth. Sea Anchor had been too backward to be trained seriously as a two-year-old but he had been improving steadily in his second season and won his last two races impressively. In the King Edward VII Stakes at Royal Ascot he had beaten Libra's Rib and Whip It Quick with Consol a distant fourth. Consol's poor display had been put down to the very firm ground and Sea Anchor may not have been quite as good as he looked. The fact that he had beaten Whip It Quick just over two and a half lengths suggested he had something to find with Grundy, but at 10–1 he looked reasonable each way value for the race, seeming certain to be staying on at the finish. Anne's Pretender had already met Grundy three times, and the closest he had yet got was at Epsom when beaten over seven lengths, so he seemed a forlorn hope, particularly as The Curragh represented a stiffer test of stamina. A 20–1 quote was fair but after him the opposition petered out and not even some fancy prices ranging from 66–1 to 200–1 should have tempted anyone to back one of the others.

Yves Saint-Martin was riding Maitland and, as he had done on Monsanto in the Irish Guineas, took his mount to the front from the start. The Curragh's terrain is not ideal for such tactics but Saint-Martin is a vastly experienced jockey and had won this race the previous year on Peter Walwyn's English Prince after making a lot of use of the colt. English Prince was always in the first three and took the lead half a mile out to win by a length and a half from Imperial Prince. Saint-Martin had come in for the ride on this occasion because Pat Eddery had been stood down by the Ascot stewards after being involved in the controversial finish to the Queen Anne Stakes that year when the first three horses were all disqualified.

Maitland was not in the same class as English Prince, however, and it soon became clear that he was under pressure and losing his place soon after turning for home. The field was well bunched at this stage and it was not easy to pick out Grundy. Eddery had decided that King Pellinore was his only danger and in consequence was tracking this horse in seventh place. What was about to happen in the next few seconds was to astound even the most hard-bitten racing observers. There was to be a glimpse of greatness; moments stamped on the mind's eye.

On rounding the turn, Anne's Pretender had been sent on by Tony Murray who, as at Epsom, was trying to poach a lead which it was hoped might see him home. But he could not get clear and Lester Piggott on King Pellinore moved up to challenge approaching the two-furlong pole. King Pellinore was obviously going the better and Piggott could take the lead whenever he wished. This he did with about three hundred and fifty yards to run, but no sooner had his mount got his head in front than a chestnut went by on the outside as if King Pellinore was marking time. Grundy had been produced by Eddery almost simultaneously. Instant, scintillating speed was switched on and Grundy shot clear. He came across on to the rails but had long since left King Pellinore trailing in his wake and there was no need for anyone to worry about a stewards' enquiry. Eddery merely applied hands and heels throughout the final furlong and a winning margin of two lengths was hardly a true reflection of his superiority.

King Pellinore stayed the mile and a half well enough to defeat Anne's Pretender by six lengths in third place. As had been expected Sea Anchor ran on but failed by half a length to land any each-way wagers. He finished fourth.

The final stages had been a procession as soon as Grundy turned on his tremendous turn of foot, which convinced many that he was a colt of the very highest class. But to put himself into that class, and into the all-time hall of fame, he had to defeat the best of the older horses. It was an issue that would not be shirked, and Peter Walwyn declared that the King George VI and Queen Elizabeth Stakes at Ascot was Grundy's next objective.

The first thing to do, of course, was to get Grundy home, a simple enough procedure in theory but not, as it turned out, in practice this time. On the same flight with him on the Sunday was a batch of fillies whose presence was detected by Grundy through smell rather than sight as they were in a separate compartment. Grundy decided he would like to have a look and pandemonium broke out when Driscoll and Johnson restrained him. A horse can normally be secured in an aircraft by putting a cow collar over his head and attaching a rope on each side to steel fittings on the floor. Attempts to get Grundy tied down in such a manner had to be given up. In all Tony Driscoll's years of travelling horses he confesses he has never been more worried than on this occasion. 'Grundy played hell all the way,' he says. Thankfully no disaster occurred but it was a nerve-racking flight, the sort of experience which makes taking a plater to Pontefract seem like bliss.

Chapter 13

Jockeys

Professional jockeys have such finely developed skill and unwitting talent that, like all craftsmen, they make what they are doing look easy. Keeping a horse straight, holding him together so that he uses his limbs correctly and rhythmically is far from easy in fact, and criticism of riders generally spills from the mouth of the uninitiated. This is not to say that jockeys never make mistakes; they do, but they make fewer than one would credit if spending an afternoon on the terraces in Tattersalls. It may be believed that the best jockeys are those who make the least number of errors but this is not strictly true. The best jockeys are those who possess all the basic skills but have the intangible quality of inspiration.

This could be described as opportunism but it is more than that. It is opportunism, determination and strength welded by moments of emotion into irresistible force to create sublime rapport between horse and rider. Seeing this chemistry come together on a racecourse is an exhilarating experience. It does not happen every day, but then not every day do beaten horses win races. When they do, the same personalities are usually involved. Lester Piggott is capable of inspired action possibly more often than anyone else. Of the two jockeys principally involved with Grundy and Bustino, Pat Eddery is definitely blessed with the gift while Joe Mercer also has moments of instinctive brilliance.

Eddery's meteoric rise to the top has been faster even than that of the 'boy wonder' Piggott in the early 1950s. Eddery did not ride his first winner until 1969 but since then has had 651 successes in seven seasons. During the comparable period of his career Piggott rode 272 winners. Eddery was champion jockey within six years of gaining a foothold whereas it took Piggott eleven years to achieve his first title.

Pat Eddery was born into racing, one of the twelve children fathered by Jimmy Eddery, who was a top-class Irish jockey in the 1950s. He achieved some notable victories in the Irish Derby, Irish Oaks and Irish 2,000 Guineas, winning the latter twice and dead-heating on one occasion. He retired in 1959, wasted his earnings in an ill-fated business venture, running an hotel in Kildare, and returned to racing. He is now back working in stables in England as an ordinary lad. There have been several poignant moments when Pat Eddery has walked from the weighing room into the paddock past his father, who has been leading round one of the runners. Young Eddery never wanted to be anything but a jockey. He left school at fourteen to work three miles from home at the stables of Seamus McGrath but he had only one ride in public in the first season and his father wrote to 'Frenchie' Nicholson at Cheltenham asking whether the lad could come to England. The answer was yes. It was a significant decision by Nicholson, who became instrumental in moulding Pat Eddery, forging a link of loyalty and mutual respect that looks as if it will last a lifetime.

There was a burning ambition in Eddery to ride winners but this was achieved only slowly at first and in his first season as an apprentice with Nicholson he had not a single success from some sixty rides. He had plenty of style and a sensible attitude, however, which convinced Nicholson that winning was only a matter of time for him. The breakthrough came at the Epsom spring meeting in April 1969. Eddery had the ride on Alvaro in an apprentice event and, as he was given a leg up by the trainer, Major Michael Pope, he was told that all he had to do was steer. The young lad looked on this advice with some scepticism but Alvaro knew what was required, was indeed a 'handicap good thing', and won easily. This was the start of a highly successful partnership and Alvaro won five races in twenty-nine days with Eddery riding. A Royal Ascot success on Sky Rocket in the Wokingham Stakes followed for Eddery,

who later won the Vaux Gold Tankard at Redcar on Philoc-
tetes. His career had suddenly blossomed and by the end of
the season he stood second to Clive Eccleston in the apprentices'
championship with 23 winners.

He was runner-up again in 1970 but with 57 winners this
time, only two fewer than Philip Waldron. Without a doubt he
would have topped the table but for two periods of suspension
each lasting seven days. His determination was making him
reckless and he had caused an accident at Chepstow when a
fellow jockey, David Yates, had had a nasty fall. But just how
much benefit he derived from his determination was seen at
Haydock Park one Saturday when he rode five winners on a
seven-race programme.

It seemed inevitable that he would win the apprentice title
the next season but he would be at a disadvantage with most
of his young rivals, having already ridden too many winners to
be able to claim any riding allowance. Thus, although still
indentured, he would be competing on equal terms with fully
fledged jockeys. This made no difference to his rate of success
and he ended the 1971 season champion apprentice with 71
winners from 655 rides.

Geoffrey Barling, the Newmarket trainer, had a gentleman's
agreement with Nicholson this season, giving him first claim
on Eddery. This meant that the youngster would be riding some
top-class horses now and he took advantage of his chance to win
the Ascot Gold Cup on Erimo Hawk. The victory had not
been straightforward, however, for Peter Walwyn's Rock Roi
had been first past the post, only to lose the race in the stewards'
room having been adjudged to have interfered with Erimo
Hawk in the final stages. This meant that Rock Roi had had
the race taken away from him in successive years – the previous
time being because traces of drugs administered on veterinary
advice had been found in the horse's system.

It was during this triumphant season that Eddery had his
first ride for Peter Walwyn and significantly it was a winner –
Silly Symphony at Wolverhampton. Walwyn had been watch-

ing the progress of the young jockey with interest and was very much impressed, so much so that, when Duncan Keith was forced to relinquish through ill-health the job as stable jockey at Seven Barrows, he lost no time in offering the position to Eddery. Thus, at the age of nineteen, the Irishman had landed possibly the top jockey's job in racing.

He never looked back, of course, and by the end of 1974 was champion jockey having ridden 148 winners. During the early part of that year he had concentrated on riding the three-year-olds at Seven Barrows and after Polygamy had come within a short-head of winning the 1,000 Guineas, the filly gave him his first success in a classic in the Epsom Oaks. Polygamy was full of courage and giving in was not her style, despite the fact that at Epsom she was outpaced almost from the start. Eddery had to ride her virtually throughout the mile and a half, his perseverance paying off as she slogged her way to the front inside the final furlong to beat Furioso. Eddery's post-race comment that day was, 'You'd have had to shoot her to stop her'.

The Seven Barrows routine demanded that he should ride work at Lambourn two mornings a week on Tuesday and Friday, and it was on one of these ordinary sessions that he first rode Grundy, having heard from Matt McCormack some time earlier that the colt was something special. He did not take much notice until this first ride, which was enough for him to start paying particular attention to Grundy. Immediately the colt gave him a great feeling: 'It's hard to describe, but when you get on a class horse it's like you're moving on ball bearings. It's so smooth but the overall feeling is power.'

Eddery has the ability to harness and maximise that power. He rides short, almost as short as Lester Piggott but it seems to go unnoticed. Piggott is constantly criticised – not that it makes a jot of difference – for his length of stirrups but Eddery, maybe because he is smaller, does not arouse any comment in this respect. He tends to perch in the saddle with his weight well forward, his hands low and his feet nearly level but with a slight tilt back at the heel. This characteristic is not as pronounced as that of Tony Murray, however, another product of the Nicholson apprentice academy. While Murray's head nods as if loose in a finish, Eddery's remains as still as possible. He uses the whip frequently but not excessively, and is happy to wave it rather than wield it when the latter is not necessary. His appearance in the saddle is neat and controlled. He looks a natural extension of the horse.

He is not a voluble character and fame has changed him little. He remains open and unassuming, friendly but shy. He is of average height for a jockey, around 5 ft. 1 in. and weighs around 8 st 1 lb, at which mark he is able to eat regular meals consisting mainly of meat, no vegetables because he does not like them and no bread. He likes to smoke a good cigar in the evening and has the occasional drink but he is not a great socialiser and his own company is often all that he seeks.

Pat Eddery is engaged to Carolyn, the daughter of Manny Mercer, who was killed in a fall at Ascot in 1959, and the niece of Joe Mercer. Joe Mercer himself is one of the most experienced and respected of jockeys, having been champion apprentice as long ago as 1952 and 1953. His style is different from Eddery's, which is something of a surprise as Nicholson regards Mercer as the model rider and tells apprentices to copy him, and he rides the length of his leg. This means he can kick: 'I am able to co-ordinate the kick and the push at the same time. I was taught this by Major Sneyd when apprenticed to him. You get far more response from a horse with hands and heels than you do by knocking spots off 'em. The Major also taught me balance and the art of being a good stableman. That's the basic start to being a good jockey. You must be able to understand horses. You've got to know what makes them tick.'

Mercer certainly knows that by now, having ridden in over 10,000 races with his first winner at Bath in 1950. He rode his first classic winner in 1953 on Lord Astor's Ambiguity in the Epsom Oaks but had to wait another twelve years before adding to his classic score on Provoke in the St Leger. He has great affection for the Astor-bred horses and has ridden five generations of them, starting under Jack Colling at West Ilsley and continuing when Dick Hern took over the stable. Economic pressures have unfortunately meant the dispersal of the Astor bloodstock except for three mares. Mercer is sad about this and believes it is a great asset to ride and train successive genera- tions, as the characteristics of the animals are so familiar.

A jockey's life is tough and the amount of travelling required is colossal. Rushing to racemeetings is something Mercer can- not escape during the season, and his Mercedes has been caught in the odd motorway speed trap before now – on one occasion in convoy behind Peter Walwyn's wife en route from Windsor. The needle was apparently around the 120 m.p.h. mark. Mercer has had some nasty experiences travelling and it was while on a weekend flight to France in 1972 that he had a narrow escape. The light plane in which he was travelling crashed as it took off from Newbury racecourse and mir- aculously he was thrown clear. But Bill Marshall, the trainer, was trapped in the wreckage until Joe crawled over to pull him clear and save his life. Within two days Mercer was back in the saddle but only a special event would have drawn him back so quickly and what was more special than Brigadier Gerard defending an unbeaten record in the Prince of Wales Stakes at Royal Ascot? In that race Mercer swears the Brigadier was aware he was unwell – he had chest injuries – and accord- ingly the horse went to post without pulling as was usual. The Brigadier did virtually everything for himself in the race and won comfortably from Steel Pulse and Pembroke Castle. Mercer was near collapse when dismounting and he retired to his bed, missing the remainder of the meeting.

Brigadier Gerard is the best horse he has ridden: 'A freak horse with tremendous enthusiasm and great speed. He won 17 out of 18 races and had the class to win beyond his distance. I still say he was not right on his only defeat. After the race there was a lot of mucus coming from his nose and he couldn't have been able to breathe properly. I suppose he was better than Bustino but then they are different types of horses. Bustino had plenty of stamina and kept on improving so that his speed got better. He'd a nice turn of foot but as we knew his stamina was so strong our philosophy was "Let's use it".'

Mercer, married to Harry Carr's daughter, speaks with a deep although slightly nasal voice. A long nose dominates his features which are beginning to take on the familiar lined look of jockeys, brought about principally by the strictures of dieting, but Mercer keeps his weight around the 8 st 4 lb mark without too much difficulty. He envisages continuing to ride until he is about fifty when he will retire, perhaps to take up training. He has never been champion jockey and the urge to achieve such distinction is no longer strong. He has reached the mature stage of life when titles mean little. He has made a comfortable living from racing and has interests outside, with a 220-acre farm near Newbury where he has two hundred head of beef. He is also in partnership in a tyre and battery business with his long-standing friend Jimmy Lindley.

He may no longer hanker after becoming champion but a more attainable ambition that he still has is to win the Derby. The Derby has been so much his unlucky race that he has hardly ever even been placed. Bustino's fourth was the nearest he has come in recent years although he did finish fourth on Remand in 1968, the year of Sir Ivor. It is hard to imagine Sir Ivor being beaten, but Remand might have come a lot closer to him if he had been at his best. Soon after the race he went down with a virus that kept him off the course for the remainder of his three-year-old career.

It is clear by comparison how fast Pat Eddery has risen to the top and how great has been his fortune, but few would say he is superior to Joe Mercer. Both are ambidextrous and able to use the whip in either hand and both possess that special brilliance which makes them able to pull races out of the fire and galvanise horses to give almost more than they are physically capable of, certainly more than the animals think they can give. Both jockeys know when they have done this and their reaction is to give the credit to the horse for showing supreme courage.

The moments to savour and the ones that are never forgotten are when two horses are subjected to simultaneous inspired pressure and respond in the same whole-hearted manner. 'When that happens you have a race on your hands, only guts count then,' Eddery says. He is right, but he gives himself less than his due, for most important of all at this crucial stage is the ability of the jockey to keep his horse balanced. If the stride pattern falters then the race is lost.

Chapter 14

Build-up

The King George VI and Queen Elizabeth Diamond Stakes was to be run over a mile and a half at Ascot on 26 July. Since De Beers Consolidated Mines Ltd, an international group whose main activities are the mining of diamonds and the marketing of rough gem and industrial diamonds, had first stepped in to sponsor the event in 1972, the race had received a much needed financial shot in the arm and was now on a par with the Prix de l'Arc de Triomphe as a valuable all aged championship.* The 1975 race was to have added money of £100,000 with De Beers contributing £44,000, the Ascot Authority £29,000 and the Horserace Betting Levy Board £27,000. De Beers was also presenting a silver cigar box inlaid with diamonds, the value of the whole being £5,000 to the winning owner and was making other diamond awards to the trainer and jockey and silver tankards to the lad responsible for the winning horse. To allow for the event of a dead-heat, the firm had taken out insurance with Lloyd's who rated the odds against such an eventuality as 220–1.

To have a runner in this year's race would cost an owner £500 – entries, closing on 23 April, costing £100 each, a further £100 being payable unless forfeit was declared by 8 July and another £300 if the horse was declared to run. Among the original entries were horses from New Zealand and the United States, although the New Zealand trainer concerned estimated it would cost £12,000 to send a horse over, in this particular case a mare, who would remain in this country until

---

*De Beers takes its name from the De Beers brothers who bought the Vooruitzicht farm in South Africa in 1860 for £50 and sold it for £6,300. About £600 million worth of diamonds have been found there.

the covering season. Not surprisingly the race is regarded principally as a European event.

It was first run in 1951 as the King George VI and Queen Elizabeth Festival of Britain Stakes for a prize of £25,000 and in that inaugural year attracted the winner of a Derby, a St Leger, a 2,000 Guineas, a 1,000 Guineas, a French Derby and a Prix de l'Arc de Triomphe. It was won by the three-year-old Supreme Court, at 100–9, ridden by Charlie Elliott in a record time of 2 minutes 29.40 seconds. This was clocked on a hand stopwatch and its reliability is open to question. Supreme Court had not run in the Derby, but trounced the Derby winner Arctic Prince at Ascot and ended the season unbeaten after four races. His Ascot performance was superb and so was Elliott's handling of the brown colt whose pedigree was uncertain – he was by either Persian Gulf or Precipitation, although for practical purposes it is always the second covering that is taken as the sire.

The race was run at a fast pace but Elliott would have nothing to do with the leaders, who were Mossborough, Belle of All and Tantieme. Sir Winston Churchill's Colonist II joined Mossborough in the straight but neither had any answer when Elliott descended on them and drew clear, chased by Zucchero, who was three-quarters of a length behind at the line with the third horse Tantieme six lengths further back. Zucchero was ridden by Lester Piggott, aged fifteen.

Supreme Court, trained by Evan Williams, retired to stud after his three-year-old career. He was not a great success as a stallion and the best horse he sired was Pipe of Peace, winner of the Middle Park Stakes and third in the 2,000 Guineas and the Derby when trained by Sir Gordon Richards.

Since 1951, English horses have won twelve of the twenty-four runnings of the 'King George'. To single out the best of these races is difficult and only emphasises that it takes a really top-class animal to win, but Mill Reef, Brigadier Gerard and Busted would be near the top of most orders of merit. Aggressor must have been a very fine horse when he won in 1960, putting up a very fast time in soft going, while Royal Palace won the accolades for courage when breaking down inside the final furlong but holding on to beat Felicio II in 1968. Ribot had registered Italy's only victory in 1956 while in the midst of his career record of sixteen unbeaten races, and he would probably rank as the greatest horse to win. France had seven successes and had won the last two runnings with Dahlia, who lowered the record to 2 minutes 30.43 seconds in the first of her triumphs in 1973. Although Nijinsky's time in 1970 was slow, he was the best of four Irish winners.

Lester Piggott was associated with him, of course, as he had been with four other winners – Meadow Court, Aunt Edith, Park Top and Dahlia. No other jockey had managed more than two victories in the race and only Bill Pyers and Roger Poincelet had achieved that score. If Piggott had stayed with Noel Murless as stable jockey for just two more years he would probably have had seven successes to his name, for Murless won with Busted in 1967 and Royal Palace the following year. Piggott's decision to go freelance at the end of the 1966 season caused a sensation at the time, but in the long term the move paid off, as it inevitably would; Murless would not remain dominant forever whereas Piggott's genius was younger and could be released to work its magic for all-comers.

Dick Hern's training success with Brigadier Gerard in 1972 had been a wonderful achievement with a horse carefully nurtured to get a mile and a half as a four-year-old. At the time the Brigadier was unbeaten and extended his sequence to fifteen victories only to fail in the Benson and Hedges Gold Cup at York. His overall record of seventeen wins from eighteen races, at distances ranging from five furlongs to a mile and a half, makes him one of the greatest horses in the history of racing.

Peter Walwyn had yet to win the race but had twice saddled the runner-up in Crozier and Ortis. Crozier did surprisingly well in 1969 to finish a length and a half behind Park Top after starting at 28–1, this being the year when a coughing epidemic mutilated the mid-season programme and for the only time in

18 Royal congratulations for Dr Carlo Vittadini.

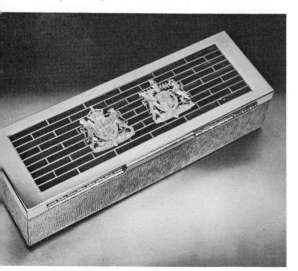

19 The £5,000 trophy designed by Gerald Benney and presented by De Beers to celebrate the 25th running of the King George VI and the Queen Elizabeth Diamond Stakes in 1975. The silver cigar box is topped by green enamel panels with 76 baguette diamonds in the lifter. The coats of arms are those of the late King George VI and of Queen Elizabeth the Queen Mother.

20 Exhaustion is etched on the face of Grundy while his lad
Charlie Johnson looks equally thankful that it's all over.

the history of the race there was not a single three-year-old runner. Ortis came up against Mill Reef in 1971 and could be excused a six-lengths defeat but his satisfactory effort was of special significance as it marked the beginning of Dr Vittadini's association with Walwyn.

Grundy could bring the partnership their first success and from the time the ante-post books opened up he was a hot favourite, varying between evens and 5–4. This augured well for his prospects, as favourites had won the race fourteen times – a success rate of 58 per cent compared to the average for all races of around 37 per cent.

Grundy had four weeks in which to recover from his Irish Derby exertions and after five races was unlikely to go to post as fresh as Bustino, who had run just the once in the Coronation Cup which gave him a breathing space of seven weeks. Bustino went into strong work around the end of June with Dick Hern concentrating on fast work rather than exercise to build stamina. Bustino galloped every three or four days after 28 June, with Kinglet a regular companion, in work-outs over six furlongs. Some of these were half-speeds but on other occasions the pair went 'a good clip' with Bustino usually giving away 12 lb to 14 lb. Everything was going well, when an accident on the gallops suddenly threw Dick Hern's plans into turmoil.

Riboson, as was now customary, was to be Bustino's pacemaker at Ascot, but he was being trained separately for the race. Although he was a thoroughly genuine racecourse performer, he had become what is kindly called 'a character' at home and some mornings he gave Jim Foggarty, his rider, hard times on the gallops. He had even been known to refuse to work but generally consented to jump off if given a lead by the four-year-old Bigribo. The two of them, therefore, became galloping companions and one morning at the beginning of July worked at speed over six furlongs. To all intents and purposes the gallop had been a routine affair and the pair finished upsides on the bridle, but as Jim Foggarty let down Riboson to begin pulling him up, the horse went lame on his near fore. Foggarty had detected nothing wrong in the course of the gallop but he quickly dismounted as it became clear that Riboson was in considerable pain – too much for the injury to be a mere strain. He was brought back home in the horsebox and the damage diagnosed as a cracked cannon bone. This meant the end of Riboson's racing career.

It also posed a tactical problem for Dick Hern who had been relying on Riboson to take Bustino into the straight at Ascot. Bustino's finishing speed was thought unlikely to be superior to Grundy's and it was, therefore, essential for the race to be run at a fast pace. In this way Grundy's sting might be drawn and it was hoped to beat him by exhaustion. There was always the possibility that such tactics might also exhaust Bustino but his courage was proven and, provided the pace was not breakneck, he had an excellent chance of lasting home. With Riboson no longer available, however, it became doubtful if there was another horse among Hern's entries for the race who could do the job.

Hern had had the foresight to leave in Kinglet, Highest and Bigribo as well as Riboson and Bustino at the forfeit stage, so he had at least three to choose from. Which of them was best? In terms of racing ability Kinglet was the pick but he needed at least a mile and a half and did not possess pace. The same was true of Bigribo, while Highest had yet to win and was proving disappointing. He was bred to be a champion, being by Crepello out of Highest Hopes, who had started joint favourite for the 1970 1,000 Guineas but ran inexplicably badly and finished last. She later showed how wrong that form was by winning the Prix Vermeille at Longchamp, the most competitive race for three-year-old fillies in Europe. Highest's optimum distance was proving to be a mile which meant that he had more initial speed than either Kinglet or Bigribo. In the circumstances Hern decided there was only one course of action – he would run both Highest and Kinglet as pacemakers, one to take over from the other at a prescribed stage. Bustino would sit in behind and strike for home as he turned into the short Ascot straight.

Meanwhile Bustino continued his preparations. On 11 July he worked over a mile on Newbury racecourse with Kinglet, and four days later he went six furlongs with Boldboy at a sharp pace. On 19 July he returned to Newbury to work over a mile and a quarter after the day's racing was over. Dick Hern was in good humour as he watched the gallop, having won the Donington Castle Stakes earlier in the afternoon with the very promising two-year-old Smuggler, a success that followed an impressive win the day before by another West Ilsley two-year-old, Relkino, owned by Lady Beaverbrook, who was running for the first time. The string seemed to be in form, therefore, and Bustino confirmed his own well-being by easily beating Kinglet and Attalus in the trial. This piece of work came a week before Ascot and was the final searching gallop, although there was one more bit of fast work to come – a six-furlongs session with the three-year-old sprinter Auction Ring. On the Thursday and Friday before Ascot, Bustino merely cantered. That was it. He was as fit now as he had ever been and Dick Hern was satisfied he had the colt ready to run for his life.

Grundy had returned to Seven Barrows in grand shape after his Irish Derby victory and ate up with his usual relish. It is by the voracity of his appetite that a horse indicates how he is feeling. Some nervous, highly-strung animals will go off their feed after just one gallop at home and it is hard to make this sort of horse put on muscle and thrive. As a general rule, the better the horse, the better the 'doer', although most stables have the seasoned old campaigner who has seen it all before, eats everything that is put in front of him, yet can hardly raise a gallop. Grundy was always a tremendous feeder. The head-lad, Ray Laing, regarded him as the least of his worries, and cannot remember him ever leaving an oat, not even after the kick in the face.

As regards work, Grundy was not asked to do much until 18 July, eight days before the 'King George', when he was taken to Derryck Candy's White Horse Hill gallop. The five-year-old Spring Stone led this mile and a quarter gallop with Red Regent and No Alimony, the others involved besides Grundy. This time Grundy showed plenty of enthusiasm and pleased Peter Walwyn a great deal more than he had done before the Irish Derby. The edge was still there.

For weeks there had been no rain to speak of and the country was sweltering under a continuous heatwave. The Ascot course had been watered but the going would certainly be fast – a surface that suited both Bustino and Grundy. Conditions were ideal for an exceptional time and when Dick Hern publicly declared on the Wednesday that Highest and Kinglet would both run as pacemakers, speculation started about whether the record would go.

By this time Hern had decided on his jockeys and had engaged Frank Durr for Highest and Eric Eldin for Kinglet. Both horses were, of course, owned by Lady Beaverbrook. Hern was hoping that Highest would be able to stay in front for at least five furlongs with Kinglet then taking over for another five. This was the blueprint to beat Grundy and, it was hoped, the remainder of the field numbering eleven runners.

Of the original entries from New Zealand and the United States, none had accepted and the foreign competition came mainly from France, with Germany being represented by Star Appeal. Star Appeal had won the Eclipse Stakes at Sandown three weeks before when beating Grundy's stable companion, Taros, by two lengths. On that form Grundy's connections were confident they would have the measure of Star Appeal but they could not be so sure about Dahlia. This mare was capable of scaling the heights and usually chose to do so in this very race, having won it in each of the last two years.

Dahlia, owned by American Nelson Bunker Hunt but trained in France by Maurice Zilber, had won races in five countries and two continents. Despite her international fame, however, she had been overshadowed in her own country by Allez France. It remained a curiosity why Allez France was not allowed more opportunities to run abroad and Alec Wildenstein had consistently refused to send her over for the 'King George'. Because of this coddling, Allez France will never earn a place among the immortals of the Turf and the name Dahlia will live longer. The name will live and so too will the memory of the brilliant speed that annihilated Rheingold in 1973. But although she possessed such abundant ability she could not produce it at will and needed time and sun on her back before finding her form. She came to Ascot this year therefore, with an uninspiring record, having failed to make the frame in any of her three previous races. Those who knew her were not being put off by that, but it seemed to be asking a lot for her to win for a third successive year.

In the Grand Prix de Saint Cloud on 6 July Dahlia had finished fifth to Un Kopeck and six lengths behind Ashmore and On My Way in second and third place. Ashmore and On My Way were in the Ascot line-up together with Card King and Dibidale, who had been unplaced in the Grand Prix. Dibidale was trained only a couple of miles from Seven Barrows by Barry Hills at the South Bank stables, once occupied by Keith Piggott. Dibidale had looked one of the unluckiest losers in the history of the Oaks the previous season, when her saddle had slipped three furlongs from home and Willie Carson had ridden her bareback to finish third. Automatic disqualification followed as Carson could not weigh in without a weight cloth, but some compensation was forthcoming when the filly won the Irish Guinness Oaks. Hills had a high opinion of Dibidale and had even been heard to remark that she was better than Rheingold whom he had trained to win the Prix de l'Arc de Triomphe in 1973. That was something to live up to, but she had been denied the chance to prove her reputation when breaking down in preparation for the Arc the previous year. Hills had done well to get her back on a racecourse at all but so far she had shown little of her previous form and on the prevailing fast ground could not be given a chance of beating the big three – Dahlia, Bustino and Grundy. She was rated a

33–1 shot along with Libra's Rib, a full brother to the classic winners Ribocco and Ribero, but not blessed with half their ability. As both Ribocco and Ribero had been late-maturing colts, their trainer Fulke Johnson Houghton was hoping that Libra's Rib had still to fulfil his potential, and there had been encouraging signs in the Princess of Wales's Stakes at Newmarket three weeks before when the colt had won in record time. But he had already met Grundy twice and been well beaten.

Libra's Rib was thus the third record breaker in the field. While Grundy had yet to push back any time barriers, it was not difficult to imagine of what he might be capable if taken to the limit.

Time was not the major consideration, however. More important was the opportunity the race would provide to compare the merit of three successive classic crops – Dahlia, five; Bustino, four; both were arguably the best of their age groups in Europe; and Grundy had proved himself supreme among the three-year-olds. On the eve of the race, the talk was of a battle of champions, but the race that took place was to exceed all expectations. It was the sort of race that takes years off a man's life; and those who had seen Quashed beat Omaha by inches in the Ascot Gold Cup of 1936 and forecast they would never see a better finish, had to revise their opinions.

Chapter 15

The Race of the Century

The alarm clock clanged out the start of another day for Ray Laing. It was 5.30 a.m., the usual time for a head lad to be up and about. But this was not a usual day. Laing's stomach told him that as a twinge of excitement knotted the nerves. This was 'King George' day and even for an experienced, hardened stableman, a big race still meant something. It rekindled some of the old magic that had magnetised him and all the young hopefuls over the years, luring them to a life which promised so much even if, materially, it yielded so little in the end.

By six o'clock Laing was in the yard and opening Grundy's stable door, which was locked top and bottom despite it being mid-summer. He found his favourite wide awake and more than ready to devour the bowl and a half of corn that was to be his only feed before the race. Laing checked the water bucket, found it was empty and replenished it to quarter full. He ran his hands over Grundy's legs. Everything was normal. He left Grundy and continued on his round.

Charlie Johnson went in to dress over Grundy and prepare him for the journey at 8.30 a.m. He bandaged all fours and greased the feet, freshly plated the evening before by the blacksmith Barry Payne; aluminium racing plates weigh between four and six ounces compared to the ten or twelve ounces of exercise plates. Grundy had been fitted with knee boots when flying but these were not regarded as necessary now, for the horsebox supplied by Lambourn Horse Transport was a modern vehicle, well padded and with sophisticated suspension. Grundy was loaded into the box around 9.30 a.m., together with other Ascot runners from Seven Barrows – Hard Day, Acquaint, Blue Raffles and Inchmarlo.

Bustino first had an inkling that a race was near when visited by David Blythe, the resident West Ilsley farrier, on the previous afternoon. Blythe always shoes prospective runners between 2 p.m. and 3 p.m. as the yard is at its quietest then and the horses at their most placid. He had shod Bustino throughout the horse's career and the two had come to know each other well, so much so that Bustino would lift his legs automatically. Bustino, like Grundy, was due to travel to Ascot on the morning of the race and he ate 4 lb of corn at 5.45 a.m. when Tom Barnes, the feeder, began his rounds. Bustino underwent a similar preparation to Grundy and the two arrived at the race-course stables within minutes of one another. But while Bustino came out of his box with decorum, Grundy was in the sort of mood that had caused so much anxiety to his handlers at The Curragh. Tony Driscoll thinks he was even worse this time and recalls Charlie Johnson slipping off Grundy's back as he reared up. After several anxious minutes Grundy was persuaded to enter his stable and once inside was muzzled up to prevent him eating – normal practice for runners before a race.

Gradually the crowds converged on Ascot and by mid-day the merciless sun was beating down, as it seemed to do continuously that summer, making the inevitable traffic jams that much harder to tolerate. Passengers became impatient and sticky, while even some of the cars cried 'Enough', puffing and panting on roadside verges. Racing might be one of the last bastions of the upper class but, with the racecourse divided into a silver ring, a Tattersalls ring and a members enclosure, all tastes and pockets are catered for and a race crowd reflects the whole spectrum of society. Fashionably dressed ladies with equally elegant escorts share a common interest with the beer and braces brigade, and even jostle with them in a rush to beat the odds. Nobody loves the bookmaker, of course, but he adds to the atmosphere which makes an English racecourse so much livelier than foreign courses.

For the Vittadinis this could be a truly memorable day for, besides Grundy, they had a vital interest in Colonel Sir Douglas

Clague's Hard Day in the Star of Sierra Leone Diamond Stakes, a race for lady riders. Hard Day was to be ridden by Dr Vittadini's twenty-two-year-old daughter Franca, who had shown herself an accomplished jockey when winning on the horse around the tight turns of Chester two weeks previously. Hard Day was a popular selection here and started a 15–8 favourite in a field of thirteen. Franca Vittadini again rode with sound judgement to lead when approaching the final furlong and win by a length. Once again the omens were good for Grundy – the Vittadini luck looked as if it was in.

Peter Walwyn went straight off to saddle Blue Raffles for the Princess Margaret Stakes, a race for two-year-old fillies, after welcoming Hard Day in the winner's enclosure, but for those wanting an advance look at the runners for the 'King George' this event had to be foregone. There was a large gathering around the tree-lined pre-parade ring and walking coolly round were all the big race runners, except Grundy. He was still in the racecourse stables at the Windsor Forest Stud – two miles from the course – not for any security reason but because it was thought best to keep him away from the excitement for as long as possible. Bustino's big bay frame looked magnificent as he was led round, without rug or saddle, between Kinglet and Highest. Dahlia was less imposing in looks and was beginning to sweat but she was fit and it seemed as if Maurice Zilber might have brought her to a peak again at just the right time. At last Grundy appeared, rugged up, and disappointingly he went straight into one of the saddling boxes where he stayed until it was time for the runners to enter the paddock.

When he emerged, the phrase pocket battleship sprang to mind. He was the smallest member of the field but, being beautifully muscled and perfectly balanced, was outstanding in looks. He attracted the eye like a twinkling star, no wonder Keith Freeman had fought prejudice and fallen in love with him that day at Overbury nearly two years ago. Apart from some sweat around his loins, Grundy was cool and his behaviour left nothing to be desired. Watching as he cantered to post – that mellifluous stride with the flaxen tail streaming, that rippling muscle and the haughty head held high – was an experience never to be forgotten. Grundy in these moments personified the glorious dignity and beauty of a thoroughbred racehorse.

Back at Lambourn Ray Laing was restless in front of his television. Time was dragging as it had been all morning. Would 3.20 never come? This terrible waiting made the stomach queasy, the knees weak and the nails short. A head lad's life is a curious existence. He misses the very moment at which weeks, months and even years of work is directed. In the end all he can do is sit and watch a television screen like millions of others powerless and remote.

Down at the start Joe Mercer on Bustino asked Yves Saint-Martin on Ashmore whether he fancied his chance. The answer was 'Non'. 'Your horse killed mine at Epsom,' said Saint-Martin. Ashmore had been beaten a length by Bustino in the Coronation Cup and on that form seemed to have an excellent chance of being involved in the finish again, but he had since run third in the Grand Prix de Saint Cloud, giving Saint-Martin the impression that he had had enough racing for the time being. The lack of confidence in Ashmore was reflected in the betting and he slipped out from 14–1 to 18–1. Only one horse 'firmed' in the market and that was Grundy, who opened at 11–10 against and started at 5–4 on. Bustino was second favourite at 4–1, having touched 7–2 at one time, while Dahlia, despite Lester Piggott's presence, was easy to back at 6–1. These were the only three in whom punters were genuinely interested, and the remainder of the runners were virtually ignored – Bustino's two pacemakers being rated 500–1 chances.

Highest was drawn number one on the outside of the field which meant he would have to come quickly across the other runners to get on to the rails and set the pace. Bustino was drawn ten, Grundy eight and Dahlia five. Dahlia had broken into a sweat and proved awkward at the start. She had to be backed up to the stalls but, once turned round, went in without objection. She had to wait little more than a minute before the last of her rivals joined her. The white flag was raised to indicate that the field was under starter's orders. Then the man in charge, Major Michael Eveleigh, pressed the lever to open the stalls.

Bustino, the first to react, shot out like a sprinter. This had not been planned but Joe Mercer had no difficulty in restraining him until passed on the outside by Highest, who was being galvanised by Frank Durr to take the lead. Within half a furlong Highest had surged to the front and he settled on the rail with Durr continuing to push. Eric Eldin went second on Kinglet followed by Star Appeal, Bustino, Grundy and Dahlia all in single file and each separated by about a length and a half. After two furlongs the field was stretched right out and the gallop could only be described as furious.

The black cap worn by Frank Durr continued to bob as the jockey pushed and pushed. Highest was being ridden right out and at such a pace it could not be long before he was done with. He lasted four and a half furlongs, and as Eric Eldin saw him begin to falter, he went straight past him on Kinglet, kicking on to ensure there was no relaxation in the gallop. Durr eased Highest to the outside and in a matter of strides the whole field swept by him. The horse had stopped to nothing.

By now the main body of the field had swung round Swinley Bottom and with less than a mile to run the order was the same apart from the change in the leader. Star Appeal was clinging to Kinglet's heels but he had chased the pace from the start and it would be a phenomenal effort if he were to keep going and take part in the finish. Behind him all the three principals were going well and Dahlia, still on the bridle, moved past Ashmore to take fourth place but some six lengths behind the leader.

Suddenly, approaching the half-mile marker, Mercer injected more speed and sent Bustino racing ahead of the gallant Kinglet whose job was now deemed to have been done. This was the moment, the crucial moment, as Bustino went for home. Pat Eddery on Grundy had been watching for it but the sudden

DAILY DOUBLE

JACKPOT PREFIX NUMBER 3

One Mile and a Half, Swinley Course, for
Three Yrs Old and Upwards

3.20 The King George VI and The Queen Elizabeth Diamond Stakes (Group 1)

£100,000 added to stakes
for three yrs old and upwards, entire horses and fillies
ONE MILE AND A HALF, Swinley Course
£100 to enter,
£100 extra unless forfeit declared by .... July 8th
£300 extra if declared to run
The second 20%, third 10%, fourth 3% of the whole stakes
Weights: 3-y-o colts .... 8st 7lb; fillies 8st 4lb
4-y-o and up colts .... 9st 7lb; fillies 9st 4lb
A piece of plate presented by Her Majesty is included in the value
of this race
DE BEERS CONSOLIDATED MINES LTD. have generously given
£44,000 included in the value of this race
The Ascot Authority have given £29,000 included in the value of this
race
The Horserace Betting Levy Board Prize Money Scheme provides for
the inclusion of £27,000 in the added money subscribed for this
race
DE BEERS CONSOLIDATED MINES LTD. will give a contribution to
the travel expenses of runners from outside Europe in special
circumstances
DE BEERS CONSOLIDATED MINES LTD. will give a Diamond award
to the winning owner value £5000 included in the value of this race
and in addition a Diamond award will be given to the trainer of
the winner and to the winning jockey
THERE WILL BE A PARADE FOR THIS RACE

A   SS

156 entries, 118 at £100, 26 at £200 and 12 at £500.—Closed April
23rd, 1975.

VALUES. WINNER £81,910; SECOND £24,100; THIRD £11,800;
FOURTH £3190

Form		Trainer	Age	st	lb	Draw

301 ASHMORE (FR) 4 9 7 (3)

10-0122
D
B c Luthier—Almyre
Mr D. Wildenstein   (A. Penna, France)   Yves Saint-Martin
DARK BLUE, LIGHT BLUE cap

302 BUSTINO 4 9 7 (10)

14211-1
D
B c Busted—Ship Yard
Lady Beaverbrook (Major W. R. Hern, West Ilsley)   J. Mercer
BEAVER BROWN, MAPLE LEAF GREEN cross-belts
and cap

303 CARD KING (USA) 7 9 7 (2)

01-1200
B or br h Cardington King—Nantua II
Mr R. Hakim   (E. Bartholomew, France)   R. Jallu
BLACK, ORANGE seams, BLACK cap

304 KINGLET 5 9 7 (7)

232-000
D
B h Pampered King—War Ribbon
Lady Beaverbrook (Major W. R. Hern, West Ilsley)   E. Eldin
BEAVER BROWN, MAPLE LEAF GREEN cross-belts,
RED cap

(Continued next page.

Form		Trainer	Age	st	lb	Draw

305 ON MY WAY (USA) 5 9 7 (11)

10-2323   B h Laugh Aloud—Gracious Me
D   Mr X. Beau   **(N. Pelat, France)**   W. Pyers
ORANGE, DARK BLUE sleeves, YELLOW cap

307 STAR APPEAL 5 9 7 (6)

4-23111   B h Appiani II—Sterna
D   Mr W. Zeitelhack   **(T. Greiper, Germany)**   G. Starkey
GREEN, YELLOW stripe, YELLOW cap

308 DAHLIA (USA) ...,..................... 5 9 4 (5)

13-0000   B m Vaguely Noble—Charming Alibi
C-D   Mr N. B. Hunt   **(M. Zilber, France)**   L. Piggott
LIGHT and DARK GREEN check, LIGHT GREEN
sleeves, WHITE cap

309 DIBIDALE 4 9 4 (4)

011-330   Ch f Aggressor—Priddy Maid
D   Mr N. J. F. Robinson   **(B. W. Hills, Lambourn)**   W. Carson
Mr R. E. Sangster
NAVY BLUE, RED and LIGHT BLUE hoop and
armlets, WHITE cap

310 GRUNDY 3 8 7 (8)

11-2211   Ch c Great Nephew—Word From Lundy
C D   Dr Carlo Vittadini   **(P. T. Walwyn, Lambourn)**   P. Eddery
DARK BLUE, YELLOW hoop, armlets and spots on
cap

311 HIGHEST 3 8 7 (1)

4-00003   B c Crepello—Highest Hopes
Lady Beaverbrook (Major W. R. Hern, West Ilsley)   F. Durr
BEAVER BROWN, MAPLE LEAF GREEN cross-belts,
BLACK cap

312 LIBRA'S RIB (USA) 3 8 7 (9)

404201   Ch c Ribot—Libra
D   Mrs Julian G. Rogers
         (R. F. Johnson Houghton, Didcot)   F. Morby
WHITE, EMERALD GREEN braces, striped sleeves,
qtd cap

NUMBER OF DECLARED RUNNERS 11

BLINKERS WILL BE WORN BY No. 7

1st.................................. 2nd..................................... 3rd.....................................

Standard Time: 2 mins. 33 secs.

1974: Dahlia (USA), 4-9-4, L. Piggott, 15-8 fav. M. Zilber (FR) 10 ran.

burst of acceleration caught him and Grundy by surprise. Grundy had been on the bit when Bustino went, but in a few strides he was off the bridle and struggling to go the pace. Eddery realised he must make every effort to go with Bustino, however, and a hard-ridden Grundy gave chase. He passed Star Appeal who was soon relegated to fourth place as Dahlia too made a forward move. But Bustino had opened a three-lengths lead in next to no time and was approaching the home turn with what looked an almost unassailable advantage. Grundy lay second, Dahlia third and the rest nowhere.

Grundy could make no ground on the turn and his position looked well nigh hopeless with Bustino still three lengths clear, and only two and a half furlongs to run. But then Grundy was seized with the spirit of combat. Eddery twice wielded the whip, which he carried in his right hand, and Grundy answered by producing that now famed speed. Bustino, on the other hand, was being ridden with hands and heels by Mercer – it was inspired, rhythmical driving that elicited the very last ounce of effort. Bustino kept on and so Grundy's spurt closed the gap only slowly, very slowly. Eddery hit Grundy again and again (nine times in all). 'I thought I'd never get to him,' Eddery said afterwards. 'Every time I got nearer he kept finding more.' After what seemed an eternity, Grundy drew level with Bustino just inside the final furlong.

That was surely it. Bustino had been mastered now and Grundy's supporters thought the race was won. But amid a crescendo of incredulous cheering, Bustino fought back. He was tired, he had drifted off the rail but amazingly he found new reserves; and now it was Grundy who was fighting off a challenge. For half a furlong the two raced head and head, locked in an awe-inspiring, epic battle. Then, a hundred yards from the post, Bustino's tongue lolled out of his mouth, and he rolled back towards the rail. Physically he could no longer respond to the call of his courage. In the last few strides Grundy pulled out half a length and that was the margin of distance when they both stumbled past the post.

Both horses were heaving and shaking as they pulled up. Grundy was noticeably unsteady on his feet, his head was bowed, his veins stood out and the walk back to the winner's enclosure looked almost too much for him. That shining chestnut body was now dark with sweat, that flashy flaxen mane was dull and damp. He looked a different horse to the one that had swept so majestically to the start only five minutes earlier.

But if Grundy looked dishevelled he was not alone. So emotionally riveting had been the battle, that women were breaking down in tears and men meandered in a daze, muttering 'What a race'. 'Did you ever see such a race?' 'Fantastic'. 'Phenomenal'. In moments such as these vocabulary and language seem totally inadequate.

The announcement of the race time confirmed what everyone had thought. The record had been smashed, and by 2.36 seconds, which meant that at 2 minutes 26.98 seconds this had been the fastest electrically timed one-and-a-half-mile races ever seen in Britain. Dahlia in finishing third, five lengths behind Bustino, had even broken her own old record of 2 minutes 30.43 seconds; while On My Way, fourth, Card King, fifth, and Ashmore, sixth, also beat that time.

Not only the clock pointed to one of the greatest races ever. The crowd had seen an amalgam of all that is best in horseracing: a brilliant tactical plan had been impeccably applied at a record-breaking pace; boundless courage had seen stirring battle joined to reveal the consummate skill of the jockey's finishing art. And all this on a shimmering afternoon before a vast, enthralled audience at a course steeped in history. This had been a perfect race, the race of the century, arguably the race of all time.

Gradually the euphoria subsided and Her Majesty the Queen presented the awards. Emotion still showed on the faces of both Carlo Vittadini and of Peter Walwyn but Pat Eddery, already changed for the next race, looked surprisingly cool and was collected enough to give his version of the race: 'Going down the back I thought, "God they're going fast". Then, approaching the turn, Bustino left me three lengths. My horse couldn't do anything on the bend. It was agony all the way up the straight. It was just inside the final furlong that I caught him and then he came and headed me again. In the last fifty yards Bustino collapsed.'

Joe Mercer said: 'Four furlongs out I was going so easy that I thought, "Right, I'm off". Turning into the straight I knew it would take a hell of a horse to beat me but in the final hundred yards Bustino faltered. Some say he's one-paced but I don't agree. I've always had a lot of confidence in him and there's no doubt he's the best four-year-old in Europe over a mile and a half.'

Bustino's performance was a tremendous credit to all at West Ilsley and in particular Dick Hern, who said: 'I'm as proud of Bustino as if he had won. I think he might just have done it if Riboson had been there to lead him into the straight. Bustino was in front a long time and it proved just too much for him in the end.' These thoughts were echoed by Lady Beaverbrook: 'He sorely missed Riboson and with the extra 14 lb on his back and Mercer not using his whip because he knew Bustino was giving his all, he filled me with pride as well as heartache.'

The 14 lb referred to by Lady Beaverbrook was the weight for age that Bustino, as a four-year-old, was required to give to the year younger Grundy. Bustino had carried 9 st 7 lb, which is a big weight, over a mile and a half. On the other hand he was a big, rangy horse who had almost reached physical maturity. He stood 16-1¼ hands compared to Grundy's 15-2½ and it would have been a formality for even a total stranger to pick out the four-year-old, if the horses had been stood side by side. Weight for age is a vital concept and there are no grounds for thinking the principle unfair. To make much of the difference in the weights carried by Bustino and Grundy is misleading; but for the 1976 season the amount of weight that a four-year-old should give to a three-year-old over a mile and a half in July has been amended to 13 lb.

After being led out of the winner's enclosure, Grundy was

taken straight to the 'dope box' by Charlie Johnson, where cotton-wool swabs were put in the horse's mouth for the purpose of a saliva test. Such tests are a routine matter after all big races. Grundy was then allowed two or three gulps of water and was washed down to remove the sweat from his matted coat. He was then allowed another quick drink and remained in the box with Johnson and the veterinary staff until a urine sample had been obtained. The results of these tests, designed to detect any trace of a 'non-normal nutrient' or dope, are not known until several days afterwards. Grundy emerged after about an hour and a quarter and was taken back to the racecourse stables by horsebox. He was given a long drink on arrival and was free to relax until it was time to make the journey home to Lambourn, an hour after the last race.

On this momentous afternoon Peter Walwyn hardly had time to receive his De Beers award before he was off to saddle Inchmarlo for the next race, to be back in the winner's enclosure yet again, having achieved a training treble in the first four races. He had had time to reflect only briefly on Grundy's performance when saying: 'What more can you ask of him. He's had a very hard race and won it on sheer guts. Obviously at the moment there are no plans.' If the Prix de l'Arc de Triomphe in October had been open to Grundy, there seemed little doubt that this would have been his next objective but, as things stood, it was to be Bustino who would carry English hopes at Longchamp and he seemed to have an outstanding chance of winning the richest race in Europe.

Back in Lambourn there was a great feeling of pride and streets that had emptied rapidly as race time approached were busy again with knots of people gathering to talk about the Herculean achievement of Grundy. Ray Laing was overjoyed; 'It gave me a hell of a lot of satisfaction. When he went past the post the winner, it was like somebody taking a hundredweight of coal off my shoulders.'

Chapter 16

York defeat

A reception committee of cheering stable staff greeted Grundy when the box bringing him home swung into the smart black and white Seven Barrows stables soon after 7 p.m. Looking tired, he accepted the affectionate slaps and pats with indifference but he could still do justice to the hot linseed mash prepared for him. The next morning, when Ray Laing opened up his box, he was still lying down asleep, which was most unusual and indicative of his exhausting experience. In the first few days after a race, Laing keeps the horses a little on the light side to relax the system and the usual quota of corn is cut by a quarter. Grundy's appetite remained unaffected and after feeding he was led out for a twenty minutes walk. On Monday the same procedure was followed and again on Tuesday, but by this time he had shaken off any signs of lethargy and Tony Driscoll returned from leading him out to tell Laing: 'I think you had better put a saddle on that horse and have him ridden tomorrow for safety sake – he's getting a bit above himself.' And so on Wednesday he was ridden out and appeared to have recovered already from his gruelling exertions.

Peter Walwyn, although not in the least anxious to hurry him, was naturally pleased by such progress. Thoughts about future plans began to formulate. Grundy's syndication agreement allowed him two more races in England. Walwyn was not attracted by the St Leger, which would only have been a possibility if the Triple Crown were at stake. As that could not be achieved, the Champion Stakes over a mile and a quarter at Newmarket in October seemed a suitable finale after a preparatory run in either the Valdo Stakes at Goodwood or the Cumberland Stakes at Ascot in September. On the other hand, there was the Benson and Hedges Gold Cup at York just three weeks away.

Walwyn summarised his thoughts: 'If Grundy was going to run in the Champion Stakes did I leave him or did I look at the Benson and Hedges and see what was going to run? If I let him down it would be very hard to get him back. Matt and Charlie both confirmed he was very well. He seemed to have made a terrific recovery and so it seemed sensible to have a look at the York race.'

The Benson and Hedges Gold Cup was to be run over a mile and a quarter on 19 August – that is 24 days after the Ascot race. Since its inception in 1972 it had produced some startling results, the first of these being the defeat of Brigadier Gerard by Roberto. The following year Moulton created a shock when beating the odds-on Rheingold into third place, but Dahlia had stopped the rot in 1974 to become the first winning favourite. Dahlia would certainly be going for the race again but although there was a suspicion that Lester Piggott had 'looked after' her at Ascot, once her chance had gone, she had over five lengths to make up on Grundy. Other likely runners were Card King and Star Appeal, both beaten a long way at Ascot, and Anne's Pretender who had already found Grundy too good on four separate occasions. The rest of the entries comprised second raters which strengthened the view that if Grundy was fit and well, he had nothing to fear.

No firm decision was taken about running at York until after Grundy had done a serious gallop. A week before his proposed race he worked over a mile and a quarter with Understudy, Spring Stone and Consol. Pat Eddery came down to ride Grundy and was delighted by the feel he got. Grundy finished on the bridle and showed plenty of enthusiasm to convince Eddery that he was as good as ever. Walwyn could see for himself that Grundy was physically fine and feeling well, so, despite a nagging doubt that mentally the horse might not be as fresh as he looked, the discussions concluded with the resolution to run.

Grundy's connections were not the only ones to do some hard

thinking after Ascot. Dahlia's owner Nelson Bunker Hunt had been a little disappointed in his mare's display in the 'King George' and was turning over in his mind the possibility of giving the ride at York to his retained jockey in France, Nick Navarro, a Panamanian rider brought over at the beginning of the season to replace Bill Pyers.

Navarro was an accomplished jockey and a fair judge of pace. If he could make the running on Dahlia at a carefully calculated speed, as his compatriot Braulio Baeza had done on Roberto when beating Brigadier Gerard, there was a possibility that Dahlia might pull off an equally sensational result. Lester Piggott's judgement of pace was not too bad, of course, and in the end he kept the ride.

Grundy travelled to York the day before the race. Tony Driscoll and Charlie Johnson were expecting the usual rodeo act when the horsebox ramp was lowered to let out Grundy. But they were wrong. Grundy came down tentatively and rather reluctantly, and stood still at the bottom. Buster Haslam, who was travelling horses for Dick Hern at the meeting, looked on and quickly shouted to Driscoll: 'That's not the same horse I've seen before.' He did not add, 'I bet he gets beaten to-morrow', but that was what he was thinking.

What was to be made of it? Grundy looked magnificent, he was eating as well as ever and he had worked to everyone's satisfaction. Because he was less high spirited was no reason to panic. Analysing the opposition which amounted to six, four of whom Grundy had already beaten conclusively, the race was well within his grasp. The additional runners were the handi-capper Jimsun and, a 100–1 chance, Meautry, from France, so there appeared to be nothing to fear from them. Withdrawing Grundy now on grounds hardly more substantial than cold feet seemed faint-hearted. It looked best to let events take their course.

The York meeting began badly for the stable. In the opening event, the Acomb Stakes over six furlongs for two year olds, Peter Walwyn saddled the filly Inchmarlo who had made a winning first appearance the same day Grundy won at Ascot. Inchmarlo was odds-on but came under pressure at half-way and was easily beaten by a Sir Ivor colt called Mid Beat, trained at Lambourn by Nick Vigors. Pat Eddery had regarded Inchmarlo as one of his bankers of the meeting along with Grundy.

The Benson and Hedges Gold Cup was worth £39,397 to the winner and if Grundy could take the prize it would push his total earnings to £351,537. He had already surpassed the previous record for an English-trained horse, the £269,117 earned by Mill Reef, with just over half having been won in France. Grundy's earnings were remarkable considering all his racing had been done in England and Ireland. As Peter Walwyn said: 'The prize money over here is all right provided you win all the top races!'

It was mainly as a spectacle that the York race made appeal, for Grundy's opposition was reduced to five when Anne's Pretender was prevented from running on technical grounds and his trainer, Ryan Price, fined £275. The colt had last run in France which meant that his passport had to be presented before he could race again in England. Unfortunately this had been forgotten and despite Price organising an air dash, the document could not be procured in time. As a result of this defection, Grundy was clearly going to start at prohibitive odds and he opened at 3–1 on. Was there any significance in the fact that by the time the runners were in the stalls he had weakened to 9–4 on? It was a curious move for there was no great confidence in Dahlia, second favourite at 7–2 or any of the other runners. Neither Dahlia's owner nor trainer were present so it seemed as if they had settled for second place. Although the weather was damp the going remained good, and there was no reason, therefore, to oppose Grundy because of any change in the state of the ground. True Dahlia was 3 lb better off at the weights compared with Ascot, but this was not of major significance as the weight for age adjustment had been taken into account. As this varies according to the time of year, the difference in weight to be carried decreases as the season progresses and the younger horses become more mature.

York has a run-in of four furlongs preceded by a long, left-hand bend. This means that much of the mile and a quarter course is on the turn and as such is suitable for front runners. When the stalls opened Piggott went straight into the lead on Dahlia, setting a sensible pace and keeping something up his sleeve in the hope of repulsing Grundy in the final stages. Card King tracked Dahlia followed by Meautry and Grundy, with Star Appeal and Jimsun bringing up the rear. This order was maintained until the field swung into the straight and Meautry began to lose his place. Piggott had not perceptibly moved on Dahlia but was gradually pressing for more pace and approaching the three furlongs from home marker it became necessary for Pat Eddery to ask Grundy to quicken.

For a few strides the response was forthcoming; but only for a few strides. Eddery drew his whip to show Grundy it was time they really got down to business. But Grundy knew. Maybe he knew too much, remembering how it had hurt last time. That lung-draining, energy-sapping effort was being called for again. This time he could not answer the call. With a quarter of a mile still to run he was obviously beaten and Eddery, not wishing to inflict pointless punishment, accepted the situation. From that stage on Dahlia was never in danger and no challenge materialised at all. Card King ran on to get within a length and a half of her at the line but Star Appeal was five lengths away third with Grundy another four lengths away in fourth place.

Grundy had thus been beaten a total of $10\frac{1}{2}$ lengths by Dahlia, who had been $5\frac{1}{2}$ lengths behind at Ascot. Card King had made up $16\frac{1}{2}$ lengths on Grundy and Star Appeal over 25 lengths. It was tragic to see Grundy reduced to such mediocrity and it was obvious now that the race had come too soon after Ascot.

Peter Walwyn was somewhat bewildered and had to face the unwelcome but naturally inquisitive press: 'I don't regret running him – if you regretted every horse that got beaten you'd go mad.' One got the impression that in his heart he did not believe what he was saying. Walwyn, although not a sentimentalist about horses, has great respect and affection for them and Grundy had been the light of his life this season. He would dearly have loved to have saved the horse this humiliation.

The defeat meant quite simply that Grundy might not now be regarded as aspiring to greatness. He was in most people's opinion a very good racehorse but would never be talked of in the same breath as Ribot or Sea Bird II or Brigadier Gerard. Even though there were obvious reasons for him running something like two stone below his form, defeat always tarnishes a reputation and highlights fallibility. A great racehorse has to be very nearly invincible. Unfortunately, due to various circumstances, Grundy had been beaten three times in his career, three times in eleven races. 'People think horses are machines you know, but they're not, they're only human,' was how one old racing salt summed it up.

So the Benson and Hedges Gold Cup had claimed another illustrious victim. While the race remains so valuable, it will continue no doubt to draw high quality runners as it deserves to do. Fields have been disappointingly small, however, and three beaten odds-on favourites in four years strongly suggests it is not a race for horses involved in the action at Ascot just three weeks before. The distance of a mile and a quarter may have contributed to some of the shock results and the overall impression to be gained is that the race is unsatisfactory. It was not originally in the scheme of the season, as worked out by those who first laid down the pattern of racing in this country, and one can begin to see why.

Grundy's failure seemed of more import at the time than Dahlia's triumph and the mare hardly received the credit she merited. She was not consistent and never had been, but on her day she was a truly brilliant performer. Piggott had handled her with perfection, of course, as he had a succession of outstanding fillies over the years. His sympathetic style is particularly well suited to the fairer sex amongst thoroughbreds. Although a tremendously strong jockey when he needs to be, he is essentially a quiet rider with wonderful balance and exquisite hands. Fillies always seem to have gone better for him than for anyone else, and a long list of them, such as Petite Etoile and Park Top, owe him much of their success.

In view of this, it is perhaps surprising to find that Piggott has won many more classics on colts than fillies, but seven St Leger victories, all on colts, are responsible for the imbalance of the overall picture. In classic triumphs, he has only once managed to win the 1,000 Guineas, however, and that was on the Peter Walwyn-trained Humble Duty in 1970. She won by seven lengths the day after Nijinsky had won the 2,000 Guineas, and Walwyn found the thought of them meeting over a mile intriguing; they never did, but Walwyn would have needed to see the result in print before being convinced of Nijinsky's superiority.

There is certainly no doubt in his mind that Grundy was superior to all those that had beaten him at York, but with the Prix de l'Arc de Triomphe out of the question it seemed to Walwyn that there was nothing much left for the horse to achieve. But Walwyn also believed that Grundy was better than Bolkonski and if Henry Cecil was thinking of running him in the Champion Stakes, then there might be a good reason for running Grundy. Otherwise the remainder of the season looked decidedly barren, so if Grundy showed, on his return home, that he had had enough, then the horse's opinion would be respected.

Chapter 17

Retirement

Twelve days after Grundy's shock defeat there came bad news of Bustino. It was officially announced that he had heat in his off-fore tendon and on veterinary advice it had been decided to retire him. Bustino, in fact, had developed 'a leg' after his first sharp canter when ridden by Bob Turner seven days after the Ascot race, but the injury had been a well-kept secret. He was on the easy list for a week after the 'King George' which meant he was merely ridden out for an hour and a half each day and this sympathetic treatment quickly enabled him to put back the 8 lb that he had lost as a result of the race. In view of the severity of the contest this was a surprisingly small amount, and an indication of how supremely fit he had been. Bustino was rested after the tendon injury first occurred, with Dick Hern obviously hoping for recovery; but immediately work was resumed, heat returned to the leg and so there was no option but to call it a day.

Joe Mercer regarded the breakdown as highly significant and the explanation of why Bustino faltered in the final stages at Ascot. His belief is that the leg went then, the trouble only coming to light when the horse was first asked to work again. This, indeed, is a common sequence of events and there is little doubt that the weakness in the tendon was a direct result of the Ascot exertions. So the race that had undermined Grundy had also claimed Bustino; proof, if it was needed, of how extraordinarily hard had been the battle.

Sadly, the bid to win the Prix de l'Arc de Triomphe was having to be abandoned, but history was repeating itself. Busted had had a similar misfortune in 1967. Like Busted, Bustino appeared to have an outstanding chance and he was the ante-post favourite at 4–1. His style of racing certainly seemed as if it would have been suited to a race that often in the past had been won by horses who had struck for home early in the straight at Longchamp. The run-in here is three furlongs, which does not allow much time to quicken, and Geoff Lewis on Mill Reef, Yves Saint-Martin on Sassafras and Allez France, Bill Williamson on Vaguely Noble and Levmoss, and Lester Piggott on Rheingold had all demonstrated that the best way to ensure victory was to be in front turning for home. Bustino would have been in his element, therefore, and would surely have proved very hard to beat, even if the ground was soft as was usually the case at this meeting. After all, as a three-year-old in the Grand Prix de Paris, Bustino had shown he could act on the soft.

It might seem that Bustino was more of an 'Arc type' than Grundy, whose ilk had suffered a string of defeats in the race, notably through Nijinsky, Park Top and Sir Ivor. These horses had all possessed great acceleration and seemed at their best when held for a late burst, but the tactics had failed in the Arc. Grundy, although possessing acceleration, was more versatile, however, and Pat Eddery had never been averse to using his speed early. Grundy did not need to be held up until the last possible moment and thus it seems, on reflection, that he would also have been suited by Longchamp. But of course there was never any intention of running him there.

The race was run without Grundy or Bustino, so it could hardly be described as a European championship. Allez France was favourite to win for the second year running but she was never going well and the race threw up a sensational 120–1 winner in Star Appeal. Two furlongs out he had been behind a wall of horses and his jockey Greville Starkey showed brilliant opportunism to switch him inside, squeeze through a narrow gap and surge clear for a breath-taking victory. It was not one of the copybook ways to win the Arc and it smacked of fluke, but it did at least pay compliments to Bustino and Grundy, both of whom had been so superior to Star Appeal at Ascot.

Star Appeal was not quite finished yet, however, and after the Arc he went to the United States to run in the Washington International at Laurel Park, where a good-class field had assembled including Dahlia, Nobiliary, On My Way, Comtesse de Loir and the 1974 Derby winner Snow Knight, now trained in America and voted grass horse of the year in 1975. This time Star Appeal made little impression and the race went to Nobiliary, ridden by the young American, Sandy Hawley, who made all the running to beat Comtesse de Loir and On My Way. This was another international result, therefore, which consolidated the reputations of Grundy and Bustino.

After the decision to retire Bustino, arrangements were put in hand for him to go to the Queen's Wolferton Stud at Sandringham. He had been syndicated as a stallion soon after his victory in the Coronation Cup in June, forty shares having been sold at 12,500 guineas, putting a capital value on him of £500,000 – an amount less than half what he would have commanded after Ascot. Not surprisingly he was over-subscribed and those lucky enough to secure a share must have congratulated themselves on their sagacity.

As a stallion Bustino has excellent credentials. On the racecourse he proved himself an outstanding middle-distance performer, being tough, courageous and able to act on all types of going. He was a strong, rangy animal without any temperamental quirks. And, of course, he was bred in the purple, coming from the famous Marchetta family. One of his first mates was to be another member of that family, Nocturnal Spree, who had won the 1975 1,000 Guineas. Nocturnal Spree was inbred to the pre-potent sire Nearco, a stallion to rank with the great St Simon. It is not hard to imagine the progeny of her mating with Bustino fetching a vast sum in the sales ring.

To maximise Bustino's chances of becoming a leading sire, however, it seems likely that he will need to be bred to speed rather than stamina which he possessed in greater measure himself. There are grounds for believing that there could be inherent unsoundness in his male line, for his sire Busted and grand sire Crepello both suffered from leg trouble, a trait which seems to stem from Blandford, the great-grand sire of Crepello. Bustino's tendon injury came after he had raced for three seasons, during which he had nine races, the last being so gruelling that it is no doubt being over-critical to condemn him for breaking down. His future at stud looks a good one and there is every likelihood of his becoming a much sought-after sire.

Grundy too was destined for stud but the decision to retire him was not made immediately after the defeat at York. There was still the possibility that he might run in the Champion Stakes at Newmarket in October although there was a gap of nine weeks before that race and no preparatory outing was allowed now under the terms of his sale. This meant that Peter Walwyn would have to let him down, then try to bring him back to peak fitness – always difficult to achieve. In any case, Grundy was a tired horse and it showed. Matt McCormack was in no doubt that Grundy's energy had been sapped, for he had now become a comparatively quiet ride: 'There was just the odd crazy moment when he was his old self again, but on the whole he was pretty lack-lustre.' On Tuesday 30 September, Pat Eddery came down to ride Grundy in a gallop, the first serious work since York, and knew immediately that the spark had been extinguished: 'He didn't give me anything like the same feel as he had. There was always a big impression of power when you rode him, the feeling that he could run forever. But that was gone. I suppose that mentally he saw there was no point in it any more.'

Peter Walwyn telephoned Dr Vittadini to discuss the situation and it was agreed that Grundy should be retired, the decision being announced publicly on 1 October. Three weeks later Grundy was on his way to the National Stud, having been examined thoroughly by the stud's veterinary officer, David Simpson, who declared him perfectly fit and sound in wind and limb.

So ended a tremendous racecourse career. Grundy had run eleven times in all, being unbeaten in four races as a two-year-old and achieving four more victories – three classics and an all-aged championship – in his three-year-old season. How good was he? His trainer thinks he was a great racehorse, using the true sense of the adjective. 'Of course he was a great little horse. Look how quickly he won all those races. The classics come right on top of one another and in the space of five weeks he won three classics and did it after a setback that would have put paid to most other horses. Without the kick in the face I am sure he would have won the Guineas as well.'

Did the York defeat detract from Grundy's reputation? 'I don't think it should make any difference. He had proved he was better than all the horses that beat him in the Benson and Hedges. In any case Mill Reef was beaten as a three-year-old and is still regarded as a great horse. Sir Ivor was beaten regularly and Nijinsky was also beaten at the end of his three-year-old days. There is no doubt in my mind that Grundy was great but that doesn't mean that someday I won't train one as good!'

It seems quite reasonable to put Grundy in the same category as Mill Reef, Nijinsky and Sir Ivor, although not one of them would be regarded as in the same class as Ribot or Sea Bird II. These two are probably the only two genuine 'greats' since the war, although the last ten years have been a vintage period when very good horses have abounded.

It is possible that Grundy might have been a genuinely great horse, who in more favourable circumstances could have remained unbeaten. Certainly the defeat in the Greenham Stakes was not his fault and neither was the York débâcle. Whether he was beaten on merit in the 2,000 Guineas, however, is an intriguing question. He reversed the form emphatically with Mark Anthony, so he had obviously put the injury behind him, but a further improvement of 2 lb would have been enough to see him triumph. Two weeks later in the Irish Guineas when he had had time to reach absolute peak fitness, he beat Mark

Anthony by two and a half lengths compared to five lengths at Newmarket. Although he won easing up at The Curragh, his diminished superiority over Mark Anthony indicates that perhaps he did run up to his best at Newmarket after all and was, in fact, beaten fair and square by Bolkonski, who, one must remember, was rated a very good miler by Henry Cecil.

To lose the 2,000 Guineas by half a length and win three other classics and the 'King George', is the record of an exceptional horse. But a great horse? Well, consider the time he clocked at Ascot – two minutes 26.98 seconds. This was over five seconds faster than Mill Reef's time in 1971, over nine seconds faster than Nijinsky in 1970. It was also 13 seconds faster than Ribot in 1956 although the race time was inevitably slow because of dead ground then. But Grundy's time was phenomenal, so fast that it must be the deciding factor in the argument. Surely he deserves the benefit of the doubt and, while racing is all a matter of opinion and one can never be categorical, it does seem realistic to talk about Grundy as a great horse.

The National Stud had pulled off a tremendous coup in buying the major shareholding in Grundy for £750,000 after his victory at Epsom. Subsequent events made this look ludicrously cheap. Like Bustino, Grundy has an excellent chance of becoming a successful stallion although it is no use pretending he is as well bred as his rival – the main reason why as a yearling he cost 11,000 guineas as against 21,000 guineas. But Grundy as a racehorse possessed the priceless quality of instant acceleration. Essentially he was a speed horse, winning over six furlongs, seven furlongs and a mile. The fact that he stayed a mile and a half was not exactly a surprise but on his breeding it was odds-against him doing so. One would expect speed to predominate in his stock and, if bred to speed, the result could indeed be a pure sprinting animal. It is unlikely that Bustino, on the other hand, will ever beget fast horses.

Speed, speed and more speed were the three requirements listed by that great trainer, Atty Persse, when asked what he thought were the three most important aspects of breeding.

That, of course, was his own highly personalised view but it illustrates how Grundy fulfils the first major requirement at least in a stallion. As well as speed he had limitless courage, a strong constitution and was perfectly sound. In fact, there was no weakness in his make-up. He was high-spirited but this vibrant quality contributed to make him almost the perfect thoroughbred. His colour may not have been considered good, but he will have gone a long way towards breaking down the prejudice against chestnuts whose courage and temperament have often been questioned.

Grundy will certainly not lack for opportunities at stud and is assured of the best mares. His first covering was of the twelve-year-old mare Palatch owned by Dr Vittadini. Palatch, by Match III out Palazzoli, was a top-class filly in 1967 when she won the Musidora Stakes and the Yorkshire Oaks. In 1972 she bred Patch who, as Grundy's stable companion, failed by only inches to win the French Derby. The offspring, if it turns out to be the first foal of Grundy, will complete a notable double for Palatch who on 8 January 1975 gave birth to a bay filly who is believed to be Habat's first progeny.

So Grundy and Bustino enter a new phase in their lives. Whatever their fate at stud, they are assured of perpetuity through the telling and retelling of their Ascot battle. It is a story that cannot be contorted or exaggerated. No race ever was more heroic; no race ever more emotional or exciting. It created an honoured place for them in the history of the Turf, for theirs was truly the race of the century.

Appendices

Explanation of race times

The figures in brackets after the race times are the number of seconds above (a) or below (b) standard time for that particular distance on that particular course. If the going allowance given at the top is taken into account an accurate idea is gained as to how good a performance was achieved.

The King George VI
and The Queen Elizabeth Diamond Stakes
(Group 1)

ASCOT, 26 July 1975

Going: firm
Wind: slight half against
Going All'ce: minus 0.20 sec per fur

Winner £81,910; 2nd £24,100; 3rd £11,800; 4th £3,190, 1 mile 4 furlongs, three-year-olds and upwards.

1	GRUNDY,	3–8–7	P. Eddery
2	BUSTINO,	4–9–7	J. Mercer
3	DAHLIA,	5–9–4	L. Piggott
4	On My Way,	5–9–7	W. Pyers
5	Card King,	7–9–7	R. Jallu
6	Ashmore,	4–9–7	Y. Saint-Martin
7	Dibidale,	4–9–4	W. Carson
8	Libra's Rib,	3–8–7	F. Morby
9	Star Appeal,	5–9–7	G. Starkey
10	Kinglet,	5–9–7	E. Eldin
11	Highest,	3–8–7	F. Durr

Distances: ½l, 5l   Time: 2 m 26.98 s (b 6.02)
                           Previous best 2 m 29.34 s

Betting: 4/5 Grundy, 4 Bustino, 6 Dahlia, 13 Star Appeal, 18 Ashmore, 20 On My Way, 33 Dibidale, Libra's Rib, 66 Card King, 500 Others.

Bustino's Races

Going: yielding
Wind: slight across
Going All'ce: 0.60 sec per fui

Acomb Maiden (at closing) Stakes, £2,460; 2nd £475; 3rd £225.
6 furlongs straight, two-year-olds.

1	CONSOLATRIX,	8–8	C. Roche
2	RADICAL,	8–11	J. Lindley
3	BUSTINO,	8–11	J. Mercer
4	Mine a Million,	8–11	A. Kimberley
5	Grey God,	8–11	B. Raymond
6	Optimistic View,	8–11	E. Hide
7	Lady Rowe,	8–8	P. Eddery
8	Appiadder,	8–11	E. Eldin
9	Royal Moss,	8–11	A. Russell
10	Blind Brag,	8–11	A. Murray

Distances: 1½ l, 1 l   Time: 1 m 16.80 s (a 5.80)

Betting: 2 Grey God, 11/4 Radical, 6 Consolatrix, 13/2 Lady Rowe,
11 Bustino, 25 Optimistic View, 33 Others.

SANDOWN, 27 April 1974

Going: firm
Wind: moderate half against
Going All'ce: minus 0.20 sec per fur

Classic Trial Stakes (Group 3), £2,910.22; 2nd £858.20; 3rd
£421.60; 4th £115.98. 1 mile 2 furlongs, three-year-olds.

1	BUSTINO,	8–9	J. Mercer
2	SNOW KNIGHT,	9–0	B. Taylor
3	UNDERSTUDY,	9–0	P. Eddery
4	Meon Hill,	9–0	B. Jago
5	Honoured Guest,	8–9	G. Lewis
6	Huzzar,	8–9	J. Lynch
7	Gerard Street,	9–0	J. Lindley
8	Martyr,	9–0	W. Carson
9	Trackers Highway,	9–0	P. Cook

Distances: ½ l, ¾ l   Time: 2 m 9.91 s (a 1.91)

Betting: 7/4 Snow Knight, 5/2 Bustino, 13/2 Understudy, 7 Gerard Street, 10 Huzzar, 11 Honoured Guest, 13 Meon Hill, 14 Martyr, 20 Trackers Highway.

LINGFIELD, 11 May 1974

Going: good
Wind: moderate half behind
Going All'ce: 0.20 sec per fur

Ladbroke Derby Trial Stakes (Group 3), £7,728.70; 2nd £2,272; 3rd £1,111; 4th £298.30. 1 mile 4 furlongs, three-year-olds.

1	BUSTINO,	9–0	J. Mercer
2	SIN Y SIN,	9–0	G. Lewis
3	SNOW KNIGHT,	9–0	B. Taylor
4	Meon Hill,	9–0	B. Jago
5	Live Arrow,	9–0	R. Marshall
6	Hope of Holland,	9–0	M. Kettle
7	Hard Choice,	9–0	E. Johnson

Distances: 1 l, 1½ l   Time: 2 m 39.88 s (a 4.88)

Betting: 13/8 Bustino, 9/4 Snow Knight, 7 Live Arrow, Sin Y Sin, 8 Meon Hill, 33 Hope of Holland, 50 Hard Choice.

EPSOM, 5 June 1974

Going: firm
Wind: moderate across
Going All'ce: minus 0.10 sec per fur

Derby Stakes (Group 1), £89,229.25; 2nd £26,355; 3rd £12,977.50; 4th £3,613,25. 1 mile 4 furlongs, three-year-olds.

1	SNOW KNIGHT,	9–0	B. Taylor
2	IMPERIAL PRINCE,	9–0	G. Lewis
3	GIACOMETTI,	9–0	A. Murray
4	Bustino,	9–0	J. Mercer
5	Northern Taste,	9–0	J. C. Desaint
6	Mistigri,	9–0	C. Roche
7	Nonoalco,	9–0	Y. Saint-Martin
8	Radical,	9–0	M. Goreham

9	Court Dancer,	9–0	W. Carson

Also ran:

	Regular Guy,	9–0	W. Pyers
	Sin Y Sin,	9–0	E. Eldin
	Arthurian,	9–0	L. Piggott
	Charlie Bubbles,	9–0	P. Eddery
	Live Arrow,	9–0	R. Marshall
	Grey Thunder,	9–0	R. Hutchinson
	Barbarie Corsaire,	9–0	R. Edmondson
	Hope of Holland,	9–0	G. Starkey
	Grand Orient,	9–0	G. Ramshaw

Distances: 21, 11   Time: 2 m 35.04 s (b 2.36)

Betting: 9/4 Nonoalco, 5/2 Giacometti, 8 Bustino, Northern Taste, 20 Imperial Prince, 25 Charlie Bubbles, Court Dancer, 28 Arthurian, 33 Sin Y Sin, 40 Mistigri, 50 Snow Knight, Live Arrow, 66 Regular Guy, Radical, 200 Others.

LONGCHAMP, 30 June 1974

Going: soft

Grand Prix de Paris £106,061.65. 1 mile 7 furlongs 110 yards, three-year-olds.

1	SAGARO,	8–11	L. Piggott
2	BUSTINO,	8–11	J. Mercer
3	KAMARAAN,	8–11	H. Samani
4	Le Bavard,	8–11	A. Gibert
5	Matching Pair,	8–11	Y. Josse
6	Ashmore,	8–11	Y. Saint-Martin
7	Poil de Chameau,	8–11	M. Depalmas
8	Battle Song,	8–11	J-C. Desaint
9	Endless,	8–11	J. Taillard
10	Court Dancer,	8–11	W. Carson

Also ran:

	Afaroon,	8–11	M. Bouland
	D'Arras,	8–11	M. Philipperon
	Salado,	8–11	G. Thiboeuf
	Little Boy Blue,	8–11	P. Paquet
	Flush,	8–11	C. Cimmino
	Grey Thunder,	8–11	B. Taylor

Social Stress,   8–11   E. Lellouche
Blue Diamond, 8–11   W. Pyers

Distances: 2 l, 1½ l   Time: 3 m 27.6 s

Betting: PM 5.70 f Pl. 2.00 f, 2.40 f, 1.70 f.

YORK, 21 August 1974

Going: good
Wind: slight across
Going All'ce: 0.20 sec per fur

Great Voltigeur Stakes (Group 2), £6,636; 2nd £1,846; 3rd £888.
1 mile 4 furlongs, three-year-olds.

1 BUSTINO,   9–0   J. Mercer
2 ENGLISH PRINCE,   9–0   P. Eddery
3 STRAIGHT AS A DIE, 9–0   L. Piggott

Distances: 4 l, 1½ l   Time: 2 m 33.23 s (a 4.23)
Betting: 4/7 English Prince, 15/8 Bustino, 10 Straight as a Die.

DONCASTER, 14 September 1974

Going: good
Wind: almost nil
Going All'ce: 0.25 sec per fur

St Leger Stakes (Group 1), £56,766.75; 2nd £16,805; 3rd
£8,302.50; 4th £2,350.75. 1 mile 6 furlongs 127 yards, three-year-
olds.

1   BUSTINO,   9–0   J. Mercer
2   GIACOMETTI,   9–0   L. Piggott
3   RIBOSON,   9–0   J. Lindley
4   Imperial Prince,   9–0   G. Lewis
5   Abide With Me,   9–0   E. Hide
6   Grey Thunder,   9–0   A. Barclay
7   Straight as a Die, 9–0   W. Carson
8   Cley,   8–11   F. Durr
9   Noblero,   9–0   R. Edmondson
10 Crash Course,   9–0   A. Kimberley

Distances: 3 l, 4 l   Time: 3 m 9.02 s (a 2.02)

Betting: 11/10 Bustino, 11/4 Imperial Prince, 11/2 Giacometti, 11 Straight as a Die, 22 Cley, 25 Abide with Me, 40 Crash Course, 66 Grey Thunder, 100 Riboson, 200 Noblero.

EPSOM, 7 June 1975

Going: firm
Wind: slight half behind
Going All'ce: minus 0.20 sec per fur

Coronation Cup (Group 1), £14,465.60; 2nd £4,276; 3rd £2,108; 4th £590.40. 1 mile 4 furlongs, four-year-olds and upwards.

1	BUSTINO,	9–0	J. Mercer
2	ASHMORE,	9–0	Y. Saint-Martin
3	MIL'S BOMB,	8–11	G. Lewis
4	Comtesse de Loir,	8–11	J-C. Desaint
5	Arthurian,	9–0	F. Durr
6	Riboson,	9–0	E. Eldin

Distances: 1 l, 6 l   Time: 2 m 33.31 s (b 3.19)

Betting: 11/10 Bustino, 4 Ashmore, Comtesse de Loir, 6 Mil's Bomb, 33 Riboson, 40 Arthurian.

Grundy's Races

Going: good
Wind: slight against
Going All'ce: nil

Granville Stakes, £1,611; 2nd £285; 3rd £135. 6 furlongs straight, two-year-old colts and geldings that had not run.

1	GRUNDY,	9–0	P. Eddery
2	NO ALIMONY,	9–0	W. Carson
3	AMERRICO,	9–0	L. Piggott
4	Jumping Hill,	9–0	G. Lewis
5	Libra's Rib,	9–0	D. Cullen
6	Fiery Ring,	9–0	J. Mercer
7	Kung Fu,	9–0	B. Raymond
8	So They Say,	9–0	B. Rouse
9	Red Fox,	9–0	B. Taylor

Also ran:

	Anne's Dream,	9–0	T. McKeown
	Gran Torino,	9–0	J. Lynch
	Great Lad,	9–0	G. Baxter
	My Revenge,	9–0	P. Waldron
	Orcis,	9–0	P. Cook
	Riva Run,	9–0	G. Starkey
	Zabaglione,	9–0	G. Rivases
	Ice King,	9–0	M. Kettle

Distances: 2l, 1½l   Time: 1 m 17.45 s (a. 1.05)

Betting: 7/4 Amerrico, 5 Grundy, 6 Fiery Ring, 7 Jumping Hill, 12 Zabaglione, 14 Red Fox, 25 Others.

KEMPTON, 30 August 1974

Going: firm (straight course)
Wind: slight half behind
Going All'ce: 0.20 sec per fur

Sirenia Plate, £621; 2nd £171; 3rd £81. 6 furlongs straight, two-year-olds.

| 1 | GRUNDY, | 9–5 | P. Eddery |
| 2 | PROSPECT RAINBOW, | 9–1 | B. Taylor |

3	GISELA,	8–12	E. Eldin
4	Ramadour,	9–5	B. Raymond
5	Sweet Reclaim,	9–1	A. Murray
6	Bam Bam,	8–11	R. Marshall
7	Sportsky,	8–11	W. Carson
8	Swallow,	8–8	J. Mercer
9	Another Pinta,	8–8	M. Thomas

Also ran:

	Vrondi,	8–11	P. Perkins
	Sky Sovereign,	8–8	G. Lewis

Distances: 2½l, Head   Time: 1 m 12.54 s (a 1.14)

Betting: 4/6 Grundy, 6 Sweet Reclaim, 10 Ramadour, 12 Sportsky, 14 Prospect Rainbow, Gisela, 20 Bam Bam, 33 Others.

DONCASTER, 11 September 1974

Going: good
Wind: almost nil
Going All'ce: nil

Champagne Stakes (Group 2), £9,443.90; 2nd £2,784; 3rd £1,367; 4th £375.10. 7 furlongs straight, two-year-olds.

1	GRUNDY,	9–0	P. Eddery
2	WHIP IT QUICK,	9–0	L. Piggott
3	BOLD PIRATE,	9–0	J. Mercer
4	Libra's Rib,	9–0	E. Hide
5	Green Belt,	9–0	E. Eldin
6	High Season,	9–0	B. Taylor
7	Berfeit,	9–0	R. Edmondson
8	Anne's Pretender,	9–0	A. Murray
9	Sir Something,	9–0	W. Carson
10	Amerrico,	9–0	G. Starkey

Distances: ½l, ¾l   Time: 1 m 27.20 s (a 2.20)

Betting: 13/8 Grundy, 2 Anne's Pretender, 8 Whip it Quick, 12 Bold Pirate, 14 Sir Something, High Season, Berfeit, 20 Amerrico, 25 Green Belt, 33 Libra's Rib.

NEWMARKET, 18 October 1974

Going: soft
Wind: strong across
Going All'ce: 0.90 sec per fur

William Hill Dewhurst Stakes (Group 1), £26,271.20; 2nd £7,772;
3rd £3,836; £1,080.80, 7 furlongs straight, two-year-olds.

1	GRUNDY,	9–0	P. Eddery
2	STEEL HEART,	9–0	L. Piggott
3	BALDUR,	9–0	J. Mercer
4	Top Level,	9–0	G. Starkey
5	Stamen,	9–0	G. Lewis
6	Berfeit,	9–0	R. Edmondson
7	Piccolino,	9–0	A. Murray
8	Big Venture,	9–0	A. Barclay

Distances: 6l, 1½l   Time: 1 m 33.67 s (a 7.67)

Betting: 6/5 Grundy, 2 Steel Heart, 8 Stamen, 12 Piccolino, 16
Baldur, 50 Others.

NEWBURY, 19 April 1975

Going: heavy
Wind: slight against
Going All'ce: 1.80 sec per fur

Clerical Medical Greenham Stakes (Group 3), £6,422.10; 2nd
£1,895; 3rd £933; 4th £258.90. 7 furlongs straight, three-year-old
colts and geldings.

1	MARK ANTHONY,	9–1	L. Piggott
2	GRUNDY,	9–1	P. Eddery
3	GREAT BALL,	8–10	W. Carson
4	Creetown,	8–10	B. Taylor
5	Highest,	8–10	J. Mercer
6	Hillandale,	8–10	G. Starkey
7	Jumping Hill,	8–10	G. Lewis
8	Town Farm,	8–10	C. Williams
9	All Friends,	8–10	P. Cook

Distances: 2l, 4l   Time: 1 m 41.71 s (a 16.31)

Betting: 4/6 Grundy, 11/2 Mark Anthony, 15/2 Hillandale, 17/2
Creetown, 14 Jumping Hill, 25 Highest, 33 Others.

NEWMARKET, 3 May 1975

Going: Good
Wind: moderate across
Going All'ce: 0.20 sec per fur

2,000 Guineas Stakes (Group 1), £36,868; 2nd £10,830; 3rd £5,290; 4th £1,412. 1 mile straight, three-year-olds.

1	BOLKONSKI,	9–0	G. Dettori
2	GRUNDY,	9–0	P. Eddery
3	DOMINION,	9–0	I. Johnson
4	Royal Manacle,	9–0	W. Carson
5	Green Belt,	9–0	E. Eldin
6	Mark Anthony,	9–0	L. Piggott
7	Prospect Rainbow,	9–0	B. Taylor
8	It's Freezing,	9–0	C. Roche
9	Auction Ring,	9–0	J. Mercer
10	Speedy Dakota,	9–0	F. Head

Also ran:

Sefton Court,	9–0	A. Kimberley
Sea Break,	9–0	Y. Saint-Martin
Amerrico,	9–0	B. Raymond
Steel Heart,	9–0	E. Hide
No Alimony,	9–0	F. Morby
Touch of Gold,	9–0	R. Marshall
Windy Glen,	9–0	J. Roe
Lord Ha Ha,	9–0	G. Curran
Anne's Pretender,	9–0	P. Cook
River Blue,	9–0	G. Ramshaw
Whip it Quick,	9–0	A. Murray
Libra's Rib,	9–0	P. Waldron
Golden Swan,	9–0	G. Lewis
Escapologist,	9–0	F. Durr

Distances: ½1, 31   Time: 1 m 39.49 s (a 0.29)

Betting: 7/2 Grundy, 9/2 Mark Anthony, Sea Break, 10 It's Freezing, 15 No Alimony, 16 Escapologist, 25 Green Belt, Steel Heart, 28 Speedy Dakota, 33 Bolkonski, Amerrico, Auction Ring, Dominion, Royal Manacle, Sefton Court, 40 Golden Swan, 66 Others.

THE CURRAGH, 17 May 1975

Going: good
Going All'ce: 0.50 sec per fur

Irish 2,000 Guineas Stakes (Group 1), £12,736.50. 1 mile, three-year-olds.

1	GRUNDY,	9–0	P. Eddery
2	MONSANTO,	9–0	Y. Saint-Martin
3	MARK ANTHONY,	9–0	L. Piggott
4	Gay Fandango,	9–0	T. Murphy
5	Golden Aim,	9–0	G. Starkey
6	Auction Ring,	9–0	E. Hide
7	Derby Court,	9–0	G. McGrath
8	It's Freezing,	9–0	C. Roche
9	Giggery,	9–0	M. Kennedy
Also ran:			
	Radiant Boy,	9–0	J. Roe
	Dempsey,	9–0	W. Swinburn
	Our Pal,	9–0	T. Carberry

Distances: 1½l, 1l   Time: 1 m 47.20 s (a 9.20)

Betting: 10/11 Grundy, 6 Monsanto, 7 Radiant Boy, 10 Mark Anthony, 12 It's Freezing, 16 Gay Fandango, 25 Golden Aim, 33 Auction Ring, Dempsey, 100 Derby Court, 200 Others.

EPSOM, 4 June 1975

Going: good
Wind: slight half against
Going All'ce: nil

Derby Stakes (Group 1), £106,465.50; 2nd £31,430; 3rd £15,465; 4th £4,289.50. 1 mile 4 furlongs, three-year-olds.

1	GRUNDY,	9–0	P. Eddery
2	NOBILIARY,	8–9	Y. Saint-Martin
3	HUNZA DANCER,	9–0	F. Durr
4	Anne's Pretender,	9–0	A. Murray
5	Whip it Quick,	9–0	P. Waldron
6	Green Dancer,	9–0	F. Head
7	Royal Manacle,	9–0	W. Carson
8	Fidion,	9–0	J-C. Desaint
9	Dominion,	9–0	I. Johnson

Also ran:

Nuthatch,	9–0	W. Swinburn
Romper,	9–0	F. Morby
Red Regent,	9–0	B. Taylor
Sea Break,	9–0	J. Roe
Bruni,	9–0	L. Piggott
No Alimony,	9–0	J. Mercer
Hobnob,	9–0	G. Lewis
Carolus,	9–0	E. Hide
Tanzor,	9–0	G. Starkey

Distances: 3 l, 4 l   Time: 2 m 35.35 s (b 1.15)

Betting: 6/4 Green Dancer, 5 Grundy, 11 Sea Break, 16 Bruni, Royal Manacle, 18 Fidion, 20 Nobiliary, Nuthatch, Hobnob, 25 No Alimony, 28 Dominion, 33 Anne's Pretender, 40 Red Regent, 50 Hunza Dancer, 66 Others.

THE CURRAGH, 28 June 1975

Going: firm

Irish Sweeps Derby (Group 1), £64,063. 1 mile 4 furlongs, three-year-olds.

1	GRUNDY,	9–0	P. Eddery
2	KING PELLINORE,	9–0	L. Piggott
3	ANNE'S PRETENDER,	9–0	A. Murray
4	Sea Anchor,	9–0	J. Mercer
5	Irish Star,	9–0	W. Swinburn
6	Maitland,	9–0	Y. Saint-Martin
7	Hobnob,	9–0	E. Eldin
8	Derby Court,	9–0	G. McGrath
9	Dowdall,	9–0	K. Coogan

Also ran:

Masqued Dancer,	9–0	R. Parnell
Phoenix Hall,	9–0	F. Durr
Giggery,	9–0	T. Murphy
Never so Gay,	9–0	M. Kennedy

Distances: 2 l, 6 l   Time: 2 m 31.10 s (b 0.90)

Betting: 9/10 Grundy, 7/2 King Pellinore, 6 Maitland, 10 Sea Anchor, 20 Anne's Pretender, 66 Hobnob, Irish Star, Derby Court, 80 Never so Gay, 100 Phoenix Hall, Masqued Dancer, 200 Others.

YORK, 19 August 1975

Going: good
Wind: slight behind
Going All'ce: nil

Benson and Hedges Gold Cup (Group 1), £39,397; 2nd £11,620; 3rd £5,710; 4th £1,573. 1 mile 2½ furlongs.

1	DAHLIA,	5–9–4	L. Piggott
2	CARD KING,	7–9–7	R. Jallu
3	STAR APPEAL,	5–9–7	G. Starkey
4	Grundy,	3–8–10	P. Eddery
5	Meautry,	5–9–7	J. Tailliard
6	Jimsun,	6–9–7	P. Cook

Distances: 1½l, 5l, 4l   Time: 2m 10.93s (a 2.43)

Betting: 4/9 Grundy, 7/2 Dahlia, 13 Star Appeal, 20 Card King, 50 Jimsun, 100 Meautry.